Understanding Teacher Stress in an Age of Accountability

a volume in
Research on Stress and Coping in Education

Series Editors:
Gordon S. Gates, *Washington State University*
Mimi Wolverton, *University of Nevada, Las Vegas*
Walter H. Gmelch, *University of San Francisco*
Christine Schwarzer, *University of Duesseldorf*

Research on Stress and Coping in Education

Gordon S. Gates, Mimi Wolverton,
Walter H. Gmelch, and Christine Schwarzer, Series Editors

Toward Wellness: Prevention, Coping and Stress (2003)
edited by Gordon S. Gates and Mimi Wolverton

*Thriving, Surviving, or Going Under:
Coping With Everyday Lives* (2003)
edited by Erica Frydenberg

Understanding Teacher Stress in an Age of Accountability

edited by

Richard Lambert
University of North Carolina at Charlotte

and

Christopher McCarthy
University of Texas at Austin

INFORMATION AGE
PUBLISHING

Greenwich, Connecticut • www.infoagepub.com

Library of Congress Cataloging-in-Publication Data

Understanding teacher stress in an age of accountability / edited by Richard Lambert, Christopher McCarthy.
 p. cm.—(Research on stress and coping in education series)
 Includes bibliographical references and index.
 ISBN 1-59311-473-7 (pbk.) — ISBN 1-59311-474-5 (hardcover)
 1. Teachers—United States—Job stress. 2. Burn out (Psychology) I. Lambert, Richard G. II. McCarthy, Christopher J. III. Series.
 LB2840.2.U63 2006
 371.1001'9
                                                                2006005236

Copyright © 2006 IAP–Information Age Publishing, Inc.

All rights reserved. No part of this publication may be reproduced, stored in a retrieval system, or transmitted, in any form or by any means, electronic, mechanical, photocopying, microfilming, recording or otherwise, without written permission from the publisher.

Printed in the United States of America

CONTENTS

Foreword
   Mimi Wolverton   vii

1. The Stress of Accountability: Teachers as Policy Brokers in a Poverty School
   P. Taylor Webb   1

2. Weighing the Risks With the Rewards: Implementing Student-Centered Pedagogy Within High Stakes Testing
   Michael M. Grant and Janette R. Hill   19

3. Teacher Stress and High Stakes Testing: How Using One Measure of Academic Success Leads to Multiple Teacher Stressors
   Sandra Mathison and Melissa Freeman   43

4. Shared Needs: Teachers Helping Students with Learning Disabilities to Cope More Effectively
   Nola Firth, Erica Frydenberg, and Daryl Greaves   65

5. Multicultural Competencies and Teacher Stress: Implications for Teacher Preparation, Practice, and Retention
   Sylvia C. Nassar-McMillan, Meagan Karvonen, and Cheryl Young   87

6. Teacher Stress and Classroom Structural Characteristics in Preschool Settings
   Richard Lambert, Jeni Kusherman, Megan O'Donnell, and Christopher McCarthy   105

7. Stress in the Student-Teacher Relationship in Dutch Schools:
A Replication Study of Greene, Abidin, and Kmetz's Index of
Teaching Stress (ITS)
Hubb A. Everaert & Kees van der Wolf — *121*

8. Sources of Teacher Demotivation
Zeynep Kiziltepe — *145*

9. Teachers' Job Stress and Human Resource Development: The
Malyasian Experience
Reynaldo Segumpan and Fazli Bahari — *163*

10. Relationship of Teachers' Preventive Coping Resources to
Burnout Symptoms
*Christopher McCarthy, Debra Kissen, Lauren Yadley,
Teri Wood, and Rich Lambert* — *179*

11. The Relationship Between Burnout and Stress Among Special
Educators
Stacey L. Edmonson — *197*

12. Helping Teachers Balance Demands and Resources in an Era of
Accountability
Christopher McCarthy and Richard Lambert — *215*

About the Authors — *227*

FOREWORD

Mimi Wolverton

In a bustling metropolitan city, a local television station runs a donation campaign to generate $1,200 worth of school supplies per teacher in the district so that teachers accustomed to digging into their own pockets to pay for these supplies will not have to. Pay is low in the district, and the district is reluctant to hire teachers with experience who move into the city from other states because they cost too much. Over 75% of its schools carry the No Child Left Behind moniker—needs improvement. Inappropriate student behavior in the district is on the rise. In response, the district has expanded it alternative programs for emotionally and behaviorally challenging students to target not only high school aged but upper elementary and middle school students as well.

These are district issues requiring district resources and district responses. Those responses, or a district's inability to respond, lead to teacher responses, which often result in teacher stress. *Understanding Teacher Stress in an Age of Accountability* is about teacher stress, teacher responses to stress, the resources that teachers employ to deal with stress, and those coping responses that are absent from their repertoires.

Although the scenario just described clearly reflects patterns found in U.S. school districts (particularly, but not solely, large ones), readers will soon discover that lack of funding, low pay, poor academic performance coupled with increased public and governmental scrutiny, and student misbehavior are not exclusively U.S. problems. In this volume, the third in a series on *Research on Stress and Coping in Education*, authors from Australia, Turkey, Malaysia, and the Netherlands sound the same alarms, post the same warnings, and draw similarly disturbing conclusions.

Webb in *The Stress of Accountability* describes how teachers and policy makers in one U.S. poverty school negotiated a set of accountability practices. Teachers became policy brokers as they attempted to educate high-risk students, some of whom came to school not to learn but to have their primary needs for food and security fulfilled. Learning came second in these instances. Implicitly, teachers changed policy to accommodate student needs rather than implement a set curriculum.

In *Weighing the Risks with Rewards*, Grant and Hill build on this notion of meeting student needs before learning can occur. However, they caution that employing a student-centered pedagogy does not always provide a sufficient return on time and energy invested, especially when teachers and students must function in a high-stakes testing environment.

Mathison and Freeman continue this dialogue about high-stakes testing and look at its relationship to teacher stress. In *Teacher Stress and High-Stakes Testing*, they delineate the changes to work environment and the nature of teachers' work that have resulted from the move toward accountability based high-stakes testing.

Firth, Frydenberg, and Greaves move the discussion about teacher stress into the realm of coping. In their chapter, *Shared Needs*, the authors report the results of research in which they examine the relationship between teaching coping strategies to students with disabilities and the levels of teacher stress once students begin to employ such strategies.

Diversity in the classroom refers not only to the abilities of students but to cultural variation as well. In *Multicultural Competencies and Teacher Stress*, Nassar-McMillan, Karvonen, and Young examine yet another special teaching setting—the preschool. They compare the demands of the job, which could prove stressful, to the physical resources that can be used to deal with these demands that schools provide to teachers. They conclude that in terms of teacher stress, children with behavior problems are the most demanding and general program resources provided by the school are the most helpful when it comes to dealing with work-related stress.

Chapter 8 moves the reader into the international arena of teacher stress. Everaert and van der Wolf replicate a U.S. study that examines stress in the student-teacher relationship to test the Index of Teaching Stress's (ITS) reliability in Dutch schools. For the most part, the ITS seems applicable in the Netherlands. Similar to several other authors in this volume, they found that problem children increase teacher stress, which in turn exacerbates the behavior of problem children.

Kzltepe catalogs the causes of teacher demotivation in Istanbul, Turkey. He suggests that the situation in Istanbul schools is representative of schools in Turkey in general and points to problems and changes over time that mirror those faced by teachers in U.S. schools.

In *Teachers' Job Stress and Human Resource Development: The Malaysian Experience*, Segumpan and Bahari replicate a U.S. study taking into account demographic variables unique to Malaysia. Even though they studied secondary teachers in the State of Malacca, their findings ring true across multiple countries. Student misbehavior followed by excessive workload, time, and resource demands, and a lack of professional recognition brought about the greatest teacher job stress. They suggest that developing better interpersonal relationships across multiple stakeholder groups can help ameliorate teacher job stress.

Burnout is endemic to the profession, especially among young teachers. McCarthy, Kissen, Yadley, Wood, and Lambert suggest that teachers attempt to cope with severe levels of work-related stress by engaging in behaviors that lead to burnout. First, they emotionally distance themselves from the situation, which manifests itself in emotional exhaustion. Second, they seek cognitive distance by depersonalizing their work. And finally, they exhibit a decline in feelings of accomplishment. The authors suggest that preventative strategies for teachers headed down this path include gaining a sense of control, maintaining perspective, drawing on a social network for support, developing self-acceptance, and acquiring the ability to scan the environment for trouble.

Edmonson conducts a meta-analysis of the literature on *Burnout and Stress in Special Educators*. The author provides a detailed description of the process and discusses the implications of the findings for both research and practice.

In the final chapter, *Helping Teachers Balance Demands and Resources in an Age of Accountability*, McCarthy and Lambert offer a summation of the issue of teacher stress and raise a substantive question that haunts both teachers and school districts: Do accountability standards conflict with the best interests of the students? In addition, they suggest that the demands placed on teachers do not necessarily increase stress levels. But whether or not teachers have the resources to meet the demands does. If resources are not available, it triggers stress responses, which taken to the extreme can lead to burnout.

I started by relating a very real scenario; I end by restating a belief that authors throughout this volume espouse: The teacher's responsibility is to educate the child. When parents and society abdicate their responsibility to raise the child so that he/she is ready to learn, teacher stress mounts. Accountability is a two-way street; over and over again, authors suggest fairly clear cut remedies for reducing teacher stress and in all likelihood increasing student learning—greater administrative support, more and better instructional materials, specialized resources targeted at demanding children, parental support, and professional recognition. I commend the authors who individually state the obvious and collectively raise the clarion call.

CHAPTER 1

THE STRESS OF ACCOUNTABILITY

Teachers as Policy Brokers in a Poverty School

P. Taylor Webb

This chapter describes how a group of teachers managed accountability stressors while teaching at a low-income school. Stressors were evident when teachers managed conflicts between expected curricular and accountability outcomes and their own diagnoses and professional expectations of students' needs. This chapter examines the reasoning and rationales behind the decisions of a small group of teachers to modify, or broker, expected accountability outcomes.

Our test scores are published. They're on the radio, on the television, in the newspapers. I'm hypersensitive to it, being it's my job at stake, but they're everywhere. They're on the Internet. They compare schools to different schools. (Maya, fourth grade teacher, Cypress Public Elementary School[1])

Understanding Teacher Stress in an Age of Accountability, 1–18
Copyright © 2006 by Information Age Publishing
All rights of reproduction in any form reserved.

Maya feels the pressure of increased accountability demands. Her "hyper-sensitivity" reveals a mix of anxiety, stress, and frustration over reported test scores. Maya knows that scores are used to judge her performance, even though those scores do not tell the whole story. Maya teaches in a high-poverty school where one quarter of the student population will transfer to and from other schools midyear.[2] Maya's admission of stress was not a subtle plea to avoid professional responsibility. That conclusion is too simple. Maya is a talented and committed teacher. Much of her stress results from the school environment that threatens her ability to reach her professional goals. She noted,

> My goal of trying to help all kids be lifelong learners can't be fulfilled for many reasons—large class size, lack of a pleasant and high quality facility for kids. Also, lack of up-to-date textbooks, and enough of them for all students. Some students are in emotionally dysfunctional homes. And finally, students with behavior problems. Some are so severe that they constantly disrupt the learning process. There are days that you go home and you think, "Why am I doing this? Should I be doing this?" It's becoming something of a drain.

In short, the demands of the job began to take their toll on Maya. Accountability demands on top of inadequate resources and community poverty weighed heavily on her. She became disillusioned at the prospect of remaining in the profession.

A serious problem has emerged in schools of the United States—teachers working within punitive frameworks of public accountability. High levels of teacher stress, amounting to demoralization, are a significant result of working under coercive threats of dismissal (McNeil, 2000). Because states have not provided requisite supports to accompany increased accountability demands,[3] problems of teacher stress have compounded into a national problem of teacher attrition (National Commission on Teaching & America's Future, NCTAF, 2003). During the last 10 years, more teachers have left the profession than have entered, with only 20% leaving for retirement purposes (Ingersoll, 2001). Attrition rates for beginning teachers are particularly steep, as nearly one third will leave teaching within their first 5 years (Ingersoll, 2001). While several factors contribute to teachers' heightened stress, a significant amount of stress results from high-stake accountability systems. Sirotnik (2002) noted that "evidence is emerging about teacher demoralization and attrition as a result of frustration with the overemphasis on mandated testing for high-stakes accountability purposes" (p. 2). Increased accountability sans adequate teacher support creates an effective policy mechanism that *thins* the teaching force, rather than effective policy that *sustains* it. Sadly, this current policy arrangement exacerbates teacher attrition in high-poverty schools—teacher attrition rates have increased by 50% above the national average in these schools (Darling-Hammond, 2003).

CHAPTER PURPOSE AND ORGANIZATION

At the heart of this discussion is a description of how Maya and her colleagues at Cypress Elementary School managed the stress of teaching at a low-income school in an era of high-stakes accountability. Participants' stress was particularly evident when they wrestled with conflicts between expected curricular outcomes and their own professional diagnoses of students' needs. This chapter examines the rationales behind the decisions of a small group of teachers to modify, and in some cases resist, expected accountability outcomes. The study had two immediate purposes: one, to better understand how teachers reconciled psychic conflicts (i.e., stress) between internally defined responsibilities and external expectations of their work, and two, to better understand how teachers coped with the stress produced by such conflicts.

In this study, the concept of stress was understood as a cognitive transaction model, that is, teachers assessed stressful situations by calculating between demands and available resources (Lazarus & Folkman, 1984). In other words, teachers made primary appraisals of accountability demands (stressors, including tests, accountability threats, and students' risk factors) and mediated stressors according to perceived resources (time, materials, study groups). Secondary appraisals defined ways teachers coped with various stressors—by assessing the available resources in their control to cope with perceived accountability stressors.

Organization

The chapter is organized into three sections. First, I review literatures on accountability intent and accountability effects. I also review emerging evidence of how educators develop endemic forms of accountability within schools—a category I describe as cultural accountability. The second section relates information about the case and reports data. Of notable importance, this section demonstrates how teachers "brokered" expected policy outcomes, evidenced in participants' mediation of mandated curricula and assessments. As such, participants' coping strategies alleviated some forms of stress but increased other forms. The final section considers the implications of such an analysis and provides recommendations for accountability alternatives that support teachers and their learning.

EDUCATIONAL ACCOUNTABILITY: HISTORICAL DEBATES

The No Child Left Behind Act (NCLB) is the most recent articulation of educational accountability in the Unites States. The federal government created NCLB, a reauthorization of the Elementary and Secondary Act, to answer questions about public education in the United States. Are educators fulfilling the expectations for which they are paid? Are students learning what they need to know? If states wish federal assistance, NCLB required lawmakers to implement assessment systems based on state standards and annual testing. Even though NCLB is the latest definition of educational accountability in the United States, it is not the first attempt to define the concept.

Accountability Intent: Teachers as Democratic Buffers or Bureaucratic Subordinates?

One axis of accountability research has tried to identify the intent of educational accountability—who holds whom accountable for what. Early intent literature distinguished professional from bureaucratic forms of accountability (Ingersoll, 2001), with the latter model closely related to market accountability (Friedman, 1962). Distinctions between these two broad forms of accountability rested on clarifying roles and responsibilities of actors in the education drama. Because educational accountability was distributed across people and space (state agencies, district offices, classrooms, etc.), researchers argued that teachers held a role *sui generis* among other education professionals (Shulman, 1983). Educators' special knowledge of pedagogy, subject matter, and students distinguished their professional duties from others in the education bureaucracy. Thus, researchers concluded that any accountability system must appropriately relate to the work of educators, not administrators (Lortie, 1975).

Researchers noted that educators' discretion provided the material from which to evaluate educators and provided an important buffer to protect communities from state and federal intrusion. Consequently, scholars argued that accountability frameworks should develop and assess educators' discretion, and, by inference, increase their professional autonomy to ensure freedom of thought in the democracy (Gutmann, 1999). However, critics argued that accountability systems controlled by educators would be ineffective because educators would protect their power rather than use it to regulate themselves (McGivney & Haught, 1972). As such, some believed a balance between professional and bureaucratic forms of accountability was needed (O'Day, 2002). Unfortunately, initial evidence of hybrid systems document an escalation of accountability politics, as educators confront an erosion of professional power from state governments (Malen, 2003) and corporate influence (Hargreaves, 2003).

Accountability Effects: Capacity Building or Disciplining Mechanisms?

A second axis of accountability research examined accountability effects. Effects literature analyzed accountability systems in order to build better policy mechanisms—mechanisms to build professional capacity (Darling-Hammond & Sykes, 1999) and/or mechanisms to punish and reward educators (Odden, 2002). Recently, effects literature switched analytic focus away from educational bureaucracies and analyzed schools and educators. A "new accountability" developed because policymakers honored earlier arguments about educators' unique roles (Fuhrman, 1999). This so-called "new" form of accountability intended to make educators' work more visible through inspections, observations, performances, and public reporting of test scores.

Critics of "new accountability" challenged assumptions about the relationships between student achievement, educator performance, and test scores. For instance, some effects literature argued that test-driven accountability policies actually increased dropout rates for marginalized students (Whitford & Jones, 2000), perpetuated racist practices for language-minority students (Wiley & Wright, 2004), increased teacher demoralization (McNeil, 2000), increased teacher stress over the legitimacy of their professional decisions (Jeffrey, 2002), and increased teacher attrition (NCTAF, 2003).

Cultural Accountability: Local and Endemic Forms of Control

An emerging third axis of accountability research is underway. This research examines educational accountability from the perspective of schools, rather than the perspective of external mechanisms that expect to influence schools (Newman, King, & Rigdon, 1997). The cultural literature assumes that schools have accountability systems already in place, albeit systems that may be unstated, ill-coordinated, and altogether different than what policymakers want. This literature examines how educators make sense of accountability issues and how schools use local concepts of accountability (Spillane, Diamond, Burch, Hallett, Jita, & Zoltners, 2002). Researchers have noted that the cultural literature differs from both the effects literature and intent literature. They stated,

Instead of asking how schools respond to policies designed to make them accountable to external authorities, we have asked how schools come to formulate their own conceptions of accountability and what role, if any, external policies play in these conceptions. Our working theory of accountability is predicated on the belief that external accountability systems operate on the margins of powerful factors inside the school, and that understanding these factors is a major precondition to understanding how and why schools respond the way they do to external pressures for accountability. (Abelmann, Elmore, Even, Kenyon, & Marshall, 1999, p. 38)

The cultural literature is an important shift in the research on educational accountability. It provides evidence of accountability systems already in place in schools. As such, the cultural literature challenges arguments that maintain that educator accountability is absent, and provides evidence of how the concept of accountability is a negotiated set of practices between educators and policymakers.

METHODOLOGY AND CASE PROFILE

The design of the study was influenced by the cultural literature and sought explanations between locally perceived responsibilities in relation to external accountability expectations. Single case study research is ideally suited to understand the intricacies of complex phenomena in order to aid the development of theory (Yin, 1994). This study describes the case in order to understand the relationships between teachers and accountability systems. Therefore, findings of this study are not generalizable to all teachers or all settings because the data were derived from a small population of teachers, in keeping with the case study methodology. However, the findings can be generalized to theories of educational accountability. Thus, the significance of this study is that it identifies social phenomena that can be used to inform, and improve, models of educational accountability. As such, the study posed three questions: (a) How do teachers resolve conflicts (cope with stressors) between their professional priorities and expected accountability outcomes, (b) what reasons supported teachers' exercise of autonomy, and (c) what impact did coping have on accountability stressors?

Case Profile

Cypress Elementary School was selected for the yearlong case study because it was identified as a "low performing" school that needed to make significant achievement gains in order to avoid sanctions from the state or district, or both. The school resides in a district that enrolls over 18,000 students and Cypress enrolls 330 of those students in grades K-6. The district has witnessed rapid changes to its student demographics over the last decade. Today, the district has nearly three times as many students eligible for free or reduced lunch as it did in 1991 (51% today)—while the district's student population has increased by 1,200 students during this time. This suggests that the average family income in the area has dropped in the last decade. Another important change in the district is that the student of color population has doubled in the past 10 years. Students of color make up 54% of the district student population today. Students who speak English as a second language (ESL) represent a total of 54 separate languages in the district. These demographic numbers suggest that White students and English speaking students are emigrating out of the district at a rate nearly equal to the immigration rate of students of color and ESL students into the district.

Cypress's demographics reflect the district's demographics. Fifty-six percent of Cypress's students are eligible for free and reduced lunch. Of the 330 students, 50% are White, 22% are Asian, 19% are Hispanic, 7% are Black, and 2% are American Indian. Compared to the district at large, Cypress enrolled greater numbers of White students and students eligible for free or reduced lunch. Over the past 3 years, Hispanics have been the fastest growing group at Cypress and Whites and Asians are the fastest declining groups at the school—numbers that are consistent with the immigration pattern of the district at large. A high mobility rate (27%) further characterized the students and their families at Cypress. Roughly 89 students did not begin or end their schooling at Cypress during the year.

Data Collection and Analysis

I spent 1 to 2 days each week at the school or district interviewing teachers, observing classes, and attending school meetings. Interviews with teachers included both focus groups and individual interviews. Approximately 15 semistructured interviews were conducted with seven teachers, and several more informal interviews were conducted to corroborate earlier statements or to extend previous conversations. Formal interviews averaged 1.5 hours. Teachers taught kindergarten, second, third, fourth, fifth, and sixth grades. Nearly 50 hours of school observations were conducted. Observations took place at faculty meetings, team-teaching meetings, school improvement meetings, classrooms, faculty lounge, hallways, playground, and school assemblies.

All interviews were audio taped and transcribed. Data were organized by identifying "patterns of generalization within a case"—themes that serve as analytic constructs among many examples of participants' actions (Erickson, 1986, pp. 148). Next, themes were compared and codes used to examine the data were developed. After reducing the number of categories from additional readings of the data, disconfirming cases were used to further distill important analytic statements. Potential problems of validity and reliability were addressed through triangulation of data—that is, observations and analyzed documents were used to provide multiple indicators of the same phenomenon (Miles & Huberman, 1994).

Documents were analyzed in relation to external expectations for teachers. Expectations included (1) what to teach, (2) how to teach it, (3) student assessment objectives, and (4) teacher accountability goals. I created a matrix that included these categories for each major document. Matrices, then, were used to compare documents to each other and to develop the stated expectations that teachers were expected to follow. In cases where a matrix did not align with a specific document (e.g., meeting minutes), I developed summary sheets that highlighted important themes related to the study. Member checks were conducted with participants, asking whether the data were accurate and interpretations plausible (Guba & Lincoln, 1989). Data were edited to assist reading.

Initial Analysis: Pressure to Improve

Initial data analysis indicated that teachers were under pressure to improve the Washington Assessment of Student Learning (WASL) scores and the Iowa Test of Basic Skills (ITBS) scores. The WASL and ITBS are standardized tests that report achievement data for students (and by inference teachers, principals, and schools). The WASL is a series of criterion-reference tests in reading, writing, listening, and mathematics that is given to elementary students in the fourth grade. These standards-based assessments incorporate three item types: multiple choice, short constructed response, and extended constructed response. The ITBS comprises the norm-referenced component of the statewide program. This measure collects achievement information about basic skills in third and sixth grades. The ITBS is used to provide independent evidence to validate the WASL while providing policymakers comparisons between state achievement levels and most other states.

Cypress Elementary needed to achieve a 3-year average of 25% improvement in meeting the mathematics standards on the WASL (40% for the reading standards) or it was subject to the following state sanctions: (1) reconstitution of school personnel, (2) removal of particular school from district jurisdiction, and/or (3) abolition of the school. Because Cypress had not improved 25% or more on the mathematics portion of the state exam for the last 3 years, it was eligible for any of the proposed interventions.

The district stipulated six additional measures to assess teachers and students. The measures included three "benchmarks" (reading, math, writing) for grades K-6 submitted three times a year, a District Reading Assessment Proficiency (DRAP) for grades 2, 3, 4, 5, and 6 submitted five times a year, a yearly District Writing Assessment (DWA) for fourth grade, and a yearly District Reading Assessment (DRA) for second grade. Cypress also implemented eight curricula mandated by the district. The curricula that Cypress implemented were: *Success for All* (reading), *Cooperative Integrated Reading and Composition*, *Open Court* (reading), *Quest* (mathematics), *Six Traits* (writing assessment), *Great Body Shop* (health), Science kits, and *Adventures in Art*.

Knapp, Bamburg, Ferguson, and Hill (1998) noted the stress created for teachers by numerous and frequent curricula reforms. The pressure to improve scores from so many "masters" necessitates a more detailed investigation of the ways teachers respond to accountability stressors. This secondary analysis extends an understanding of how teachers coped with the stress produced from the accountability pressure.

RESULTS

At Cypress, teacher stress was apparent when participants accounted for risk factors in students' lived experiences. Emotional and physical abuse, alcoholism, drug dependency, divorce, and truancy were somber factors that challenged participants' capacity to fulfill expected instructional outcomes. Hence, participants felt their abilities to fulfill accountability criteria were threatened. Interestingly, participants "brokered" instructional policies (altered, modified, resisted) to better align students' experiences with curricular and instructional expectations. However, such a coping strategy created additional stressors when participants wrestled with the accuracy and legitimacy of their professional diagnoses.

Sources of Teacher Stress: Conflicts Between Student Needs and Expected Outcomes

Stress was evident when participants wrestled with expected policy outcomes in relation to students' needs. As noted, Cypress faculty mediated severe risk factors that adversely affected students. Steve, fifth grade, noted how teachers coped, or tried to cope, with the stress produced by aspects of students' lives. He stated,

> Teachers absorb and deal with children's lives that aren't pleasant, and it rips us up. You have to understand that these kids have problems and we're going to do the best we can with them. But you can't heal everybody, and you do the best you can and teach as much as you can while you have them.

Steve's use of the word "heal" indicates the severity of risk factors that participants negotiated in the classroom. His testimony identified a tension between facets of students' lives that jeopardized instructional expectations, hence ramping-up potential for accountability sanctions. Because of the "unpleasant" aspects of some students' lives, the act of teaching was a process that required (more) time and patience if teachers and students were to meet policy demands. Joanne discussed the impact this had on teaching. She stated,

> I take time out because of the children. Some of their backgrounds are tough and some of them have really been in some traumatic things. Others have extreme anger problems, so I'm sorry, but teaching has to wait a few minutes while we calm down and we review lessons about what we value and what we don't as a class. I mean Quest [math curriculum] can say you have to be this far and this far and this far, but man, you have to work with what you've got and if students aren't ready for it, they're not ready for it.

The instructional calendar that regulated participants' curriculum—in particular, the dates to report scores—failed to consider students' individual learning needs. Instead, policy outcomes were designed for the "typical," "generic," or "aggregated" student. However, participants *did* account for individual needs—at the risk of not fulfilling accountability expectations on time.

Participants remarked that students who spoke English as a second language needed additional time, attention, and curricular adaptations to meet policy outcomes. Sarah, the third grade teacher noted,

> In my reading group, we're supposed to finish the story in 5 days so we can turn in the scores. Well, because I have 10 students who don't speak English very well, there's no way I can get through it in 5 days. It takes me longer. I can't cover as much curriculum. I teach in depth so they really learn, and not just zoom over the material.

Accountability pressure reduced the act of teaching to a dichotomy of breadth versus depth for Sarah. This dichotomy was created because external accountability pressure did not account for students who were not fluent in English.

Participants used an endemic form of accountability at Cypress, and external forms of accountability only provided additional sources of stress for participants. Participants' unique form of accountability accounted for local risk factors negatively impacting students' learning. That is, participants *were accountable to students* by attending to factors that placed their learning at risk, rather than being accountable to scores and calendars. In the midst of 16 separate instructional policies, participants accounted for risk factors in students' lives and modified instructional policy to help students meet instructional goals. Modifications were most easily observable when participants took "more" time to teach than what was allocated by the testing schedule. Thus, participants *did not* fit the mold of a technician, assigning work in regimented ways on a prescribed schedule assigned by policymakers. This is often reported as the phenomena of "teaching to the test." Rather, participants made diagnoses of student needs and modified instructional policies to address those needs. Here, participants were "policy brokers," not curriculum implementers (Schwille et al., 1986).

Policy brokering was a resource, or strategy, participants used to cope with stress produced from policy expectations. Policy brokering was also a unique form of accountability and professional responsibility *in place* at Cypress. While somewhat implicit, teachers developed a form of accountability at the school—a commitment to student learning. They did so even at the risk of losing their jobs. They practiced several forms of professional development to aid their diagnoses; however, the act of policy brokering created an additional source of stress for participants as they wrestled with the accuracy and legitimacy of their professional diagnoses.

Sources of Teacher Stress: Policy Mediation and the Legitimacy of Professional Reasoning

The idea that participants brokered policies, instead of implementing policies, marked a coping strategy participants used to alleviate accountability stress. In fact, two participants used similar phrases to express the idea that teacher's professional identity at Cypress was more aligned with being a policy broker than a curriculum implementer: "I'm not going to tell you that I teach to a curriculum. That doesn't work. I teach to the child" (Julep, sixth grade), and, "You have to teach the child, not the curriculum" (Martha, second grade).

A good example of how participants brokered policy to alleviate stress was evidenced in the talk of Martha. Martha made a decision about the appropriateness of the reading program in relation to her students needs.

After having assessed the students' abilities, she decided that changing the curriculum would better serve her students. She stated,

> You just can't say, "here's the book and we're going to follow this, this, and this." If it's not going to work for the kids then I'll say, "okay, we're going to do something different." For instance, we're supposed to start at the beginning of the year doing reading groups where they had reading books that they would take home. Well, it's way too soon, way too soon. So it was like "why would I do that? The kids are not ready." So you have to modify the curriculum to work for the kids.

Here, Martha possessed a large degree of talent and skill, evidenced in her abilities to identify students' learning needs ("The kids are not ready."). Martha also used a body of developmental knowledge that supported her work, knowledge about how students learn to read ("Well, it's way too soon."). Finally, Martha made a decision to marry skills with this knowledge to solve complex problems of student learning, displayed in her brokering of the reading policy ("So you have to modify the curriculum to work for the kids."). Participants' diagnoses of students were combined with a form of reasoning that modified expected policy outcomes. Hence, participants brokered policies in order to improve students' learning, rather than to just satisfy accountability demands. This often placed participants in binds when they decided to re-teach topics, thereby placing them at risk for reporting delayed scores for accountability purposes. Steve stated,

> I taught the health curriculum but the kids crashed on the test. It got to a point where I said, "ok, three people passed, three people got over 80%. Wad up your papers and throw them in the recycle bin. We're not going to use this test for your grades." However, it was important material about personal safety issues and emotions and so I re-taught it. It might have been that my teaching style didn't match well with their learning styles. I figured out another way to get to them. But I was pretty much following the rules and it didn't work.

Steve's testimony provides further evidence of participants' pedagogical reasoning in relation to gaps within the stated curricula (the "rules" for Steve). His testimony also provides evidence that teachers at Cypress used assessment to improve instruction; contra to the policy environment which used assessment data inappropriately for accountability decisions (Sirotnik & Kimball, 1999).

The choice to broker instructional policy meant participants forsook some curricular material for the sake of student learning. In fact, participants skipped material (further example of brokered policy) for which they would be held accountable. Anne stated,

> If the assessment doesn't assess what it should, then it's not going to work for the kids. My ideas are ideas for the kids, not for the WASL, and not for the administration. I'm teaching the student. If I am supposed to use an assessment form that is not appropriate for the children, then I won't use it. I'll find another assessment.

Anne's testimony provided evidence that teachers did not teach to the test, but instead, *disregarded the test altogether* when their professional discretion and judgment led them to a more appropriate instructional method and more appropriate form of assessment. In fact, knowledge about students' needs as learners led one participant to treat some prescribed policy as mere contrivance, a hide-and-seek game. He noted,

> If I don't truly believe what I'm teaching then I will subvert it and change it. When the doors are open they will see something different than when they doors are closed. If I don't believe that what I'm teaching, or what I'm being told to teach, will help the kids, then I won't do it. I'll do two sets of lesson plans. Kind of like keeping two sets of books. You have the set of books for the auditors and then you have the set of books that you're really doing your stuff. I think teaching is like that. If you truly don't buy into what the curriculum is telling you to do, you are going to subvert it to some degree.

Even in a district that stipulated an enormous amount of instructional policies, participants felt obligated to mediate these directives. However, what emerged from this discussion were questions about the viability of participants' decisions. For instance, would other teachers be as confident about curricular resistance? Because participants relied on their professional decisions to help students learn, they reflected on the accuracy and legitimacy of their diagnoses. For instance, Joanne described the stress caused by the cacophony of accountability pressure that challenged her own professional discretion. She stated,

> It takes so much time to prepare district curricula and how valuable is it really? Some people say, "they're not being tested on the WASL right now so don't worry about that" and other people are saying, "forget the science, do the writing, spend your time on writing, reading, and math." And then some people say, "drop that." Others say, "no you need to do this because it's informational writing." All I hear is, "do this, no back off you can't do that—you don't have time to do that." Who do you listen to?

When asked to clarify how she made decisions amid the accountability cacophony (Interviewer, "*who* do you listen to?"), Joanne responded,

> My background. I have a good background in reading. I was a Title One reading teacher for about 20 years in Michigan. I have my masters in ele-

mentary reading instruction from Michigan State. And I've been to two International Reading Association [IRA] conventions. I've been to over 15 years worth of the Michigan State conferences.

Joanne reflected on her education at Michigan State, her participation in IRA, and her knowledge developed from years of experience working with students when she discussed reasons for exercising her professional discretion. Joanne's decisions were based on her affiliation with reputable organizations and her experience teaching students living in conditions of poverty.

In another example, Martha used action research to help her better cope with the stress of making decisions about students' needs and policy outcomes. She believed that participant inquiry helped her understand her practice and her students, and it provided her with benefits associated with collegial interactions. She reflected,

> Action research helps because it makes me more aware of my teaching. By systematically studying my teaching, I learn how to improve. Another reason action research has been beneficial is not just reflecting about your practice, but I'm getting a chance to meet with teachers in our grade level [across district]. This has been extremely beneficial because we are all able to share how we've learned to teach. For example, there's one teacher that I got this great idea from about how to teach fractions. That ability to share with colleagues has been beneficial.

Action research enabled Martha to tailor investigations to their immediate classroom situation. Classroom study was not aimed at generic skill acquisition, but rather, it allowed her to meet individual student's needs by systematically examining students' needs and curricular content. Another benefit of classroom inquiry was evidence of student achievement. Knowledge about students' performances was immediate and evidentiary. Martha assessed students on their performances *of the material* (not of a constructed test question). As such, participants made curricular adaptations quickly and with more precision. Waiting for standardized test results would take months. The use of action research to broker policy buttressed Martha's pedagogical decisions.

DISCUSSION AND CONCLUSION

Teachers at Cypress were accountable and committed to student learning. This *sine qua non* of teaching, however, was characterized by participants' sophisticated knowledge of how to mediate risk factors negatively impacting student learning—including truancy, abuse, and family addictions.

Thus, teacher knowledge, discretion, and reasoning were significant variables mediating student learning amid threats from the external accountability system.

Returning to the theoretical framework, participants appraised the accountability demands (primary appraisals: accountability pressures, administrative demands, community poverty, threats to professional discretion). From that, participants made secondary appraisals to cope with primary stressors. Secondary appraisals were evident when participants brokered instructional materials to better serve students (individualized instruction). Finally, primary coping resources were evident when participants mediated and brokered accountability policies. Secondary coping strategies included the kinds of professional development practices participants used to justify threats to their professional discretion. External accountability pressure (the reporting of test scores) only exacerbated participants' work-related stress by questioning the legitimacy of their professional decisions—an additional layer of stress characterized as "professional-identity" stress.

Based on this study, the external accountability system was symbolic rather than a well-crafted instructional policy. The accountability system assured the public that policymakers were interested in questions of educational quality and would "get tough" if schools and teachers failed in their work. Unfortunately, external accountability communicated an incorrect message to the public—that teachers were not committed to students' learning. In fact, participants had knowledge about students that improved their learning. Thus, participants drew upon knowledge that policymakers did not have to improve student learning. The notion that teachers needed a "fire lit beneath them" was a message that was antiquated, arrogant, and unhelpful—although it may have assuaged public perception.

The external accountability system was simply too broad and generic to provide participants instructional support with the student population they worked with, and thus, the external system of accountability paled in comparison to the local form of accountability practiced at Cypress. In fact, the external system "got in the way" of some participants' work and exacerbated the stressors already produced by helping students learn. The punitive nature of the accountability policy added insult to injury. The teachers in this study were activists who smartly brokered policy mandates and did so with legitimate professional activities that generated credible knowledge to act upon. When attempting to understand the reasons for using generic instructional materials, the principal explained,

> I don't care what curriculum you use, it's good teachers that make the difference. All the focus on these curriculums and tests, really. If a teacher's good

at teaching reading, she's going to teach reading well. But right now there's such a shortage of good teachers that the assumption is what curriculum would support *anyone* in teaching (my italics).

The corollary premise is that punitive accountability frameworks increase adherence to mandated curricula because of fear of losing one's job.

It was apparent that not every teacher at Cypress was committed to practicing the kinds of professional endeavors that support curricular revisions. It was also clear that participants' professional development activities (action research, curriculum study, professional conferences) were just the beginning of complex knowledge acquisition. However, a growing literature insists that school districts should play an important role in developing conditions for teacher learning, rather than teacher obedience (Darling-Hammond & Sykes, 1999). The portraitures presented herein provide evidence that participants understood and applied best practices. Questions about best practices were not simply questions for policymakers and curriculum developers. States and local school districts need to support teacher learning instead of devising more and more ways to eliminate it through adherence to accountability threats. Governmental bodies that continue to neglect the idea of quality professional development run a serious risk of liability when they breach the public trust about schooling. States and school districts breach a moral imperative when they infer that the problems of education fall squarely on "non-compliant" teachers. This breach is exacerbated when teachers are excluded from developing initiatives aimed to improve the conditions for schooling at their local sites—sites where teachers may in fact know more about students' "needs" than do policy-makers. Policy practices that sublimate the interests of those closest to the issues, indeed, the very people held accountable for the issues, are morally dubious. It is time that school districts and governments become accountable to teachers and their power. School districts and governments are also accountable to the reform literature that exists and should quickly facilitate opportunities for teacher learning.

NOTES

1. Maya and Cypress are pseudonyms. All names have been changed to protect participants' anonymity.
2. At Cypress, 56% of students are eligible for free and reduced lunch and the school has a 27% student mobility rate.
3. Better salaries, support for student discipline problems, better opportunities for professional advancement are examples of some requisite supports (Ingersoll, 2001).

REFERENCES

Abelmann, C., Elmore, R., Even, J., Kenyon, S., & Marshall, J. (1999). *When accountability knocks, will anyone answer?* (CPRE Policy Brief No. RR-42). Philadelphia, PA: University of Pennsylvania, Consortium for Policy Research in Education.

Darling-Hammond, L. (2003). Keeping good teachers: Why it matters and what leaders can do. *Educational Leadership, 60*(8), 6-13.

Darling-Hammond, L., & Sykes, G. (1999). *Teaching as the learning profession: Handbook of policy and practice.* San Franciso: Jossey-Bass.

Erickson, F. (1986). Qualitative methods in research on teaching. In M. C. Wittrock (Ed.), *The handbook of research on teaching* (pp. 119-161). New York: MacMillan.

Friedman, M. (1962). *Capitalism and freedom.* Chicago: The University of Chicago Press.

Fuhrman, S. H. (1999). *The new accountability.* (CPRE Policy Brief No. RB-27). Philadelphia, PA: University of Pennsylvania, Consortium for Policy Research in Education.

Guba, G., & Lincoln, Y. (1989). *Fourth generation evaluation.* Newbury Park, CA: Sage.

Gutmann, A. (1999). *Democratic education.* Princeton, NJ: Princeton University Press.

Hargreaves, A. (2003). *Teaching in the knowledge society: Education in the age of insecurity.* New York: Teachers College Press.

Ingersoll, R. (2001). Teacher turnover and teacher shortages: An organizational analysis. *American Educational Research Journal, 38*(3), 499-534.

Jeffrey, B. (2002). Performativity and primary teacher relations. *Journal of Education Policy, 17*(5), 531-546.

Knapp, M. S., Bamburg, J. D., Ferguson, M. C., & Hill, P. T. (1998). Converging reforms and the working lives of frontline professionals in school. *Educational Policy, 12*(4), 397-418.

Lazarus, R. S., & Folkman, S. (1984). *Stress, appraisal, and coping.* New York: Springer.

Lortie, D. (1975). *Schoolteacher: A sociological study.* Chicago: The University of Chicago Press.

Malen, B. (2003). Tightening the grip? The impact of state activism on local school systems. *Educational Policy, 17*(2), 195-216.

McGivney, J., & Haught, J. (1972). The politics of education: A view from the perspective of the central office staff. *Educational Administration Quarterly, 8*(3), 18-38.

McNeil, L. (2000). *Contradictions of school reform: Educational costs of standardized testing.* New York: Routledge.

Miles, M., & Huberman, M. (1994). *Qualitative data analysis.* Thousand Oaks, CA: Sage.

National Commission on Teaching & America's Future (2003). *No dream denied: A pledge to America's children.* Washington, DC: Author.

Newmann, F., King, B., & Rigdon, M. (1997). Accountability and school performance: Implications form restructuring schools. *Harvard Educational Review, 67*(1), 41-74.

O'Day, J. (2002). Complexity, accountability, and school improvement. *Harvard Educational Review, 72*(3), 293-329.

Odden, A. (2002). *Paying teachers for what they know and do: New and smarter compensation strategies to improve schools.* Thousand Oaks, CA: Corwin Press.

Schwille, J., Porter, A., Belli, G., Floden, R., Freeman, D., Knappen, L., & Kuhs, T. (1986). Teachers as policy brokers in the context of elementary school mathematics. In L. Shulman & G. Sykes (Eds.), *The handbook on teaching and policy* (pp. 370-391). New York: Longman.

Shulman, L. (1983). Autonomy and obligation: The remote control of teaching. In L. Shulman & G. Sykes (Eds.), *Handbook of teaching and policy* (pp. 484-504). New York: Longman.

Sirotnik, K. (2002). Promoting responsible accountability in schools and education. *Phi Delta Kappan, 83*(9), 662-673.

Sirotnik, K., & Kimball, K. (1999). Standards for standards-based accountability systems. *Phi Delta Kappan, 81*(3), 209-214.

Spillane, J., Diamond, J., Burch, P., Hallett, T., Jita, L., & Zoltners, J. (2002). Managing in the middle: School leaders and the enactment of accountability policy. *Educational Policy, 16*(5), 731-762.

Whitford, B. L., & Jones, K. (2000). *Accountability, assessment, and teacher commitment: Lessons from Kentucky's reform efforts.* New York: State University of New York Press.

Wiley, T., & Wright, W. (2004). Against the undertow: Language-minority education policy and politics in the "age of accountability." *Educational Policy, 18*(1), 142-168.

Yin, R. (1994). *Case study research: Design and methods.* Thousand Oaks, CA: Sage.

CHAPTER 2

WEIGHING THE RISKS WITH THE REWARDS

Implementing Student-Centered Pedagogy Within High Stakes Testing

Michael M. Grant and Janette R. Hill

There is a growing research base to support teacher use of student-centered learning strategies. However, this research comes at a time when high-stakes testing is the focus of much of the work in schools in the United States. This chapter examines the risks teachers take when implementing student-centered pedagogy within these contexts. Based on previous and current research we describe a framework for understanding these risks, emphasizing the challenges teachers face. Additionally, we examine how each of these factors affects teachers, offering examples from teachers and the literature where appropriate. Finally, recommendations for the successful implementation and reduction in teacher stress are presented.

Many researchers exploring teacher education have called for more constructivist (Applefield, Huber, & Moallem, 2000; Harel & Papert, 1991), student-centered learning approaches in the classroom (Olson, 1999).

These include the completion of in-depth projects (e.g., project-based learning (Blumenfeld, Soloway, Marx, Krajcik, Guzdial, & Palinscar, 1991)) solving real-world problems (e.g., problem-based learning; Barrows & Tamblyn, 1980), and learning situations defined and constructed by learners (e.g., open-ended learning environments; Hannafin, Land, & Oliver, 1999). Standardized testing seems to counter these educational goals. The assessment movement, bolstered by requirements in the No Child Left Behind Act of 2001, has created an atmosphere in some schools that reinforces teacher-centeredness, encouraging use of "lots of skills and drill" activities (Barksdale-Ladd & Thomas, 2000, p. 389) that are incongruous with the aims of student-centered learning. Nieto (2003) contends that high-stakes testing may in fact be restricting pedagogy. For example, instructional practices indicative of student-centered learning, such as collaborative writing, science experiments, and thematic integrated units, are being suspended in some schools (Barksdale-Ladd & Thomas, 2000).

A loss of diversity in instructional practices is not the only product of an increased focus on high standards through testing. Teachers are feeling the pressures of these learning contexts, and the effects can be destructive. In a seminal synthesis of research on teacher stress, Wiley (2000) reports:

> As a consequence of their job conditions, many teachers are finding that their feelings about themselves, their students, and their profession are more negative over time. These teachers are susceptible to developing chronic feelings of emotional exhaustion and fatigue, negative attitudes toward their students, and feelings of diminishing job accomplishments ... these feelings are aspects of stress and often result in absenteeism, which may lead to student absenteeism and a lack of academic achievement. (p.81)

Powerlessness to implement pedagogy that extends beyond mandated curriculum standards and a lack of autonomy could contribute as stressors for teachers, impacting teachers' self-efficacies. Lazarus and Folkman (1984) characterize stress as an individual's interpretation of interactions with environmental events. Stress is appraised in terms of previous harm, future threats, and optimistic challenges. Hancock Ward, Szalma, Stafford, and Ganey (2004) assert that "the negative effects of stress are most likely to occur when individuals view an event as a threat, and when they assess their coping skills as inadequate for handling the stressor" (p.1). Social factors, like role conflict, role ambiguity, and resource overload (Lazarus & Folkman, 1984), are grave factors in generating stress for individuals and specifically teachers (Wiley, 2000).

There is, however, growing literature to support student-centered learning strategies. For example, Lord (1999), George, Hall, and

Uchiyama (2000) and Secker (2002), report improved student achievement with student-centered instructional strategies. Likewise, advocates for meaningful technology integration emphasize consistent student-centered learning as the strategies necessary to leverage the computer as a powerful tool for student learning (Bickford, Tharp, McFarling, & Beglau, 2002; Lowther, Ross, & Morrison, 2003).

But what are the risks for teachers to employ these strategies? While much as been reported about the successes of employing these techniques, little discussion has focused on the challenges teachers face in student-centered learning environments (Brush & Saye, 2000). It is important for teacher educators to paint a complete picture of the details associated with student-centered learning, including the issues associated with teacher stress, classroom management, and school cultures. Moreover, it is equally essential for inservice teachers to comprehend the advantages and challenges they and their students may face when implementing student-centered approaches.

In their extensive review of teacher autonomy, Pelletier, Séguin-Lévesque, and Legalt (2002) summarize:

> that when authorities impose restrictions about a curriculum, make teachers responsible for their students' performance, and pressure or reward teachers to produce good student performance, and teachers believe that their students are extrinsically motivated or possibly not motivated toward school, it is likely that teachers will become controlling with students. (p. 187)

It is easy to see that these factors, often indicative of high-stakes testing, may promote little student-centered learning.

In our joint and independent work with preservice and inservice teachers across Georgia, Tennessee, and Kentucky, we have observed in classrooms and discussed in depth the successes to implementing student-centered learning strategies. Similarly, we have seen the conscious decisions by teachers to continue didactic pedagogy. In a study of a laptop integration project in Georgia (Hill, Reeves, Grant, Wang, & Han, in press[1]), one secondary English teacher noted, "Projects don't provide a good return on investment when I have limited time to cover a large number of objectives." This representative quote highlights one of the disadvantages often cited by educators when discussing student-centered approaches: too risky. Other concerns that were often voiced in studies we have conducted include: time limitations, resource demands, and lack of self-regulation skills of learners. In addition to the concerns, several benefits were also mentioned by educators in our research, including: more in-depth knowledge of the subject, more engagement by the learners, and an increase in the overall value of the end product associated with ownership of the project.

Overall, we advocate using a variety of pedagogical methods. Moreover, we acknowledge the pressures teachers confront in order to succeed and survive with an increased focus on high-stakes testing. This article examines the risks teachers take when implementing student-centered pedagogy within these contexts. From our professional development and collaborations with teachers, teacher interviews, focus groups, classroom observations, and surveys, as well as an extensive review of the related literature, we interpret our aggregate findings (see e.g., Grant, 2002, 2003; Grant, Key, & Abdi, 2004; Grant, Ross, Wang, Potter, & Wilson, 2005; Hill et al., in press) in order to offer a framework for understanding these risks, emphasizing the challenges teachers face.[2] Additionally, we examine how each of these factors affects teachers, offering examples from teachers and the literature where appropriate. Finally, recommendations for the successful implementation and reduction in teacher stress are presented.

INFLUENTIAL FACTORS IN STUDENT-CENTERED PEDAGOGY

We have identified five factors that influence teachers' decisions as they use student-centered pedagogy. Although other areas of impact may exist, these factors seem to cover the broadest range of concerns, highlighting the psychological, pedagogical, and physical effects to teachers. Descriptions for and examples of the five categories are included below (see Table 2.1 for a summary).

Describing the Factors

Recognition and acceptance of new roles and responsibilities is the first set of dynamics impacted in the adoption of a student-centered approach. Roles and responsibilities represent the functions performed in a student-centered environment by the teachers and students. This factor includes the obligations for which each participant in the environment is held accountable, as well as the implicit and explicit expectations teachers have for learners and learners have for teachers. Wiley (2000), along with Gold and Roth (1993), identified role conflict and role ambiguity as potential factors contributing to teacher stress. The abilities of teachers to recognize the shifts in their functions, obligations, and expectations in the new environment, subsequently accepting and adapting to these changes, can influence the success of a student-centered learning strategy.

Comfort level in the learning environment is another factor influenced when employing a student-centered learning pedagogy. Elements, such as

Table 2.1. Description of Factors

Factors Influencing a Student-Centered Learning Environment	Description	Examples in Student-Centered Learning
Recognition and acceptance of new roles and responsibilities	Recognition and acceptance of obligations each participant in the environment is held accountable for, as well as the implicit and explicit expectations.	• Teacher's role is de-centered. The teacher is a facilitator of learning and a partner in learning with students. • Instruction includes group negotiation, time management and project-management skills. • Assessments are integral to learning, performance-based and collaborative.
Comfort level	Level to which the teacher and learners are comfortable with the physical dislocations inherent to student-centered pedagogy.	• To observers, the classroom may seem out of control. • Student discussions are occurring simultaneously. • Students are moving in and out of groups, sometimes teacher-directed and often student-directed. • Physical layout of classroom may appear messy with furniture, computer technologies and print resources.
Tolerance for ambiguity and flexibility in management	Extent to which teachers manage the ambiguity and flexibility characteristic of student-centered learning.	• Teacher is not the sole source of knowledge. • Many lines of inquiry may be underway by students. • Student progress may be more difficult to discern.
Confidence in integrating technology	The teacher's self-efficacy to successfully integrate software, hardware, and networks into teaching and learning.	• Technology is used as a tool for authentic learning not for acquisition of basic skills. • Technology is an integral resource. • Instruction will include technology training.
Integration of the new pedagogy with realities beyond the classroom	The student-centered learning is situated within a larger context of the school, district, state and national cultures. The teacher's ability to negotiate the new pedagogy within these realities will also affect the success.	• Students may be ill-prepared to accept new roles and responsibilities. • Standardized tests are not sensitive to project-based work. • Mandated curriculum competes with in-depth inquiries. • Individual teacher epistemologies must mesh with school climate.

noise, collaborations, movement (Muir & Tracy, 1999) and classroom reconfigurations (Windschitl & Sahl, 2002), change the tone and character of the learning environment. The level to which the teacher is comfortable with a more dynamic environment, as well as the physical dislocations inherent to student-centered learning, may also impact its success.

The third factor influenced in student-centered learning is *tolerance for ambiguity and flexibility in management* of the new learning environment. The comfort level factor concentrated on the physical aspects of the learning environment; this factor, however, addresses the psychological and social facets of integrating student-centered pedagogy. The extent to which teachers and learners manage the uncertainty of student-centered learning will determine how well they perform (DeRoma, Martin, & Kessler, 2000). The teacher must design lessons where "students must struggle to understand their environment and that for true growth to occur must learn to endure a period of mental discomfort or cognitive dissonance ... embrace uncertainty and learn to enjoy the struggle to make sense of their environment" (Applefield, Hubert, & Moallem, 2000, Ms. Blake's Classroom section, para. 3).

The fourth factor, *confidence in integrating technology* into the new learning environment, centers on the teacher's self-efficacy to successfully integrate software, hardware, and networks into the curriculum and their daily work. No Child Left Behind legislation has mandated meaningful use of computer technologies to support learning, and student-centered pedagogy has been identified as the strategies that make best use of computers for higher order and critical thinking (e.g., Bickford et al., 2002; Lowther, Ross, & Morrison, 2003). However, teacher epistemologies and philosophies about teaching and learning can impact the use of computer technologies (Windschitl & Sahl, 2002). Blending these technology tools with other more familiar resources in the classroom, such as globes, textbooks, and calculators, requires significant confidence in each teacher and student's reliance on the processes, methods, and knowledge to interact with these systems.

The fifth and final factor we will explore, *integration of the new pedagogy with realities beyond the classroom*, represents the current "state of affairs." This final factor situates the teachers' experiences of the student-centered pedagogy within a larger context, reflecting the broader educational culture's emphases on appropriate pedagogy, assessment, and student activities (Rovegno, 1994). The existing realities are the combined everyday challenges learners and teachers negotiate as new roles and responsibilities become evident, comfort levels fluctuate, tolerance for ambiguity and flexibility is managed, and confidence for integrating technology strengthens.

Interaction of the Factors

Although the five factors can be examined independent of one another, it is important to recognize that constant interaction is present—both within the new learning environment (i.e., classroom) and between the larger educational culture (i.e., school, district, state). As depicted in Figure 2.1, teachers in the learning context are influenced by the larger educational culture (arrows pointing in) and are also influencing the larger educational culture (arrows pointing out). The interaction and interplay between these two contexts is important to take into consideration when adopting a student-centered pedagogy. It is important the teacher understand that the learning environment in which the new ped-

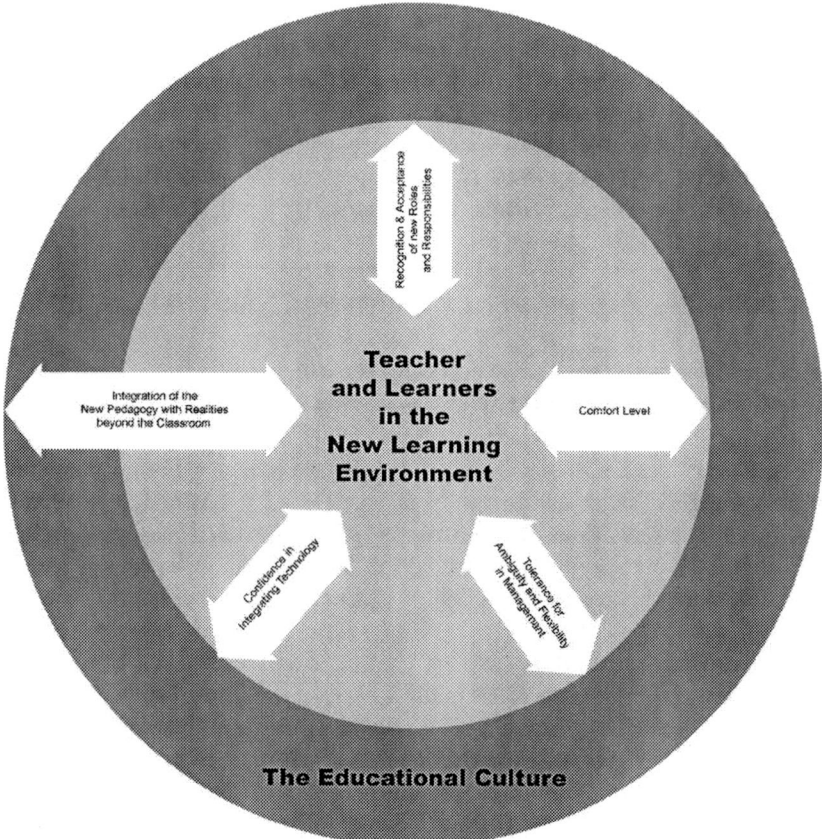

Figure 2.1. Interaction of the factors influencing the transition from a teacher-centered pedagogy to a student-centered pedagogy.

agogy will be implemented does not stand alone from the larger context, and that the larger context can have a constructive or damaging impact on the successful implementation of the student-centered pedagogy. For example, a teacher may be interested in adopting a new role for herself, and/or her students, but the larger school culture may not be willing or able to accept these new roles, such as with resistance from school or district administrators (see e.g., Passman, 2001; Rovegno, 1994).

It is also important for the teacher to recognize that the larger educational culture may also be making demands on the classroom learning environment, which the teacher is not prepared to implement. For example, the larger educational culture may expect that teachers be confident and capable in the area of technology integration, such as with a school-wide laptop program or the nationwide No Child Left Behind Act of 2001 requiring technological literacy by eighth grade. As such, the demands placed on the teachers may be perceived to be extensive—particularly if the teachers are not highly confident in their technological competence and/or are not provided with the professional development vital to sustain these initiatives. Understanding the influence of the factors for the teachers—within and outside of the learning environment—is critical if the student-centered pedagogy is to have a chance to be successful. The next sections explore these influences and discuss their implications.

EXAMINING THE INFLUENCE OF THE FACTORS ON TEACHERS

Recognition and Acceptance of New Roles and Responsibilities in Student-centered Learning

Some teachers are very successful and dynamic in a role that has come to be known as "sage on the stage" (King, 1993), where teachers lecture and students engage in passive learning activities, such as note taking and worksheets (Morrison & Lowther, 2005). In this teacher-centered model of instruction, the teacher directs the decisions of learning in the classroom.

The transition from directed teaching to a facilitator of learning in student-centered pedagogy, often called the "guide on the side" (King, 1993), may make some teachers feel less professionally satisfied. When teachers begin to move from the *director of learning* to a *collaborator for learners*, their responsibility for and control of learning is reduced. Hence, the value teachers place on the significance of their role in the classroom may also be reduced.

Moving to a facilitator of learning also shifts what the teacher teaches. The teacher now also teaches more self and group management skills in addition to the content (Tiene & Luft, 2001-2002). These "soft skills" include time management, project management, cooperation, and collaborations. Even as these skills are used in didactic instruction, they are perhaps less obvious to the learner because the teacher directs many of the learning activities. As the learner takes on more responsibilities, the teacher has to supplement the instruction with management skills if learners are to be successful.

In many instances, it may be difficult for the teacher to "give away" the responsibility for learning. One teacher's sentiment, published in a paper by Passman (2001), summarizes this position: "But still, underneath it all, I am responsible for scores and grades" (p. 196). As students take more responsibility and control over topic and means, the transactional distance (Moore, 1993) between teacher and learner may increase. Or more simply, a teacher may feel disconnected from her learners. While meeting one-on-one in a 50-minute class period with learners can help address this, a teacher may not be able to meet with each student each day.

In a teacher-directed classroom, the teacher has a firm grasp of the body of content the students must negotiate, because the teacher has determined the curricular content ahead of time. Student-centered classrooms may have students directing their own investigations into areas that are unfamiliar to the teacher. During instances when the content is unfamiliar, the teacher may be uncomfortable in making suggestions to guide students and facilitate the learning, receding into the background of the classroom (Brush & Saye, 2000).

Many student-centered pedagogies also employ in-depth investigations, where different areas of content are researched (e.g., Blumenfeld et al., 1991; Levstik & Barton, 2001). The broad scope of content may place additional pressures on the teacher (see e.g., Tiene & Luft, 2001-2002). This shift in content may further emphasize the differences in responsibilities and may result in uncertainty regarding expertise. Currently, however, teachers feel little flexibility to experiment or implement these types of inquiry. For example, during an on-going study in Tennessee, one seventh grade science and pre-algebra teacher in an email noted,

> I fear that the investigations would take students away from the state measured skills. I do believe that students should be able to explore their own interests about a given topic; however, with the amount of material needed to be covered and the strict guidelines set forth by the school district, there is very little time for this.

Finally, assessment strategies also differ between teacher-centered and student-centered classrooms. In teacher-centered instruction, Hirumi (2002) suggests that "assessments are (a) used to sort students, (b) primarily paper-and-pencil tests, (c) where the teacher determines the level of performance, and (d) where students must seek out what the teacher wants them to learn" (p. 11). Student-centered classrooms conversely have the potential to offer a different perspective: "Assessments are (a) framed and critically linked to learning; (b) performance-based, emphasizing the application of knowledge and skills; [and] (c) built through collaborations between teachers and students to determine levels of performance" (Hirumi, 2002, p.11). Surprisingly, some teachers currently feel they have quite a bit of autonomy and flexibility to implement various forms of assessments. In the Tennessee study mentioned previously, one fifth grade science teacher, representative of many others, said,

> Basically, we are told to use all forms of assessments: classwork, quizzes, homework, projects, presentations, tests, and unit tests. We are encouraged to use a format that appears on the [state-mandated test] so that the children will not be confused by the appearance of this test. However, we are given a tremendous amount of flexibility.

Comfort Level in Student-Centered Learning

Many teacher-centered classrooms organize students and desks into neat columns and rows, promoting order and physically separating the students from one another (Passman, 2001). This structure discourages group collaborations, peer reviews, sharing resources, movement, and noise. A teacher-centered classroom may appear to place value on isolating the individual within the learning environment.

A student-centered environment, however, is not dictated by the instructional space. Classroom structures in student-centered learning are variable (Applefield et al., 2000). A classroom may be configured as a large circle of desks, or a teacher may organize the classroom into clusters of two to five students. Learners in a student-centered environment are often collaborating and discussing activities with others in their grouping or another set, fluidly moving in and out of clusters.

As students move about the classroom, discussing content with one another and accessing resources, such as computers and the Internet, reference books, and calculators, a teacher could easily feel her classroom is out of her control. For example, one fifth grade social studies teacher paired students to create electronic presentations of events and people from the mid to late twentieth century (see Grant et al., 2005). Each dyad chose their own topic; however, the pairs sought out help with information-seeking and technical assistance from other individuals in the class. The numerous simultaneous student activities and discussions can lead to increased noise levels as well (Moursund, 1999). This level of movement and activity can be disquieting and uncomfortable to a teacher more accustomed to a controlled learning environment.

In some instances, the physical layout is insufficient to accommodate student-centered pedagogies. Teachers may direct students to meet in corners of the classroom for discussions or to work on the classroom floor in order to spread out their materials and resources. In other circumstances, the classroom itself is inadequate; and teachers may lead students to computer labs, the media center, or borrow spaces like corridors, the cafeteria, art room, or auditorium.

Tolerance for Ambiguity and Flexibility in Management of Student-Centered Learning

In directed classrooms, the management of learning is often highly controlled. As mentioned previously, learners are typically interacting with content that the teacher has command of, so questions about the content are often limited in scope. Learner-centered classrooms have students investigating areas that may be unfamiliar to the teacher, and many areas may be under investigation within one classroom. The range of questions about content, learning decisions, relevancy, and importance can be quite broad.

The teacher has to be confident in the process of managing this dynamic environment while continuing to aid learners in becoming critical thinkers. Teachers must also be comfortable working with ill-defined, ambiguous contexts. As stated by DeRoma and colleagues (2000), teachers need "ambiguity-tolerance in the classroom to teach students how to better interface with unavoidable ambiguities in everyday life" (p. 107). Along with facilitating problem solving associated with curricular content, teachers must model, scaffold, and coach (Collins, Brown, & Newman, 1990). Teachers model learning strategies, providing support (i.e., scaffolding) as needed, gradually fading the support (i.e., coaching) as students become more knowledgeable.

In a teacher-centered classroom, the teacher is the primary instructional resource. In contrast, the resources available for student-centered investigations are endless, coming from a variety of sources. Hill and Hannafin (2001) classify resources as print, electronic, and human. Resources may include books, museum artifacts, photographs, maps, Web sites, CD-ROMs, videos, and interviews and/or discussions with experts or more knowledgeable peers. Access, time, and imagination may be the only limits to the resources used for any particular task. The use of a variety of resources is not without challenges. Locating and reviewing existing resources, as well as developing original ones, that promote and support higher-order thinking skills in a student-centered approach can be a consuming task.

Student-centered classrooms also try to integrate authentic tasks that are practical and relevant to the lives of learners or reflect the activities of practitioners in the field (e.g., Herrington & Oliver, 2000; Honebein, Duffy, & Fishman, 1993). The complexities of these tasks typically require more instructional time, competing with the efficiency of learning (Lee, 2003). For example, seventh graders at Scott Middle School designed and produced scale drawings of their dream homes, including justifying the cost of constructing their home with average costs per square foot, salaries, and mortgages (Weidemann & Braddock Hunt, 1997). Additionally, these tasks can be more difficult to manage because they are not segmented, decontextualized pieces of instruction. Instead these tasks cover concepts that are regularly more challenging, or they may include steps normally excluded in direct instruction. The students at Scott Middle School, for example, needed practice reading commercial builder's plans before they could begin designing their own homes.

Confidence in Integrating Technology into Student-Centered Learning

Many student-centered pedagogies include technology as integral to the learning process or project investigations. Project-based science serves as one example where technology is fundamental to the authentic tasks (Blumenfeld, Krajcik, Marx, & Soloway, 1994; Blumenfeld et al., 1991). Teachers guide student investigations reflecting the actual work of scientists in the field. As such, they use processes and tools like scientists. A Colorado environmental education program, for example, used handheld data collection devices to test soil characteristics, such as surface temperature, pH, porosity, permeability, and percolation during the construction of a wetlands project (Orey, Winward, & DiStephano, 2001).

Emphases from the No Child Left Behind Title II, Part D legislation have also increased the focus on educational technologies for K-12 teachers. While the proceeding example illustrates the advantages of using technology in the classroom, the use of technology can also bring the need to adopt additional roles, such as compelling an instructor to be a teacher of technology and/or a troubleshooter. Often in adopting the use of technology, the teacher may be viewed as an advocate for technology (i.e., a "technology-using teacher").

Integrating technology as part of the curriculum may mean less time for other curricular content. If an English instructor chooses to include hypermedia presentations as the final product of a project, then other curriculum content, such as discussing the novel *To Kill a Mockingbird*, must be shortened or removed from the curriculum altogether in order to accommodate the learning and use of the software. The advantages of learning these new skills may be reaped later in the course, but the teacher must make instructional decisions about the value of content and the need to spend more time on specific areas of content over others.

Integration of Student-Centered Learning with Realities beyond the Classroom

As with any educational innovation, success is not guaranteed. Some students may learn more with a student-centered pedagogy; some students will struggle with the added responsibilities. "A real challenge in developing extended project and thematic units is that it takes a great deal of time and effort" (Lee, 2003, p. 455). Teachers must make instructional decisions about breadth versus depth of curricular content.

Another reality often faced in student-centered learning relates to the assessment structure. The extra effort teachers put forth to employ student-centered pedagogy may not be rewarded. Standardized test scores may not change; or worse, they could go down. Standardized tests cover a broader scope of curricular content and may not be sensitive enough to reflect the more thorough in-depth study of specific subjects often associated with student-centered strategies, such as project-based learning and problem-based learning.

In addition, sources of resistance to using student-centered pedagogies come from a variety of sources. Tensions can develop among teachers who are using student-centered pedagogies and those who are not. Bickford et al. (2002) contend that teachers feel pressure to stay on schedule with grade-level colleagues. Pelletier et al. (2002) suggest pressures exist from colleagues, administrators, and the curriculum. Barksdale-Ladd and Thomas (2000) argue that teachers express stress and shame for low-performing students, specifically when their names are public record in local newspapers.

IMPLICATIONS FOR EVERYDAY TEACHING AND LEARNING

Certainly, there are challenges associated with student-centered learning. The challenges depicted above echo stress factors from previous findings (e.g., Wiley, 2000), including role conflict, role ambiguity, time demands, and inadequate training. These challenges are not trivial, nor are they isolated; the teacher and learner share them. The risks and potential stressors may take teachers interested in using student-centered pedagogy aback.

At first glance, the list of challenges can appear so daunting that the reaction may be to recoil from a student-centered approach. However, the potential benefits to students are significant, including: learning to learn, metacognitive strategies promoting self-directed and self-regulated learning, desires for lifelong learning, task and process management, higher-order and critical thinking skills, and team and group dynamics in addition to academic achievement with fundamental curricular content. We must find ways to address the risks and stress in order to reduce the psychological, physical, and work-related effects (Wiley, 2000) that harm teachers and reduce the quality of education for learners. In the following paragraphs, we present ways to address the challenges and to take the steps necessary to move forward with the successful implementation of student-centered approaches. Many of these methods are indicative of coping strategies reviewed by Lazarus and Folkman (1984). Examples of the strategies include problem-focused forms of coping centered on the environment and the self, and the emotional-physical, psychosocial, and personal-intellectual needs identified by Gold and Roth (1993). Lazarus and Folkman also describe emotion-focused coping strategies, where teachers receive social support from other teachers to help them deal with stress-produced emotions in implementing student-centered environments.

Recognition and Acceptance of New Roles and Responsibilities in Student-Centered Learning Revisited

Although role conflicts and role ambiguity are sources of stress, teachers must identify their roles and responsibilities in student-centered learning and continue to be the instructional leaders in their classrooms. Confidence in these responsibilities could help reduce their perceived stress.

The responsibility changes demanded in a student-centered approach create a need for new skills. For the teacher, it means an increased awareness of management strategies at the individual and group level. It also means an understanding of how to assist learners with acquiring *soft skills* (e.g., group interactions, time management). As learners move through the various stages of group formation—forming, storming, norming, and performing (Tuckman, 1965)—teachers will need to help guide the process and give direction. The benefits of cooperative and collaborative learning (see e.g., Johnson & Johnson, 1989) are not a given, and literature (e.g., Socha & Socha, 1994) suggests learners need practice.

As students begin to direct their own investigations, teachers must remain confident in their ability to facilitate learning and the decisions associated with learning. The teacher may be one of a number of resources in a student-centered context. However, that does not mean the teacher does not have a role. Teachers must remain visible in the classroom to help individuals and groups successfully negotiate the many possible paths through the content.

Within these role and responsibility shifts, assessment also transforms. Teachers now can collaborate with students to develop formal and self assessments (Hirumi, 2002). Also, as group negotiation skills are taught, critical peer assessment skills can also be incorporated into student-centered learning.

Another area of need relates to soft skills (e.g., negotiation, small group interaction). While the ability to teach soft skills may not be difficult to acquire, it may not be a part of preservice education on a widespread basis (Bouas, 1996). We need to provide additional outlets so that inservice teachers can acquire these skills once they are in the classroom, as well as incorporate these skills into preservice teacher programs. Learning new skills is one method for coping with stress (Lazarus & Folkman, 1984). So, feelings of inadequacy to implement these strategies may be overcome.

Comfort Level in Student-Centered Learning Revisited

Student-centered pedagogy does not dictate the learning environment or the classroom organization (Applefield et al., 2000). Teachers can offer learners the opportunity to work in a variety of environments, including computer labs, science labs, library/media centers, and drama rooms. Teachers and learners will also need to become comfortable in working individually, as well as in teams. As individual work continues to play a role in student-centered approaches, group work is also an important component. Working to acquire skills related to team-based approaches is an important activity in student-centered environments.

Teachers may also choose to be cognizant of environmental factors associated with learning styles (e.g., Dunn & Dunn, 1978; Dunn & Price, 1997), such as lighting and noise levels. Elementary teachers and secondary teachers with block schedules or extended periods may find it beneficial to offer a variety of learning environments, such as quiet times, music, and soft lighting. These may be associated with specific recurrent tasks, such as music with testing (see e.g., Muir & Tracy, 1999), or soft lighting with free reading.

Tolerance for Ambiguity and Flexibility in Management of Student-Centered Learning Revisited

It is important to emphasize that, as mentioned above, ambiguity and flexibility inherent to student-centered learning does not denote a lack of structure within instruction (Applefield et al., 2000). For example, teachers are very accustomed to providing summative feedback to learners as they complete assignments and projects. Formative assessment feedback—feedback that comes as a project is developed and used to adjust teaching and learning (see e.g., Black & Wiliam, 1998)—becomes an integral part of the equation in student-centered learning. Even though the learner plays a central role in defining many of the parameters in student-centered learning, the teacher continues to facilitate the process, helping the learners with refining goals, selecting resources, creating elements in the project, and so forth. In the laptop project study described earlier, a seventh grade math teacher explained this role as, "Students do not have 100% autonomy. I still have to monitor and assist as they complete their projects and/or investigations." Many of the teachers participating in the studies continued to see the importance of their role in the process, even in student-centered contexts. Feedback, important in any educational setting, is critical in more student-centered environments, where traditional roles and responsibilities may be shifted and comfort levels may not be as stable (McCown, Driscoll, & Roop, 1996).

Another skill that is fundamental in student-centered learning is the ability to *know what you know* and *know what you don't*—in short, having a robust set of metacognitive strategies to manage the learning process. Research has indicated that possessing a robust set of metacognitive strategies can assist the learner when working in more ill defined contexts (see e.g., Hill & Hannafin, 1997), helping mitigate the innate ambiguity for learners. Reflection is one strategy that has proven effective for enhancing metacognition (Palinscar & Brown, 1984; Scardamalia, 1984). Teachers can employ monitoring methods, ranging from open writing and reflecting on the process (e.g., reflective journaling; Spaulding & Wilson, 2002) to posing questions and answering the questions (e.g., double entry journals [Hughes, Kooy, & Kanevskym, 1997]) to reflecting on what is known and what I want to learn (e.g., KWL strategies; Carr & Ogle, 1987; Ogle, 1986).

Because of the open-ended nature of student-centered work, it can be difficult to put well-defined parameters around how much time should be committed to any one part of the project. However, practitioners suggest that establishing a schedule can help significantly with the completion of a project (see e.g., Stephens, 1996). Carefully thinking through the tasks associated with the project and assigning specific deadlines to accomplish individual tasks substantially increases the chances of project completion. Whole-class progress charts may also help the teacher monitor individual student progress.

To aid in tolerating the ambiguity, teachers may also use instructional strategies that specify roles for the learners, such as WebQuests (Dodge, 1995, 1998) and jigsaw teams (Aronson & Patnow, 1997; http://www.jigsaw.org). These strategies identify tasks for each member of teams in order to increase student accountability.

Confidence in Integrating Technology Into Student-Centered Learning Revisited

The central role that the computer plays in teaching and learning continues to increase. Teachers often teach technology skills as a part of adopting a student-centered model, but technology itself is not the focus of the lesson. For example, an elementary school that used Hypercard®, a multimedia development tool created by Apple®, with a project to learn geography discovered teachers viewed the technology as a mediator for learning—a means to an end to facilitate finding, manipulating, organizing and, presenting information—while students viewed learning the technology as an end in itself (Lundeberg, Coballes-Vega, Standiford, Langer, & Dibble, 1997). Working to reconcile these differing perspectives is a challenge that needs to be met.

The capabilities of and desirability for technology tools also dictate the need for a stable infrastructure in which the technology can operate. It is no longer sufficient to rely upon the out-dated, often inefficient, technology found in many schools. Schools continue to be plagued by inconsistent network access (e.g., Grant et al., 2004; Grant et al., 2005). To succeed with student-centered learning, teachers and students need up-to-date, robust, and reliable computer technologies. Specifically, teachers need commitments from school and district personnel for dependable networks. This will enable teachers to not only locate the resources they need for curricular tasks, it will also enable them to do their work with greater efficiency.

The expertise in using technology does not necessarily rest on the teacher alone. Technology in the classroom can be regarded as a tool that is everyone's responsibility to use, maintain, and support, including learners. Leveraging the learners' knowledge and skills about the technology can motivate the learners and advance the teacher's own knowledge and skills, developing a classroom learning community (Wenger, 1998), alleviating the teacher's perception she must be the *only* computer expert in the classroom.

Integration of the New Pedagogy with Realities Beyond the Classroom Revisited

One of the everyday realities of the classroom is that there are real constraints on time. Multiple topics are covered and myriad activities occur within the 7 to 8 hours that a teacher and student are together. Working to maximize the time spent on any one given topic or activity becomes critical.

As we have already discussed, student-centered learning takes more time than traditional, lecture-type delivery of information. And even though many teachers would like to do all instruction from a student-centered perspective, this may not always be realistic. Scott (1994) recommends that proactive management of the learning environment can assist with this challenge. For example, rather than doing many projects back to back, Scott recommends integrating student-centered approaches around other kinds of activities, with the potential goal of completing two large projects during one academic year.

Some of the strongest coping resources available to teachers may be outside themselves and their classrooms. Pressures to maintain pace with other teachers may prevent the implementation of student-centered approaches (Bickford et al., 2002). Teachers may find it beneficial to use team teaching and participative decision making (Wiley, 2000) within grade levels to accomplish multiple curricular objectives within a larger project. Social and peer supports (Lazarus & Folkman, 1984; Gold & Roth, 1993) from colleagues and administrators may mitigate some of the demands to match other classrooms, and it may work to relieve some of the stresses associated with colleagues. Brewer and Daane (2002) assert that teachers who share the same philosophy and epistemology "offer each other a strong support system, encourage professional growth and provide a sounding board for one another" (p. 421).

Equally important, school administrators must endorse the time and efforts necessary to realize student-centered pedagogies. Administrative support as an example of social support can help teachers reduce their perceived stress (Lazarus & Folkman, 1984; Wiley, 2000). Other social supports, such as study groups, mentoring programs, and induction programs help to address the emotional-physical needs and intellectual needs of teachers, potentially alleviating stress (Gold & Roth, 1993).

Integrating student-centered approaches within the context of other activities will also address another reality teachers face in the current educational climate: the value placed on standardized testing as the primary assessment mechanism. Having students complete two or three projects during an academic year will give them the experience of working in a more open-ended, student-driven learning environment without sacrificing the need to attend to other content. A middle school math teacher from Tennessee explained, "Our investigations are based upon the constructivist approach and have very clear objectives." In striking a balance, the teacher and students are empowered to explore a variety of pedagogical methods and at the same time continuing to meet the demands of the larger educational culture.

Finally, it is important to acknowledge that as with any pedagogy, student-centered instruction will empower some learners and disempower others. Students who are accustomed to success in the teacher-centered classroom may be disenfranchised with student-centered learning. As "A students" and "the smart kids," these learners may struggle with their increased roles and responsibilities in the new learning environment. The teacher must pay extra attention to these to make sure they continue to succeed and be leaders in the classroom.

CONCLUSION

Dede (2004) summarizes current perspectives and future prospects for education:

> The most important challenge the U.S. education system faces is not preparing students to do well on high-stakes tests, but rather fostering 21st century skills and knowledge in learners so that they are prepared to participate in our global, knowledge-based civilization [and].... Current professional development that focuses on how to optimize teachers' knowledge and skills within the current high-stakes testing environment is tactically useful but strategically inadequate. (pp. 12, 16)

These statements underscore the significance for implementing the types of pedagogy indicative of student-centered learning and essential for the Information Age. However, innovative pedagogy comes with risks, and risks have the potential for stress. We must find ways to mitigate these risks and the stress associated with the teaching and learning environment. By identifying and exercising coping resources, such as more positive personal beliefs, problem-solving skills, social skills, and social supports (Lazarus & Folkman, 1983), teachers have the potential to overcome the challenges that prevent them from implementing student-centered learning strategies.

Some suggest that student-centered learning only benefits the students. However, teachers have an opportunity for gains as well. Increased professional satisfaction, self-confidence, and pride in their work and students can contribute to their emotional-physical needs (Gold & Roth, 1993) and well-being. Teachers need to understand the risks they assume with student-centered pedagogy within high stakes testing—for their learners and themselves. The simple acknowledgment of these risks may in fact help relieve stress as well.

AUTHOR'S NOTE

Correspondence concerning this article may also be addressed to Janette R. Hill, Instructional Technology, The University of Georgia, 604 Aderhold Hall, Athens, Georgia, 30606. Email: janette@coe.uga.edu

NOTES

1. See Hill et al. (in press) for a more detailed description of the methods used for these studies.
2. While we understand that other stakeholders, such as administrators, students, and parents, influence and are also affected by instructional decisions, discussing these in depth are beyond the scope of this chapter.

REFERENCES

Applefield, J. M., Huber, R. L., & Moallem, M. (2000). Constructivism in theory and practice: Toward a better understanding. *High School Journal, 84*(2), 35-53.

Aronson, E., & Patnoe, S. (1997). *The jigsaw classroom: Building cooperation in the classroom* (2nd ed.). New York: Addison Wesley Longman.

Barksdale-Ladd, M. A., & Thomas, K. F. (2000). What's at stake in high-stakes testing: Teachers and parents speak out. *Journal of Teacher Education, 51*(5), 384-397.

Barrows, H. S., & Tamblyn, R. M. (1980). *Problem-based learning: An approach to medical education.* New York: Springer.

Bickford, A., Tharp, S., McFarling, P., & Beglau, M. (2002). Finding the right fuel for new engines of learning. *Multimedia Schools, 9*(5), 18-26.

Black, P., & Wiliam, D. (1998). Inside the black box: Raising standards through classroom assessment. *Phi Delta Kappan, 80*(2), 139-144.

Blumenfeld, P. C., Krajcik, J. S., Marx, R. W., & Soloway, E. (1994). Lessons learned: A collaborative model for helping teachers learn project-based instruction. *Elementary School Journal, 94*, 539-551.

Blumenfeld, P. C., Soloway, E., Marx, R. W., Krajcik, J. S., Guzdial, M., & Palinscar, A. (1991). Motivating project-based learning: Sustaining the doing, supporting the learning. *Educational Psychologist, 26*(3 & 4), 369-398.

Bouas, M. J. (1996). Are we giving cooperative learning enough attention in preservice teacher education? *Teacher Education Quarterly, 23*(4), 45-58.

Brewer, J., & Daane, C. J. (2002). Translating constructivist theory into practice in primary-grade mathematics. *Education, 123*(2), 416-426.

Brush, T., & Saye, J. (2000). Implementation and evaluation of a student-centered learning unit: A case study. *Educational Technology Research & Development, 48*(3), 79-100.

Carr, E., & Ogle, D. M. (1987). A strategy for comprehension and summarization. *Journal of Reading, 30*(7), 626-631.

Collins, A., Brown, J. S., & Newman, S. E. (1990). Cognitive apprenticeship: Teaching the crafts of reading, writing, and mathematics. In L. B. Resnick (Ed.), *Knowing, learning, and instruction: Essays in honor of Robert Glaser* (pp. 453-494). Hillsdale, NJ: Erlbaum.

DeRoma, V. M., Martin, K. M., & Kessler, M. L. (2000). The relationship between tolerance for ambiguity and need for course structure. *Journal of Instructional Psychology, 30*(2), 104-109.

Dodge, B. (1995, May 5). *Some thoughts about WebQuests*. Retrieved August 7, 2001, from http://edweb.sdsu.edu/courses/edtect596/about_webquests.html

Dodge, B. (1998, June 22-24). *WebQuests: A strategy for scaffolding higher level learning*. Paper presented at the National Educational Computing Conference, San Diego, CA.

Dede, C. (2004, September). Enabling distributed learning communities via emerging technologies—Part one. *T.H.E. Journal, 32*, 12-22.

Dunn, R., & Dunn, K. (1978). *Teaching students through their individual learning styles: A practical approach*. Englewood Cliffs, NJ: Prentice Hall.

Dunn, R., & Price, G.E. (1997). *Learning styles inventory*. Lawrence, KS: Price Systems.

George, A. A., Hall, G. E., & Uchiyama, K. (2000). Extent of implementation of standards-based approach to teaching mathematics and student outcomes. *Journal of Classroom Interaction, 35*(1), 8-25.

Gold, Y., & Roth, R. A. (1993). *Teachers managing stress and preventing burnout: The professional health solution*. London: Falmer Press.

Grant, M. M. (2002). *Individual differences in constructionist learning environments: Qualitative inquiry into computer mediated learning artifacts*. Unpublished doctoral dissertation, The University of Georgia, Athens, GA.

Grant, M. M. (2003). *Supporting technology integration onsite: Theory, cases and lessons learned* (Policy and Planning Series No. 106). Alexandia, VA: Appalachian Technology in Education Consortium.

Grant, M. M., Key, S. G., & Abdi, S. W. (2004, October). *Zoocam and real time Internet video: Zoological observations with classroom computers*. Paper presented at The Association for Educational Communications and Technology annual conference, Chicago, IL.

Grant, M. M., Ross, S. M., Wang, W., Potter, A., & Wilson, Y. (2005, April 11-15). *Computers on wheels (COWS): An alternative to 'each one has one.'* Paper presented at the American Educational Research Association annual conference, Montreal, Canada.

Hancock, P. A., Ward, P., Szalma, J. L., Stafford, S., & Ganey, H. C. N. (2004, November 29-December 2). *Stress and human information processing: A descrip-*

tive framework presented in a novel manner. Paper presented at the 24th Army Science Conference, Orlando, FL.

Hannafin, M., Land, S., & Oliver, K. (1999). Open learning environments: Foundations, methods, and models. In C. Reigeluth (Ed.), *Instructional design theories and models, Volume II*. Mahwah, NJ: Erlbaum.

Harel, I., & Papert, S. (Eds.). (1991). *Constructionism*. Norwood, NJ: Ablex.

Herrington, J., & Oliver, R. (2000). An instructional design framework for authentic learning environments. *Educational Technology Research & Development, 48*(3), 23-48.

Hill, J. R., & Hannafin, M. J. (1997). Cognitive strategies and learning from the World Wide Web. *Educational Technology Research & Development, 45*(4), 37-64.

Hill, J.R., & Hannafin, M. J. (2001). Teaching and learning in digital environments: The resurgence of resource-based learning. *Educational Technology, Research & Development, 49*(3), 37-52.

Hill, J. R., Reeves, T. C., Grant, M. M., Wang, S. K., & Hans, S. (in press). Learning in a wireless environment: The successes and challenges of ubiquitous computing in a school. In C. Vrasidas & G. V. Glass (Eds.), *Current perspectives on applied information technologies: Preparing teachers to teach with technology* (Vol. II). Greenwich, CT: Information Age.

Hirumi, A. (2002). Student-centered, technology-rich learning environments (SCenTRLE): Operationalizing constructivist approaches to teaching and learning. *Journal of Technology and Teacher Education, 10*(4), 497-537.

Honebein, P. C., Duffy, T. M., & Fishman, B. J. (1993). Constructivism and the design of learning environments: Context and authentic activities for learning. In T. M. Duffy, J. Lowyck, & D. H. Jonassen (Eds.), *Designing environments for constructive learning* (pp. 87-108). Berlin: Springer-Verlag.

Hughes, H. W., Kooy, M., & Kanevsky, L. (1997). Dialogic reflection and journaling. *The Clearing House, 70*(4), 187-190.

Johnson, D. W., & Johnson, R. T. (1989). *Cooperation and competition: Theory and research*. Edina, MN: Interaction.

King, A. (1993). From sage on the stage to guide on the side. *College Teaching, 41*(1), 30-35.

Lazarus, R.S., & Folkman, S. (1984). *Stress, appraisal and coping*. New York: Springer.

Lee, J. O. (2003). Implementing high standards In urban schools: Problems and solutions. *Phi Delta Kappan, 84*(6), 449-455.

Levstik, L. S., & Barton, K. C. (2001). *Doing history*. Mahwah, NJ: Erlbaum.

Lord, T. R. (1999). A comparison between traditional and constructivist teaching in environmental science. *Journal of Environmental Education, 30*(3), 22-27.

Lowther, D. L., Ross, S. M., & Morrison, G. M. (2003). When each one has one: The influences on teaching strategies and student achievement of using laptops in the classroom. *Educational Technology, Research & Development, 51*(3), 23-44.

Lundeberg, M. A., Coballes-Vega, C., Standiford, S. N., Langer, L., & Dibble, K. (1997). We think they're learning: Beliefs, practices, and reflections of two teachers using project-based learning. *Journal of Computing in Childhood Education, 8*(1), 59-81.

McCown, R., Driscoll, M. P., & Roop, P. (1996). *Educational psychology: A learning-centered approach to classroom practice* (2nd ed.). Needham Heights, MA: Allyn & Bacon.

Moore, M. G. (1993). Theory of transactional distance. In D. Keegan (Ed.), *Theoretical priciples of distance education* (pp. 22-38). New York: Routledge.

Morrison, G. M., & Lowther, D. L. (2005). *Integrating computer technology into the classroom* (3rd ed.). Upper Saddle River, NJ: Pearson Prentice Hall.

Moursund, D. (1999). *Project-based learning using information technology*. Eugene, OR: International Society for Technology in Education.

Muir, S. P., & Tracy, D. M. (1999). Collaborative essay writing. *College Teaching, 47*(1), 33.

Nieto, S. (2003). Challenging current notions of "highly qualified teachers" through work in a teachers' inquiry group. *Journal of Teacher Education, 54*(5), 386-398.

No Child Left Behind Act of 2001, Pub. L. No. 107-110, § 2204 (2002).

Ogle, D. M. (1986). K-W-L: A teaching model that develops active reading of expository text. *Reading Teacher, 39*(6), 564-570.

Olsen, D. G. (1999). Constructivist principles of learning and teaching methods. *Education, 120*(2), 347-355.

Orey, M., Winward, S., & DiStephano, B. (2001, November). *A project-based environmental education program using hand-held data collection technology with Denver area high school at-risk students*. Paper presented at the annual meeting of the Association for Educational Communications and Technology, Atlanta, GA.

Palinscar, A., & Brown, A. (1984). Reciprocal teaching of comprehension-fostering and monitoring activities. *Cognition & Instruction, 1*(2), 117-175.

Passman, R. (2001). Experiences with student-centered teaching and learning in high-stakes assessment environments. *Education, 122*(1), 189-199.

Pelletier, L. G., Séguin-Lévesque, C., & Legault, L. (2002). Pressure from above and pressure from below as determinants of teachers' motivation and teaching behaviors. *Journal of Educational Psychology, 94*(1), 186-196.

Rovegno, I. (1994). Teaching within a curricular zone of safety: School culture and the situated nature of student teachers' pedagogical content knowledge. *Research Quarterly for Exercise and Sport, 65*(3), 269-280.

Scardamalia, M. (1984). Teachability of reflective processes in written composition. *Cognitive Science, 8*(2), 173-190.

Scott, C. (1994). Project-based science: Reflections of a middle school teacher. *Elementary School Journal, 57*(1), 1-22.

Secker, C. V. (2002). Effects of inquiry-based teacher practices on science excellence and equity. *Journal of Educational Research, 95*(3), 151-160.

Socha, T. J., & Socha, D. M. (1994). Children's task-group communication. In L. R. Frey (Ed.), *Group communication in context: Studies of natural groups*. Hillsdale, NJ: Erlbaum.

Spaulding, E., & Wilson, A. (2002). Demystifying reflection: A study of pedagogical strategies that encourage reflective journal writing. *Teachers College Record, 104*(7), 1393-1421.

Stephens, K. R. (1996). Product development for gifted students. *Gifted Child Today Magazine, 19*, 18-21.

Tiene, D., & Luft, P. (2001-2002). Classroom dynamics in a technology-rich learning environment. *Learning & Leading with Technology, 29*(4), 10-13.

Tuckman, B. W. (1965). Developmental sequence in small groups. *Psychological Bulletin, 63*, 384-399.

Weidemann, W., & Braddock Hunt, J. (1997). Using house plans to teach ratio, proportion and more! *Mathematics Teaching in the Middle School, 3*, 14-18.

Wenger, E. (1998). *Communities of practice: Learning, meaning, and identity*. Cambridge, England: Cambridge University Press.

Wiley, C. (2000). A synthesis of research on the causes, effects and reduction strategies of teacher stress. *Journal of Instructional Psychology, 27*(2), 80-87.

Windschitl, M., & Sahl, K. (2002). Tracing teachers' use of technology in a laptop computer school: The interplay of teacher beliefs, social dynamics and institutional culture. *American Educational Research Journal, 39*(1), 165-205.

CHAPTER 3

TEACHER STRESS AND HIGH STAKES TESTING

How Using One Measure of Academic Success Leads to Multiple Teacher Stressors

Sandra Mathison and Melissa Freeman

In a naturalistic study exploring the impact of outcome-based accountability on teaching and assessment practices in 3 school districts, teachers identify increased stress as a prime effect. The teachers' experiences and their perspectives on stress are analyzed as being the result of transactions between themselves and the workplace environment. This chapter identifies and outlines some of the changes made to the workplace and to the nature of teachers' work brought about as a result of a high stakes accountability environment.

The spiraling demands of government initiatives, incessant record-keeping, education plans, targeting and inspections, have left teachers reeling. A working week of 50 hours is average. Many are doing 70. This is not only bad for teachers; it's harmful to children. (It's Time, 2001).

Our culture harbors romantic conceptions of teachers and teaching. We employ a rhetoric about teaching as both art and science, as a matter of the head and the heart. And it is. But, so too is teaching work, teachers are workers, and schools are workplaces. In the seminal study on teaching, Jackson (1968) describes the complex of essential and trivial events that make up life in classrooms including the many demands on teachers. In their analysis of Jackson's work, Vinson and Ross (2003) identify school as a workplace for teachers and students characterized as crowded, shaped by episodes of evaluation and praise, and inherently marked by hierarchical power relations. These attributes offer but a glimpse into the nature of schools that results in two thirds of teachers describing their work as "extremely stressful" (Proctor & Alexander, 1992).

This chapter analyzes the manifestations of teacher stress in elementary and middle schools, particularly as it relates to high stakes mandated student testing. Stress is not, in and of itself, a bad thing. Organizational researchers have long believed that modest amounts of workplace stress lead to greater senses of accomplishment and performance levels among employees (Quick, Quick, Nelson, & Hurrell, 1997; Selye, 1976). The relationship between stressors in the environment and the stress responses of individuals, however, is complex. Focus on this interaction originated in the work of Yerkes and Dodson (1908) who showed that learning and performance declined if the stressors became too great. Quick et al. (1997) explain: "[P]erformance increases with increasing stress loads up to an optimum point, and then the stress load becomes too great, resulting in depressed performance" (p. 4). This research suggests stress is best understood as the result of a complex of interactions, or transactions (Lazarus, 1990), between people and their environments, and that these interactions can have negative consequences when the environmental stressors exceed the physical, psychological or ethical propensities of the individual (Fontana & Abouserie, 1993).

In our own explorations of the impact of outcome-based accountability on teachers' teaching and assessment practices, teachers identified increased stress to be a significant effect. Although the work teachers essentially do (e.g., teaching the curriculum and assessing student progress) has not changed, the presence of high stakes testing has altered the nature of this work and has radically changed teachers' roles and relationships to others within the workplace. Teachers' experiences with high stakes mandated student testing point to the importance of understanding the manifestation of teacher stress in outcome based accountability as a relationship between environmental pressures and individual performance. Outcome based accountability rides on the belief that an increase in pressure and clear consequences for failure will increase teachers' ability to improve the performance of their students. While coping with stress depends to some extent on the individual capacity of teachers, we found that environmental conditions and the nature of the requirements played a significant role in whether the increased demands were perceived by teachers to be a positive source of motivation or to produce largely negative effects. The teachers' experiences revealed that high stakes accountability creates consistent responses across districts where stress is manifested in similar ways, but there are also district-specific differences that result in different levels and types of stress. In this chapter, we identify and describe some of the multiple stressors evidenced in this high stakes accountability environment and then show how particular workplace relationships and demands exacerbate these stressors in different ways.

THE STUDY AND CONTEXT

Elementary and middle school teachers from three demographically different school districts in upstate New York have been participating in our research on the impact of high stakes testing on teaching and learning.[1] The study is based on ethnographic case studies of schools, the aim of which is to develop an understanding of the actions, perceptions, beliefs, and ideas of participants within a shared setting and around a common issue, in this case the presence of high stakes testing. Over the course of a school year, we conducted weekly classroom observations, engaged in formal and informal interviews with teachers, and organized teacher focus groups around emerging themes.

Our research approach is naturalistic. We did not employ a preordinate design that directed our focus on any one aspect of the work of teachers and others. Instead, our data collection processes were open-ended and probing, and pursued themes that emerged within the context of our work with teachers. An inherent assumption in naturalistic research methods is that understanding any topic within a context begins by gathering the understandings, themes, and issues about the topic through close and multiple observations of and interviews with the people working within that context. Since the majority of the elementary and middle level state tests are given in fourth and eighth grade, our case study work has focused primarily on teachers in those grades. Teachers in other grade levels were invited to participate in focus groups and included in observations and interviews in limited ways. On average, 13 teachers from each case study school participated. In some cases, teachers from other schools within a district participated in a focus group. In total, 63 teachers from case study schools and 35 teachers from district-wide focus groups participated in this study.

Table 3.1. District and Case Study School Demographics 2001-2002

	\multicolumn{5}{c}{Districts}
	\multicolumn{2}{c}{Park City}	Willow Valley	\multicolumn{2}{c}{Orchard Hill}
Case study schools	Hemlock	Oak Ridge	Willow Elementary	Cherry Grove	Orchard Central
Total students	\multicolumn{2}{c}{8,338}	1,470	\multicolumn{2}{c}{3,342}
Grade level	PK-5	6-8	K-6	K-5	6-8
Enrollment	360	682	817	474	808
Total teachers	30	46	52	28	51
Other staff	3	4	5	6	9
Student Demographics					
Free lunch rates	90.3%	41.3%	47.6%	3.3%	2.5%
Reduced lunch rates	11.7%	10%	15.5%	1.3%	2.2%
American Indian, Alaskan, Asian, or Pacific Islander	0.3%	6.2%	2.6%	0.2%	1.4%
Black (not Hispanic)	34.7%	32.8%	16.4%	1.1%	0.7%
Hispanic	15%	8.2%	3.8%	0%	1.0%
White (not Hispanic)	50%	52.8%	77.2%	98.7%	96.9%

Note: Free and reduced lunch rates may exceed 100% when added, however, that is how the data are reported in New York State's Comprehensive Information Report for these districts.

The districts[2] vary in their size and demographics. Park City can generally be described as urban, largely minority, and poor; Willow Valley as urban, White, and working class, and Orchard Hill as suburban, White, and upper middle class. In each district, except for Willow Valley where only the elementary school participated, one elementary and one middle school were selected as case study schools (see Table 3.1 for district and case study school information).

Throughout the data collection process, we analyzed the data using a constant comparative approach to organize participant responses around common themes and perspectives. The constant comparative method is an inductive data coding process used for organizing and comparing qualitative data for analytical purposes, usually associated with the methodology of grounded theory. A theory is considered "grounded" when it is derived from everyday experience as constituted by the empirical data (Glaser & Strauss, 1967). Since the data represent multiple perspectives, this approach provides a way to systematically organize, compare, and understand the similarities and differences each case offers on the topic of inquiry as well as differences and similarities across cases. Through this process relationships between themes and constructs are built and a conceptual theory begins to take shape.

It is through this naturalistic research approach and iterative data analysis that our understanding of the nature of teacher stress in a high stakes testing environment has developed. Our findings support Cox, Griffiths, and Rial-Gonzalez (2000) suggestion that the conditions causing stress can be better understood through an analysis of workers' perceptions of that environment. So although stress was not a specific focus of our study, we have been able to identify specific themes and issues offered by teachers about the nature of their work as well as the nature of their workplace that produce significant stress responses. We chose the examples and quotes provided in this chapter because they most fully and explicitly describe the range of experiences shared by teachers in regards to stress. Other explanatory theories about work-related stress are incorporated to assist in the development of a comprehensive and grounded theoretical understanding of the empirical evidence provided by the teachers.

SITUATING TEACHER STRESS

Because teachers are workers, the stress they experience can and ought to be understood as occupational in nature, a result of both the nature of the workplace (i.e., schools) and the nature of their work (i.e., teaching). The literature on workplace stress reflects in significant ways the situations teachers in our study identified as causing stress. The examples from this literature provide a context for better understanding the experiences shared by teachers in our study.

In a study of teachers in British Columbia, Naylor (2001a, 2001b) found that teachers reported that their work is stressful. Reasons included the increased complexity of their work, such as working with students who speak English as a second language, those with special needs, or students living in poverty; the increased volume of work (dealing with curriculum changes, increases in state accountability through student testing, or work intensive periods, such as report card time or parent-teacher conferences); as well as a lack of time, respect, resources, and support.

A common stress-inducing condition that serves as a useful example is flat management structures. In many industrialized countries, schools have moved from a centralized organizational structure to one that is decentralized and referred to as site-based management. Site-based management and decision making thrusts teachers into new roles, ones they may not want or be comfortable with. As its name suggests, site-based management asks teachers to assume non-classroom, managerial duties, such as budgeting, hiring, purchasing, work scheduling, and so on. This flattening of the management of schools as workplaces has generally had deleterious effects on teachers (Smyth, 1993, 2002) by creating role overload.

Furthermore, occupations dominated by women show a high prevalence of stress. In a study on work-related appeal processes, Lippel (1999) describes how the dual roles for women (as workers and caregivers/homemakers) and their greater victimization from overt and covert violence (including sexual harassment) contribute significantly to greater workplace induced stress. She also shows that assumptions about women and women's work make it much more difficult for women to get their stressors attended to or dealt with by management, colleagues, and the legal system. "The very nature of women's work provides opportunity for both the development of psychological stressors and the nonrecognition of their consequences" (Lippel, 1999, p. 80). Teaching is done primarily by women, and even when men do it teaching remains largely women's work. And so because teaching is gender-based work, at least in our culture, this predisposes teachers to greater workplace stress.

There is a body of literature suggesting teachers have a vulnerability to stress because of their expectations, motivations, and coping styles. For many teachers there is an expectation they need to deal with whatever their workplace asks of them (Chorney, 1998), but it is equally plausible that stress results from the nature of the workplace. In particular, stress-inducing workplaces rely on external and controlling mechanisms, such as task contingent rewards, surveillance, evaluation, and threats of punishment (Deci, Connell, & Ryan, 1989). Such mechanisms run counter to what Deci and Ryan (1985) propose humans, and thus teachers, need—choice, noncontrolling feedback, and acceptance or acknowledgement of each other's perspective—to be motivated. Deci and Ryan's self-determination theory (SDT) suggests that workplace stress is the result of a collision between human nature and organizations.

> SDT is based on an organismic-dialectical meta-theory, which begins with the assumption that people are active organisms, with innate tendencies toward psychological growth and development, who strive to master ongoing challenges and to integrate their experiences into a coherent sense of self. This natural human tendency does not operate automatically, however, but instead requires ongoing nutriments and supports from the social environment in order to function effectively. That is, the social context can either support or thwart the natural tendencies toward active engagement and psychological growth. (Deci & Ryan, 1985, p. 35)[3]

In a study of teacher identity transformation under stress, Woods and Carlyle (2002) demonstrate the difficulties teachers have in maintaining a positive self-image during times of intense restructuring.

> Extreme, profound, and unsettling emotions are experienced at times of stress. Elsewhere, we have set out the connections between the onset and nature of these emotions and the restructuring of education and schools that has dominated the last decade or so, from the rational-technocratic discourse of performativity, heavy duty accountability, hierarchical managerialism, and intensification.... It can be no coincidence that stress in teaching (and in other occupations) has risen markedly over the last 10-15 years. (p. 170)

Woods and Carlyle show that while most teachers are able to recreate a new, positive sense of self, few do so within the workplaces that instigated the intense stress. They conclude that this may be reassuring from a mental health standpoint, but the losses and disruptions to educational systems are extremely disturbing and need to be addressed.

New demands placed on teachers everyday and an increased focus on the outcome of their work, makes understanding the nature of their work and workplace crucial. Table 3.2 provides a summary of the literature on workplace stress (Cox, Griffiths, & Rial-González, 2000). We have italicized the stress-inducing conditions that were repeatedly brought up by teachers in our study.

STRESS-RELATED CONDITIONS IN OUTCOME BASED ACCOUNTABILITY

The particular stress-related conditions we have analyzed here are manifest in a particular environment—an outcomes based accountability environment. Generally, outcomes based accountability is the establishment of externally formulated goals with content standards and a strict accountability system (that usually relies on high stakes tests) that taken together are presumed to lead to improvements in education. The logic is that if teachers know what goals they are aiming for and are equipped with the proper information they will be well positioned to increase the performance of students as measured by standardized tests. So, outcomes based accountability systems alter the workplace (in terms of reward structures, teacher professionalism, messages regarding goals, relationships) and the nature of teachers' work (fragmentation and deskilling of teachers).

Table 3.2. Summary of Conditions Creating Work-Related Stress

Elements of Work	Conditions Creating Stress
Nature of workplace	
Organizational culture and function	Poor communication, *lack of clear or conflicting organizational goals,* lack of problem-solving, lack of support for personal development, lean production, downsizing, *flat management structure.*
Leadership style	Controlling, bullying, inconsistency.
Role in organization	*Role ambiguity, role conflict, role overload,* responsibility for others, working outside skill level.
Career development	*Career stagnation, under and/or over promotion, low pay,* lack of job security, use of contingent labor.
Decision control	*Lack of control, lack of choice, low participation in decision making.*
Interpersonal relationships	*Social or physical isolation,* poor relationships with superiors, interpersonal conflict, lack of social support, *lack of personal safety.*
Role of union	*Focus on economic conditions, lack of focus on workplace conditions, little advocacy for worker autonomy.*
Quality assurance	*High levels of surveillance and accountability, summative rather than formative performance feedback.*
Home-work interface	*Conflicting demands,* low support at home, dual career families, *predominantly female workers.*
Nature of work	
Environment/ equipment	Low reliability, availability, suitability of equipment and space, informationization.
Task design	Lack of variety, *fragmented and/or meaningless work,* high time pressure.
Workload/pace	*Intensification, doing more with less.*
Work schedule	Shift work, inflexible schedules, unpredictable hours, *long hours.*

Source: Adapted from Cox et al. (2000).

We discuss, in this section, the stress teachers felt that is directly related to this outcomes based accountability environment. We have organized the stress inducing circumstances and teacher responses around the framework summarized in Table 3.2 (i.e., the nature of the workplace and the nature of work). In the discussion of the changes in the nature of the workplace associated with outcomes based accountability we discuss: teachers' lack of voice and choice, the excessive demands on teachers and students, unclear or hidden goals and objectives, and the high level of surveillance and risks of exposure associated with outcomes based accountability. The nature of teachers' work is discussed around two themes: the fragmentation of work, and its consequent meaninglessness, and the intensification of teachers' work.

Nature of Workplace

Lack of Voice and Choice

Teachers may have never really had much decision-making power over choice of curriculum (see, for example, Vinson & Ross, 2003), however, the teachers in this study relate that previous to the state tests they had a lot more freedom, flexibility, and autonomy in deciding how they covered, delivered, and assessed the curriculum. For some teachers this freedom is associated with a lack of leadership and professional support, but for most teachers the freedom to make pedagogical decisions within their own classrooms was an essential part of their self-perception as professionals.

For these teachers, the absence of choice and flexibility to make decisions about one's teaching means that teaching as a profession is being threatened. Previous to the adoption of state mandated testing, teachers felt they played a vital role in making decisions about what to teach and how to teach to meet state or district standards. The nature of high stakes, standardized testing, however, has created a chain of accountability that links the work of teachers and administrators in new ways. Low test scores do not just impact teachers; they hold real consequences for schools and districts. As a result, all three districts responded to this new measure of success by adopting textbooks aligned to the format of the tests and pushing for uniformity of teaching across grade levels. A third grade teacher in Park City described this change:

> Everything is done for you. My first two years it wasn't like that because they didn't have the math or the reading [texts]. Then two years ago they got all the programs and it completely changed. This is what you do, this, this, this. And they keep track of it, they make sure you're doing it, so you're doing everything from the book ... you have to tell [district office] what lesson you're on, they come and check now and then. So they're babysitting us.

A third grade teacher in Orchard Hill agreed:

> I don't think it's right that we have to cram so much curriculum into a small amount of time.... To be fair to the students they need to be familiar with the [test] format ... but I wish that wasn't there. I wish we could just be teaching and not having the pressure of understanding the format. We lost a lot of choice. I think that's the bottom line with this whole thing.... You used to be able to do what you thought was valuable and your philosophy of what was important for kids to learn. Really you don't have that freedom of choice that we used to have.

Teachers in all three districts witnessed a reduction of control over decisions that directly impact their work, which resulted in teachers reorienting themselves toward their work. They resented this change because there was no clear indication, from either the state or their district, of the purpose for these changes. A fourth grade teacher in Orchard Hill asked:

> I'm still not understanding why we're doing this and what it's going to be used for. I mean are we just giving kids assessments just to give them assessments or is there a purpose behind this?... Are we giving this just because New York State says we have to give the test each year or are we giving this because we're using it as some sort of measurement? I think it needs to be a little bit clearer as to what these are for. ... because I don't think everyone is clear as to why.

Excessive Demands on Teachers and Students

Teachers' frustration with having their professional judgment bypassed by the district and state was exacerbated by demands for compliance with curricular policies and practices they felt were not in the best interest of their students. Teachers in all three districts described the content to be covered in preparation for the state tests to be excessive, stressful, and harmful to students' learning and well-being. A fourth grade teacher in Orchard Hill explained:

> Because our math test is given in May our entire curriculum has to be taught and covered by spring break, and you can't get around that. When we sit down as a team during the summer we start at the test date and work backwards. And if you don't feel ready to give a certain test, you have to. It doesn't matter if you feel ready to. If you feel you need a couple more days, you can't because you are scheduled to cover it.

An eighth grade teacher in Park City agreed:

> There's plenty of pressure [to cover the curriculum]. A lot of times it makes you forge on, to get to the next topic, without waiting for the old, do I dare say mastery, until everybody learns it. You can't wait anymore. You've just got to keep going. You have to expose the children to every single thing that you're supposed to. Most of them will get it, many of them will not.

Furthermore, teachers were not only pressured, if not mandated, to increase their curricular content, they were required to give more assessments as well. These were usually built into the textbooks as end of unit benchmark tests, but districts also increased the number of standardized tests they give to students for diagnostic (typically a prediction of how students will do on state mandated tests) purposes. In Willow Valley, K-3 teachers were caught off guard when they were suddenly required to administer a battery of literacy assessments at the end of the year. A second grade teacher expressed her displeasure at the additional task thrown her way:

> I'm sure the literacy committee worked very long and hard on this. Was there a lot of teacher input or were they all reading specialists? And from a reading specialist standpoint it's a fabulous measurement for the kids, the reading, the writing, the listening. It's all there. From a classroom teacher, 27 children perspective, you just gave me a whole other set of work for the last six weeks of school that I didn't need and I'm not even sure how and why you're going to use it. Since April I have tested my students in Terra Nova's, Theme 5 reading test, Theme 6 reading test, Literacy Assessment Test, not to mention your other benchmark tests in science, social studies, and math. The last eight weeks of school, my children have done nothing but take tests. Fabulous if you're going to use these assessment tools to see where my program is going and where I should be. Kill them with tests if no one is going to use these assessments for where we're going with these kids.

Unclear or Hidden Standards and Goals

Despite alignment, increases in curricular content, and extensive test oriented work, teachers found administering the state tests a stressful and uncertain event. The reason for this is simple: the state does not describe which content will be emphasized on the state tests and so teaching the curriculum is a gamble with uncertain results. Practice tests can prepare students for a certain format but the actual content and emphasis may vary considerably from one year to the next. A fourth grade teacher in Willow Valley explained how this uncertainty hits you hard. When she saw the math test one year she felt so sick she had to excuse herself to go to the bathroom because she felt she was going to vomit. She commented:

> I just feel like no matter what you do with these tests you cannot win. I don't know. Maybe it's just us being paranoid, you just never, ever feel like you've prepared the kids enough no matter what. No matter how much you've put out there. I've done centers last year and this year in math just trying to find another way to review more skills in one set amount of time and make it child-oriented as much as possible and hands-on as much as possible. But still when you come to that test you're kind of like shaken up a little thinking, oh my God, I don't think I did that the right way.

Teachers were discouraged and they were scared. They felt they played their part just to have the state arbitrarily decide the cut-off scores, which determine who passes and who fails. An eighth grade teacher in Orchard Hill commented:

> We don't know how [the state] gets from the 68 points on the math test to that scale that they publish. I don't know where those numbers come from.

They don't share that. I guess that's a secret. Or the dividing line between the levels. How they do it? I have no idea. I wish they'd share that."

These feelings were intensified during the scoring of the tests, in which the teachers were expected to participate. The regulated and scripted nature of these events hides the ambiguous nature of the task—a task that results in high stakes consequences for teachers and students. Teachers found themselves sitting in crossfire, wanting to give the students every possible point while also abiding by the state scoring rubric. An example of this dilemma happened in Willow Valley when four teachers were scoring the fourth grade science test 3 weeks before the end of the school year. The teachers were quickly trained by a veteran teacher before beginning. On one of the questions involving a multistep sorting activity, a first-year teacher began to question her interpretation of the rubric. After scoring a pile of responses to this question, she goes back over the directions and looks back over some of the students' responses. The more she attempts to understand the scoring rubric, the more she had doubts that she had scored the responses correctly and consistently. She explains to the others that the way the rubric is worded, they have to go back and check at each step what the students had originally included or excluded in their sorting boxes. She felt that in their haste to get scoring, they did not do that. She did not get the response she was hoping for from the other teachers, however. Instead she was gently chastised for having fallen so far behind. The day was coming to an end and the teachers explained the principal had only allotted 1 day for this task and they could not ask him for more time. Instead, they helped the teacher who has fallen behind by pitching in and scoring her pile, but they did not want to revisit the tests they had already scored and pressured her to move faster and not be so concerned. The teacher complied, but was noticeably upset for the remainder of the session.

High Level of Surveillance, Accountability, and Exposure

Public exposure is another feature of outcome based accountability that has dramatically increased the stress level for teachers. A fourth grade teacher in Willow Valley explained:

The problem with the numbers [test score reporting] is that it seems like a lot of what we do is test-driven. They tell you you're not supposed to teach to the test, but in effect that's what ends up happening. You have to teach to the test because if these scores are not good enough, then it's reflected back on you. It's reflected back on the students. It's reflected back on the administration, and that's *not* a good thing.

An eighth grade teacher in Park City agreed:

> The day the grades come out, the local paper will have a huge headline, which will say "53% of our district's students fail ELA test." There will be so and so's column about how you pay teachers $70,000, and they only teach 180 days, and what the hell is going on, kids can't write, kids can't read ... and I've been here 33 years, and I've never felt pressure before, and the last 3 years I've felt pressure.

Teachers admitted the consequence of being publicly responsible for scores that they have little control over has made them afraid of teaching certain grade levels: "I am not going to go back to eighth grade without being tenured because I'm afraid. I'm afraid to be the person responsible for the eighth grade ELA and be a non-tenured teacher."

They also admitted to receiving messages from their colleagues to act in ways that are immoral or illegal. For example, a remedial teacher in Park City reported having been under increased pressure to "assist" his students during the tests:

> [When] I conducted resource room ... every time we'd take these tests the teachers come up to me and say, "you could help them, read it to them, tell them what" and they're basically telling me, tell them how to pass or help them pass it, word it how they can pass it. And that's not really what you are supposed to do, so a lot of times, I'm under pressure because the teachers are like squeezing in on us, that we have to have them pass.

Nature of Work

Meaningless, Fragmented Work

Teachers in all grade levels find themselves pressured to keep students moving though the content even when the students have not mastered a previous lesson. A third grade teacher in Willow Valley explained:

> I get stuck between a rock and a hard place every single time, I feel like I'm rushing through my math series, that there's times that I know they don't necessarily get it because there's so much I have to get through. And I've gone to the fourth grade teachers and said help me out. Do you want them to at least be like, oh I've seen that before and not necessarily have it down, or do you want them to come to you with less and have it down?' And they've said that they would like them to have at least the exposure. So I feel like a lot of times I'm not giving them the time to master a concept in math before moving on.

And teachers commented that test-oriented work takes away from other, often more essential, learning experiences. A fourth grade teacher in Park City commented:

> There's a lot of stress not being able to let the students spend time on necessary skills. Our kids are missing a lot of Piaget stuff.... They lack kinesthetic experiences with blocks or Legos. You can't teach them that. They need hands-on."

An Orchard Hill teacher explained how the assessments increased fragmentation rather than promoting integration of the curriculum:

> [Preparing for the tests has] definitely made you give up some of the great things that we were doing.... The push for so long was to integrate the curriculum areas and I think somehow the assessments have forced us to pull them apart. I think it is the assessment because the assessment then drove the purchase of all these new materials including the new reading ... and math series and that then drove [the curriculum] apart.

Intensification

Teaching to the test has altered the priorities of teachers. Teachers felt they not only lost control over the way they teach, but that the way they were being required to teach contradicts what they learned as professionals. They felt the intensification of a test-oriented curriculum was occurring at the expense of the academic, psychological, social, and emotional needs of students. A fourth grade teacher in Park City expressed her anger:

> I resent what I perceive as the politicians and the powers that be. I resent the strain that they've put on me, because I still feel it's important to take care of children, because that is what we do. We don't just teach; we take care of children. That is a huge part of what we do. And they seem to have devalued that completely.

And most of the teachers felt the consequences for students who are already struggling might be devastating. A fourth grade teacher in Park City explained:

> We're putting a lot of pressure on nine-year-olds. And the students who are not as capable ... become very frustrated because we're asking them for higher level thinking skills when they are still having trouble even reading. And that's very frustrating for them and I think leads to anxiety and acting out and certainly low self-esteem. It can't be anything but for them.... I liken it to taking a beginner down a double diamond trail, after that that person

will never ski again and so for the students who are behind, this is the problem.

Even in districts where students normally do well on state assessments, teachers noticed the impact these tests are having on the attitudes of students. A fourth grade teacher in Orchard Hill described her students between the math and science tests:

> Their behavior has been horrible. The students are tired. Their behavior is distracted and they are having difficulty focusing. My usually very mild-mannered class is very testy, tattling, and short tempered. Even a simple mother's day project has them befuddled.

ONE MEASURE OF SUCCESS—MULTIPLE CONTEXTUAL STRESSORS

Outcome based accountability has increased the stress level experienced by teachers by altering the nature of the workplace and the nature of the work as illustrated by the preceding analysis. While this analysis illustrates common responses to outcomes based accountability across districts, there are also particular ways the relationships of people within districts have been altered. In this section, we describe how the stress conditions described above are further exacerbated by the way the accountability structure has altered the way people relate and work together.

"We Are Being Watched, That's for Sure"

The teachers in Park City have been required to follow a rigid reading and math program for K-5 students. Unlike other districts in our study, however, this one comes with a district mandate not to pull students out of the classroom and group them by ability. This mandate has been particularly difficult for one group of fourth grade teachers who had disobeyed this mandate the previous year.

> We were told to teach the reading program in a certain way and many of us tried. But some people did start doing pull out. And a good teacher is going to enhance a program with what he or she feels the children need. But we weren't supposed to be doing that and our scores went up and then our principal spoke with the superintendent and told him what we were doing and the superintendent flipped out, was yelling at him because we didn't follow protocol.

Hours of curriculum work had been put in over the summer and on weekends, often without pay, to create a literacy program for third and fourth graders especially geared toward the ELA. The teachers were proud of their work, thought it was top notch, and more importantly had felt particularly resourceful since it was successful and no other program was available at the time.

> Now I wouldn't dare pull a student out to help a student improve. We were told in no uncertain terms that we had to follow policy. The removal of the principal was a message to staff. First, we got the news of how well we had done. We were shocked and ecstatic, and then totally demoralized.... Our superintendent has never congratulated us.

The consequences associated with this event altered the relationship teachers at Hemlock Elementary have with their district administrators. Whereas before they had felt supported in their efforts, now they feel disgraced and under intense scrutiny. Demoralized and with no alternative plan to adapt their program effectively, they began the year running what they believed was a less effective and more relentless program to whole classrooms of students.

From September to January, the stress of conducting a program the teachers believed was failing to adequately prepare students, their increasing resentment over the district's condemnation, and their rising fear of what might happen if their scores drop (and they were certain that they will) was taking its toll. Two weeks before the test, the teachers panicked. "It's simply stupid not to have been able to group. We've wasted so much time and the students aren't prepared." Not knowing if extra review sessions fall under the "no ability grouping" mandate, the teachers increased test preparation time and began grouping.

> As we got closer [to the test] it was very apparent that the students were nowhere near where our fourth graders were last year at the same time, nowhere near ... and I would say we all fel ... a sense of failure. And we were terribly worried that even our better students wouldn't pass.... And so in the last few weeks there was this frantic struggle...and that's when we broke into groups because we needed to have the students who had the capability of passing work together, they had so much to accomplish.

The Friday before administration of the English language arts test, the teachers met for one last planning session. The strain was evident in their bloodshot eyes. Knowing, however, that there was nothing more they could do, they reminded each other not to push the students over the edge, knowing they had already fallen over that edge themselves.

"He's a Former Coach. He Keeps Score. That's What They Do, Keep Score"

Stress occurs when people are pressured by their supervisors to engage in practices they do not believe are in the best interests of those they serve, and is increased by being held solely responsible for the results of those practices. "I get extremely nervous with all of the tests. The principal looks at all the grades. He keeps track of who is doing what. He's got a list: Ms. X, science this many 3s, this many 2s, you know," a teacher in Willow Valley explained.

In a discussion about what a supportive and proactive administrator might look like, a Willow Valley teacher commented:

> They don't go by and say, "I saw a lot of twos [from your room]." They don't walk around and right in the middle of the test your door opens, yea right in the middle of the test "how do you think they're doing?" Oh my God, get out of my room!

Supportive and resourceful leadership was not what teachers in Willow Valley felt they were receiving. Several fourth grade teachers described what planning with their principal looked like:

> There's an awful lot of 'who do you think is going to make it through and who do you think isn't?' What can you do to help them? It pretty much comes down to the fourth grade teachers and it starts right after the first report card. "What if I give this aide for an extra half an hour a day?" "Why don't we get this person tested?" And then all of a sudden that person is lifted from the bottom of the testing schedule to the top and while I admire the effort and I think it's noble, it's not the right way to go.... It's the mad dash to what are we going to do to get these kids ready? Sometimes I just feel like saying stop! It's not what are we going to do to get these kids ready. What have we been doing and how can we keep doing that? And when we sit in the fourth grade team meeting room and we're all sitting there and "what are you going to do?" What can we do? And it's like saying, it's not completely our responsibility.... And that's what happens every month we have a meeting and we hear the same thing.

> And I get a sick feeling in my stomach because it's like how am I going to get 4s out of some of these kids?

> It hurt our relationship when the administration made it clear, you know, we want to get those twos to be threes. We want those threes to be fours. We don't want any ones, ok? We have those same goals, but at the same time I have several remedial reading students in my class and ... nothing has been done to meet the needs of those children. And all I hear from administration is the scores, the scores, the scores. But I don't see anything done for

the needs of our children.... We still have those stresses on us and we don't see the standards addressing programming needs and staffing needs and things like that. We haven't seen it driving that.... It's still us that's providing everything.

In these two situations stress is a manifestation of a complex interaction between the relationships of people in the workplace, resources, and the demands of meeting the needs of students, who because of poverty and other life situations present multiple challenges to teachers. But even in successful suburban districts, such as Orchard Hill, where students for the most part successfully pass the state exams, teachers talked of stress.

"We Know We Have Bright Kids. We Want to Make Sure That's What Is Seen"

In a district that prides itself on meeting the high expectations of the community, the state standards and tests have added a new and, according to many Orchard Hill teachers, "questionable" standard of measurement. The pressure on the teachers included maintaining a high level of success and making sure the community did not misinterpret the test scores. This was because, in successful districts with high parental involvement, the parents were an additional source of stress for teachers.

> Parents, if they notice, for instance let's say I didn't really teach note taking in my class and my class has a lower grade score on the ELA test ... so there's that pressure of you don't want your scores to drop as a person, as a grade level, as a district to significantly go down one year. And that's a huge pressure.

The problem with explaining to parents what the state scores mean was created both by the teachers' lack of involvement in and understanding of how the state determines the test scores, and by the limited scope of this form of measurement.

> The thing I see with the standardized tests is that unfortunately [they] become too often, in the public eye, the sole measure of the school, sole measure of a program.... That's my one fear. There's so much other stuff that goes on, and a lot of time that's the sole measure that they get to see.

The concern raised by these teachers was not that parents were interested in the test scores (they were used to that kind of scrutiny); it was in knowing the parents will be interested in the scores and that these scores do not fairly or accurately represent what students are capable of.

I guess looking at anywhere between 60-70% of the kids passing in English or math, that's fairly good, although I'm sure people looking at that in the public and saying "40% of the kids can't read and write." I see that, but it's just one particular score.... It's not broken down enough to say anything about the kids' skills or what their abilities are."

CONCLUSIONS

Conditions that cause anxiety, tension, fear, helplessness, anger, and frustration cause stress (Kyriacou, 1987). When these feelings result in negative perceptions of one's work and workplace, they result in helplessness rather than productivity, uncertainty rather than assurance, and dependency rather than autonomy. Outcome-based accountability, such as practiced by New York State Education Department, has created a uniformity of responses across school districts regardless of the level of student achievement, the quality of the teachers, and other district resources. These responses have in turn created new sources and levels of stress that have tipped the scale from what might have been healthy pressure to unhealthy stress experiences for teachers.

The teachers' experiences suggest that outcome based accountability creates a domino effect that has resulted in the disintegration of the physical, social, and emotional context meant to support the work of teachers. Excessive, unrealistic, and ambiguous demands of the workplace, a reduction in support, trust, and respect for the capabilities of teachers with regard to their work, and the public exposure of the results of that work have resulted in an increase in the amount of ethical, psychological, and physical conflicts experienced by teachers. When those conflicts are perceived to be impossible to resolve in a way that maintains the integrity of the responsibilities teachers have to their superiors, themselves, their students, and the public, the inevitable result is intense and unhealthy stress.

The three districts in our study are different in the populations of students they serve, the amount of professional development teachers receive, and the style of leadership displayed by principals and superintendents. Yet, the practices teachers engaged in as a result of the presence of high stakes tests and the conditions they related as inducing negative stress responses were remarkably similar. This suggests that outcome based accountability produces responses across schools and districts that exacerbate the conditions within teachers' work and workplace that produce stress. What seems evident from the teachers' accounts, however, is that stress becomes aggravated in situations where opportunities for professional judgment and input, flexibility of approach, and strong interpersonal relationships are thwarted, and where the multiple and complex objectives of schooling are reduced to one narrow measure of success. Furthermore, these findings are supported by Deci and Ryan's (1985) self-determination theory—that healthy work environments support the active engagement of humans with complex and challenging social roles and experiences, indicating that situations that lack personal input, coherence, and meaning are more likely to produce unhealthy stress.

Schools as workplaces are complex and demanding social contexts. Teachers' experiences suggest that outcome based accountability structures result in practices that restructure the nature of teachers' work as well as the nature of their workplace. What is also suggested is that these accountability structures are more likely to thwart teachers' tendencies for active engagement in their work, and psychological well being and growth. Indeed, they are likely to have unhealthy effects and lead to stressed teachers who struggle along, get sick, or leave the profession.

NOTES

1. This publication is based on research supported by the National Science Foundation (Grant # ESI-9911868). The findings and opinions expressed herein do not necessarily reflect the position or priorities of the sponsoring agency.
2. Pseudonyms are used as district names.
3. more information on Self-Determination Theory is available at http://www.psych.rochester.edu/SDT/theory.html

REFERENCES

Chorney, L. A. (1998). Self-defeating beliefs and stress in teachers. *Dissertation Abstracts International, 58,* 2820.

Cox, T., Griffiths, A., & Rial-González, E. (2000). *Research on work-related stress.* Luxembourg: Office for Official Publications of the European Communities. Retrieved January 15, 2006, from http://osha.eu.int

Deci, E. L., Connell, J. P., & Ryan, R. (1989). Self-determination in a work organization. *Journal of Applied Psychology, 74*(4), 580-590.

Deci, E. L., & Ryan, R. (1985). *Intrinsic motivation and self-determination in human behavior.* New York: Plenum Press.

Fontana, D., & Abouserie, R. (1993). Stress levels, gender and personality factors in teachers. *British Journal of Educational Psychology, 63,* 261-270.

Glaser, B. G., & Strauss, A. L. (1967). *The discovery of grounded theory.* Chicago: Aldine.

It's time to limit the load [Editorial]. (2001, April 13). *Times Educational Supplement,* p. 10

Jackson, P. W. (1968). *Life in classrooms.* New York: Teachers College Press.

Kyriacou, C. (1987). Teacher stress & burnout: An international review. *Educational Research, 29*(2), 146-152.

Lazarus, R. S. (1990). Stress, coping and illness. In H. S. Friedman (Ed.), *Personality and disease* (pp. 97-120). Chichester, United Kingdom: Wiley.

Lippel, K. (1999). Workers' compensation and stress: Gender and access to compensation. *International Journal of Law and Psychiatry, 22*(1), 79-89.

Naylor, C. (2001a). *What do British Columbia's teachers consider to be the most significant aspects of workload and stress in their work?* Vancouver, British Columbia, Canada: British Columbia Teachers Federation. Available at: http://www.bctf.ca/researchreports/2001wlc03/report.html

Naylor, C. (2001b). *Teacher workload and stress: An international perspective on human costs and systemic failure.* Vancouver, British Columbia, Canada: British Columbia Teachers Federation. Available at: http://www.bctf.ca/researchreports/2001wlc01/report.html

Proctor, J. L., & Alexander, D. A. (1992). Stress among primary teachers: Individuals in organizations. *Stress Medicine, 8*, 233-236.

Quick, J. C., Quick, J. D., Nelson, D. L., & Hurrell, J. J., Jr. (1997). *Preventive stress management in organizations.* Washington, DC: American Psychological Association.

Selye, H. (1976). *The stress of life.* New York: McGraw-Hill.

Smyth, J. (Ed.). (1993). *A socially critical view of the "self-managing school."* Bristol, PA: Falmer Press.

Smyth, J. (2002). Unmasking teachers' subjectivities in local school management. *Journal of Education Policy, 17*(4), 463-482.

Vinson, K. D., & Ross, E. W. (2003). *Image and education: Teaching in the face of the new disciplinarily.* New York: Peter Lang.

Woods, P., & Carlyle, D. (2002). Teacher identities under stress: the emotions of separation and renewal. *International Studies in Sociology of Education, 12*(2), 169-189.

Yerkes, R. M., & Dodson, J. D. (1908). The relation of strength of stimulus to rapidity of habit-formation. *Journal of Comparative Neurology and Psychology, 18*, 459-482.

CHAPTER 4

SHARED NEEDS

Teachers Helping Students with Learning Disabilities to Cope More Effectively

Nola Firth, Erica Frydenberg, and Daryl Greaves

Relationships with students who have learning disabilities are especially likely to cause teacher stress as these students are at risk of behavior problems and of resorting to the use of nonproductive coping strategies. A study involving 77 adolescent students with learning disabilities investigated the effect of a 10-week coping program and a teacher feedback intervention. Both interventions aimed to increase students' sense of control and productive coping and to decrease nonproductive coping. Pre- and postprogram data on perceived control and coping were collected from parents, teachers, and students. It was analyzed with a one-way analysis of covariance. Results showed significant changes in the coping program group to a greater internal locus of control. The teachers reported the use of fewer nonproductive coping strategies for the teacher feedback and for the concurrent teacher feedback/coping program recipients. Teachers also reported stress reduction due to improved relationships with students and to increased self-efficacy in regard to effective teaching methods for these students.

Both current and historical accounts of teacher stress show that the management of problematic student/teacher relationships is an important contributor to teacher stress (Kyriacou, 2001; Otto 1986). Problematic teacher/student classroom relationships manifest as difficulties in controlling the negative behaviors of students (Friedman, 2004), difficulty teaching students who lack motivation, and a perceived inability by the teacher to cater to the special needs of some students (Shoho, 2002). A significant group of students who have special needs is students who have learning disabilities. As many of these students are also at risk of having a passive learning style (Dweck, 2000) and others present with behavior problems (Chan & Dally, 2000), working with these students is likely to expose teachers to increased levels of stress (Westwood & Graham, 2003). Teachers and students share a common difficulty in this situation. While the causes may differ, both teachers and students experience stress in the classroom (Kyriacou, 2001; Otto, 1986). This shared stress may be an opportunity to effectively focus on concurrent reduction of stress by both teachers and students.

There is some debate in regard to terminology and definitions of learning disabilities (Louden, 2000). For the purposes of this chapter a student who has learning disabilities has an IQ score greater than 80 and deficits in at least one area of academic achievement, such as reading, spelling, or mathematics, as well as specific processing difficulties, such as short-term memory problems or poor auditory discrimination ability (Prior, 1996). Learning disabilities affect a greater proportion of the community than is generally recognized. According to Prior's (1996) definition, perhaps 10% of the population is affected and it is likely that there are two or more students who have learning disabilities in most school classes. The intractable and genetic nature of the processing difficulties inherent in learning disabilities implies that, despite teachers' best efforts, many of these young people will always find aspects of reading, spelling, and mathematics problematic (Reiff, Ginsberg, & Gerber, 1995; Raskind, Goldberg, Higgins, & Herman, 1999). Furthermore these students are at risk of leaving school earlier and experiencing fewer career opportunities with lower remuneration, more unemployment, mental health problems, and increased risk of criminal prosecution than would otherwise be expected (Prior, 1996).

Behavior problems are characteristic of perhaps 50% of these students from early childhood onward (Chan & Dally, 2000; Prior, 1996). Students with learning disabilities are at risk of low perceived control and often resort to the use of nonproductive coping strategies. While perceived control in general is likely to be important for students who have learning difficulties, for the purposes of this study "perceived control" refers to locus of control and "productive" and "nonproductive" coping strategies refer to coping responses from the Adolescent Coping Scale (Frydenberg & Lewis, 1993). Examples of productive coping strategies are working hard and thinking positively and examples of nonproductive coping strategies are ignoring the problem and self-blame.

Low perceived control manifests for many of these students in three important facets: namely high external locus of control (Bender, 1987; Wehmeyer & Kelchner, 1996); low self-regulation (Prior, 1996); and passive learning style (Dweck, 2000; Peterson, Maier, & Seligman, 1993). Coping profiles for these students also frequently include high use of nonproductive strategies, such as self-blame, worry, and failing to apply any active strategies to combat the stressor, and low use of productive coping strategies, such as working at solving the problem and positive thinking (Cheshire & Cambell, 1997). It is the influence of associated behavioral responses rather than the specific learning difficulties themselves that have the greatest influence on poor outcomes in adult life (Prior, 1996). Furthermore such nonproductive coping responses create major challenges for teachers (Westwood & Graham, 2003).

In contrast, several studies show that successful adults who have learning disabilities take control and use effective coping strategies despite their difficulties. These adults use a proactive coping style. They persevere, access help when they need it and are creative in finding alternative strategies in the face of difficulty. The success achieved by these people has occurred in spite of continuing difficulties with reading, spelling, and some areas of mathematics (Raskind et al., 1999; Reiff et al., 1995). It is clear that, although some academic skills are resistant to development due to the processing skill difficulties inherent in learning disabilities, taking control and developing effective coping skills in the face of these difficulties is crucial for life success (Raskind et al., 1999). Furthermore, development of these skills is also likely to benefit teachers. Students' passive and/or nonproductive behavior is likely to decrease and teaching adaptive coping behavior to students will enhance the teacher's own coping skills (Huxley, 2004).

In response to an increasing awareness of the difficulties faced by many adolescents (Resnick et. al, 1997) programs have been developed that aim to assist both "at risk" groups as well as other students to develop skills, such as conflict management, positive thinking, goal setting, and relaxation (e.g., *Best of Coping*, Frydenberg & Brandon, 2002; Bright Ideas, Brandon & Cunningham, 1999). Recent research into teachers' experiences of teaching coping programs to regular classes in schools indicates that teaching such programs causes teachers to reflect on and build their own coping strategies (Cunningham, 2002; Frydenberg, 2004). Teachers involved in implementing these programs are likely to benefit through modelling and teaching students in their classrooms to adopt positive, proactive coping strategies. One teacher of the *Bright Ideas* positive thinking program remarked, "It wasn't only the kids who got the message. We also got the message for helping us deal with our lives" (Cunningham, 2002). Finally, as teachers empathize with the stress of their students and experience less depersonalization towards them, they are likely to experience the success of knowing they have an effective strategy to offer these students.

This chapter reports two programs that targeted the needs of students with learning disabilities to determine the level of assistance provided to them in regard to coping with the inevitable stressful situations that arise. The two programs, a coping skill program and a teacher feedback program, were designed to increase perceived control and productive coping and to decrease nonproductive coping of adolescent students who had learning disabilities. The programs were based on research with adults in regard to the importance of the perceived control for people who have learning disabilities (Raskind et al., 1999; Reiff et al., 1995). The coping program taught the importance of taking control, awareness and choice of coping style, assertiveness, and positive thinking. The teacher feedback program involved teachers individually encouraging students to use effort and find alternative strategies in the face of difficulty. It was expected that students who took part in the programs would be less likely to be overwhelmed by their learning disabilities. With this increased internal control the student would then be more likely to choose a productive coping strategy than experience negative emotions. Their responses might be asking assertively for use of a computer spellchecker, or for the teacher to modify the task so it had less reliance on print media, or for his/her neighbour to spell the word. Such responses are in contrast to the nonproductive responses frequently used by many students with learning disabilities, such as giving up work on the project, talking to class mates instead of working, getting angry at the teacher, being overdependent on the teacher's help, or becoming withdrawn and feeling a failure.

THE CURRENT STUDY

In the study, the efficacy of the coping program and the teacher feedback program and their impact on perceived control and coping style of students with learning disabilities was considered from the point of view of the students and their teachers, and their parents. These programs were also evaluated with regard to how they might affect teacher stress. The research questions for the study were: (1) Do the coping program and/or the teacher feedback interventions increase internality of locus of control of the sample of students who have learning disabilities? (2) Do the coping program and/or the teacher feedback interventions increase use of productive and decrease use of nonproductive coping styles of the sample of students who have learning disabilities? (3) Do the coping program and/or the teacher feedback intervention make positive changes to the level of stress experienced by teachers in this study who implement these programs?

METHOD

Participants

Seventy-seven adolescent students from three school groups ($n = 24, 26, 27$) who had been diagnosed with learning disabilities took part in the study. The three schools were a high socioeconomic independent regional school, a government regional school, and a Catholic rural school. Students and their parents were primarily Australian born and of Anglo/European background. Exceptions were one student with Chinese background, one Middle Eastern migrant student and parent, and one student with a migrant parent of Italian origin. Teachers were Australian born and of Anglo/European background. Student ages ranged from 12 to 16 years (mean = 13.8) and 29 were female and 48 were male. School timetabling and teacher commitments influenced the grouping process such that numbers in the groups varied slightly from school to school. Groups were made up of combinations of intact class groups and/or students from different classes. Attrition also occurred in some groups if students who were originally included in the groups were discovered through individual testing not to have learning difficulties.

Instruments

Learning Disabilities Screening
All students included in the study were assessed for an IQ score greater than 80 and scores of 2 or more years below chronological age in at least one area of academic achievement, such as reading, spelling, or mathematics. Results of The Weshcler Intelligence Test for Children were available through school records for many students and these were used to establish IQ scores. This test is administered by qualified psychologists and remains stable over time (Prifitera & Saklofske, 1998). Results from normed, individually or group administered spelling, reading, or mathematics tests undertaken by teachers within the past 2 years were used to establish levels in reading, spelling, or mathematics (e.g., The Neale

Analysis of Reading Ability, Neale, 1988; Tests of Reading Comprehension, Australian Council of Educational Research, 2003; The South Australian Spelling Test, Westwood, 1999). For all the students at one school and about a third of the students at the other two schools a learning disability was suspected, but students were not already fully tested. These students were assessed by the researchers. Tests used by the researchers were the Kaufmann Brief Intelligence Test (Kauffman & Kauffman, 1996) and The South Australian Spelling Test (Westwood, 1999).

The Adolescent Coping Scale (ACS)

Student coping strategies were measured pre- and postprogram by self-report, parent-report, and teacher-report versions of the ACS (Frydenberg & Lewis, 1993). Students completed a long (60-question) version of the scale. To allow triangulation and reduce reliance on student self-report, teachers and parents were also asked to complete a short (13-question) version of the scale. Teachers who completed the scale taught the student concerned for at least four lessons per week. Responses on these scales were on a 5-point Likert scale that ranged from *never* to *often* and related to how the student dealt with his/her concerns. Examples of items from this scale were: work at solving the problem to the best of my ability and worry about what will happen to me. Productive coping strategies included in the scale were working hard, working at solving the problem, relaxing, keeping fit and healthy, and thinking positively. Nonproductive coping strategies were ignoring the problem, self-blame, not having a way of coping, tension reduction activities such as drinking alcohol, worrying, keeping problems to oneself, and wishful thinking. The scale contained between three to five questions on the long form for each strategy and one question for each strategy on the short form. The original 89-item version of the long form of the ACS includes a third coping style entitled reference to others. Over the first 3 years of its use with adolescents in Australia this scale showed a median Cronbach alpha figure of 0.70. However the coping styles of productive and nonproductive have shown reliabilities above 0.80 (Frydenberg & Lewis, 1996). The stability of responses as measured by test-retest reliability coefficients have been moderate and range from .44 to .81 (Frydenberg & Lewis, 1996). The original 18-item version of the short form of the ACS also includes the third coping style of reference to others. Reliability for this scale has ranged between 0.67 and 0.79 (Frydenberg & Lewis, 1996). In this study the Cronbach alpha for the long form completed by the students was 0.90 and for the coping styles of productive and nonproductive it was 0.80 and 0.86 respectively. The

Cronbach alpha for the short form completed in this study by teachers was low at 0.45 with the coping styles of productive and nonproductive higher at 0.64 and 0.75 respectively. For the short form completed by parents the Cronbach alpha was also low at 0.47 with productive coping measures at 0.57 and nonproductive at 0.74.

Locus of Control Scale for Children

Students completed the Locus of Control Scale for Children (Nowicki & Strickland, 1973) pre- and postprogram. This scale measured the extent to which the child felt she/he had control over her/his life (internal locus of control) as distinct from being controlled by external circumstances (external locus of control). Higher scores reflected a higher sense of external control while lower scores indicate a higher internal sense of control. Example items from the scale were: Do you believe that wishing can make good things happen? When you get punished does it usually seem that it's for no good reason at all? Test-retest reliability for the test has measured between 0.63 and 0.71 (Nowicki & Strickland, 1973) and in a recent Australian study it was 0.73 (Gomez, 1997). Internal consistency reliability was 0.75 in Kline's (1993) review of the instrument. This test has been used extensively with adolescents (Mamlin, Harris & Case, 2001). The Cronbach alpha in this study was 0.67.

Questionnaires and Interviews

Students and teachers involved in the programs answered short questionnaires in regard to their responses to the programs (e.g., Has this program helped you feel more in control over what happens to you? Has this teacher's help led you to feel more in control of your schoolwork? Do you believe the coping program helped students to take on more control? Have you noticed any change in (student name)'s sense of personal control since the beginning of the program?). Interviews followed questionnaire schedules but allowed further depth of responses.

The teachers' stress response schedules asked teachers to comment on their stress responses in relation to the programs (e.g., Did using the coping/teacher feedback program affect your stress level in either direction in regard to teaching your classes? Do you think that using the coping/teacher feedback programs may preempt or resolve difficulties in your classroom?).

Procedures

Teachers initially identified students whom they believed had learning disabilities. Information about the project was sent by the schools to parents of these students. Consent for participation in the study was obtained from both parents and students. If a learning disability was suspected, but students were not already tested, these students were assessed by the researchers. The researchers assessed all the students at one school and approximately a third of the students at the other two schools.

The students were divided into four groups: a wait-list control group ($n = 24$); a group that received the teacher feedback program ($n = 17$); a group that received a coping skills program ($n = 21$) and a group that received both teacher feedback and the coping skills program ($n = 15$).

The two programs continued concurrently for a 10-week period to allow sufficient exposure to change behavior and thought patterns (Gresham, 1998). The teacher feedback intervention was delivered by 11 core class teachers who taught the students at least four times each week. These teachers participated in a 2-hour professional development program that introduced the theory and methodology of the intervention. Teachers were directed not to change the number of times they interacted with students. The special education teacher delivered the coping program in each of the three schools. These special education teachers also received at least two hours of professional development on the theory and methodology of the coping program. Each teacher was also given on-site weekly support during the 10-week intervention period and the researcher was present for at least one lesson by each teacher delivering the feedback program and for at least two of the coping program lessons.

Students completed The Children's Locus of Control and the ACS before and after the 10-week programs. Teachers and parents also completed a short form of the ACS at both these times. At the end of the programs students and teachers who were involved in the programs also completed questionnaires on their responses to the program. Additionally nine of the teachers who delivered the teacher feedback program (three of whom also taught the coping program) also responded to a brief questionnaire on teacher stress in regard to the programs. Interviews were also conducted with the three teachers who taught the coping program, two teachers who taught the feedback program, and at least one student from each of the intervention groups.

The Teacher Feedback Program

The teacher feedback program involved feedback from class teachers to individual students to encourage them to develop similar coping strategies to those used in the studies by the successful adults who had learning difficulties (Raskind et al.,1999; Reif et al. 1995). In particular the teacher feedback program aimed to encourage students to be aware of their own use of successful coping strategies, to use effort, to see difficulty as a challenge, and to look for alternative strategies. Instead of immediately giving solutions to students experiencing difficulty, teachers asked questions (e.g., What strategy could you use to help you here?), or drew students' attention to successful strategies (e.g., What did you do to achieve that?), or praised them for use of effort (e.g., Your hard work paid off!).

These interventions were based on the work of Dweck (2000) who discovered that in contrast to high achievers many underachievers have a helpless orientation toward learning. Dweck concluded that this orientation is likely to have originated from early global praise or blame by adults and that this resulted in a belief by children that ability is a fixed entity, that use of effort is a shameful proof of lack of cleverness, that there are few alternative strategies available, and that the appropriate response to failure is negative emotive rumination rather than active pursuit of alternative strategies. In contrast, feedback from teachers that conveyed an explicit expectation of and praise for use of effort and strategy rather than negative rumination on poor ability was expected to begin to reverse this orientation and encourage students to take on more of a mastery orientation in response to difficulty.

The Coping Program

The coping program was a modified version of the program *Best of Coping* (Frydenberg & Brandon, 2002) that has been successfully used in general classrooms to increase productive coping and decrease nonproductive coping patterns (Frydenberg, 2004). *Best of Coping* is a 10-session program that utilizes the Adolescent Coping Scale (Frydenberg & Lewis, 1993) to enable students to gain an awareness of their individual coping style and to gain skills, such as time management, asking for help, getting along with others, decision making, and goal setting. To incorporate best practice for students who have learning difficulties (e.g., extra revision time and direct instruction, Vaughan, Gersten, & Chard, 2000) and an intensive focus on perceived control, the program was reduced to include only awareness and choice of coping strategies, positive thinking, and assertiveness training. Additionally, print content was reduced to a minimum to accommodate the literacy abilities of students who have learning disabilities. Personal goals, such as passing a subject or being selected for a sports team, were added to the program to increase student motivation and generalization of strategies and each component was introduced and interspersed with direct teaching of the efficacy of taking control. The assertion component incorporated elements of an assertion program previously developed for students who had learning disabilities (Firth, 2000). These were an emphasis on goal clarity (e.g., What do you really want in this situation?), use of role-plays, and use of a home practice schedule. Students attended the program over 10 weeks for one hour per week.

RESULTS

Participation Rates

Consent to participation was obtained from 77 students, parents, and teachers. However participation in completion of some measures was incomplete. Some teachers experienced difficulty completing several of the questions about students on the Adolescent Coping Scale resulting in 50 of the 77 teacher-report Adolescent Coping Scales available for analysis. These were fairly evenly spread across the four groups. Fifty-one of the 77 parent Adolescent Coping Scales responses were returned. However only six of these were from parents in the feedback/coping group. See Table 4.1 for participation rates in the ACS across the four groups in the study. Additionally, due to logistical problems at one school 23 of the 32 students who received the teacher feedback program returned their post-program response questionnaire and the feedback program teachers returned postprogram response questionnaires for 26 students.

Data Examination

Prior to analysis, the quantitative data was screened for out of range and missing values and outliers. Outliers were checked for accuracy of entry but not removed. Missing values were replaced with the mean score

Table 4.1. Participation Rates in the ACS by Parents, Teachers and Students

Group	Students	Teachers	Parents
Control	24	12	17
Coping program	21	14	16
Teacher based feedback	17	9	12
Coping program and teacher feedback	15	15	6
Total	77	50	51

for all cases (Tabachnick & Fidell, 1996). If more than 10% of items were missing from a scale response it was not included. The data were screened for the assumptions of normality. As there were known differences in the groups, analysis of the data were then undertaken using a one way between groups analysis of covariance (ANCOVA). The pretest measure in each case adjusts for the pretest differences in subjects on the relevant measure so that the analysis reflects the adjusted group differences in the posttest measure. The model fitted was a main effects model with group as a factor at four levels and the pre-test score as a covariate. The assumption of constant variance was tested. A test for interaction was also carried out. In all cases, the tests for normality and constant variance were acceptable, and the test for interaction was not statistically significant. The means at time 2 are presented, adjusted for time 1 scores using ANCOVA. In addition, the estimates of effect (compared to control) are provided, together with significance tests comparing each treatment to control; no adjustment has been made for multiple comparisons.

Research Question 1: Do the coping program and/or the teacher feedback interventions increase internality of locus of control of the sample of students who have learning disabilities?

The Locus of Control Scale responses showed that in comparison to the control group, there was a trend toward increased sense of control for those who undertook the coping program and/or the teacher feedback program. Locus of control scores remained the same for the control group but decreased for the groups who were in the two programs. Change in this direction indicates a more internal locus of control and higher sense that control comes from internal sources rather than external circumstances. The greatest effect within the three scales occurred for the coping program group. A one way between groups analysis of covariance showed the differences between the means for the control and intervention groups and the results of comparisons between the intervention groups and control, adjusted for pre-program levels for each group. Mean scores thus adjusted were 16.9 for the control group, 13.8 ($p < 0.05$) for the coping group, 15.2 ($p < 0.27$) for the teacher feedback group and 15.4 ($p < 0.38$) for the group that received both interventions $F = 1.339$ ($df = 3, 68, p = 0.27$).

The teacher feedback postprogram response questionnaires indicated that teachers believed that 19 of 26 students receiving the teacher feedback showed increased sense of personal control. Students' evaluations of the feedback program indicated that 16 of the 23 students felt more in control of their schoolwork as a result. Twenty of the 36 students in the coping program indicated this program helped them feel more in control. Of the three teachers teaching the coping program, two believed that the program assisted most students to develop increased control and one believed that it may have assisted some students in this regard.

Research Question 2: Do the coping program and/or the teacher feedback interventions increase use of productive and decrease use of nonproductive coping styles of the sample of students who have learning disabilities?

While means on productive and nonproductive coping on the ACS moved in the expected direction, only two were statistically significant ($p < 0.05$). These were the teacher-reported decrease in nonproductive coping for the feedback group and for the feedback/coping group.

Tables 4.2 and 4.3 illustrate the changes in nonproductive and productive coping as measured on the Adolescent Coping Scale pre- and post-programs for all groups and by each reporting group (i.e. teachers, parents and students). A one way between groups analysis of covariance showed the differences between the means for the control and interven-

Table 4.2. Results of Analysis of Covariance Post Program for Productive Coping on the Adolescent Coping Scale (ACS)

| | \multicolumn{5}{c}{Productive coping (ACS)} |||||
Group	Time 1 Mean	Time 2 Mean	Adjusted Means[a]	P-value	Estimate of Effect
Teacher report					
Control	17.3	17.7	17.0	—	—
Coping	16.9	18.8	19.0	0.75	1.9
Feedback	16.9	18.1	18.4	0.23	1.4
Coping and feedback	15.1	17.9	18.7	0.12	1.7
Parent report					
Control	17.4	17.2	16.8	—	—
Coping	16.8	16.3	16.5	0.73	0.3
Feedback	17.7	17.7	17.0	0.79	-0.2
Coping and feedback	14.5	16.9	17.2	0.70	-0.4
Student report					
Control	17.4	16.8	16.7	—	—
Coping	17.1	16.9	17.3	0.41	0.5
Feedback	18.1	17.0	16.6	0.89	0.1
Coping and feedback	17.6	17.7	17.7	0.18	1.0

[a]Mean scores at Time 2 adjusted for Time 1 scores on the ACS.
*$p < 0.05$.
Teacher report productive coping ACS: F =1.31 (df =3,47, p = 0.283).
Parent report productive coping ACS: F = 0.19 (df =3,47, p = 0.901).
Student report productive coping ACS: F =0.87 (df =3.68, p = 0.461).

tion groups and the results of comparisons between the intervention groups and control, adjusted for pre-program levels for each group.

Mean scores thus adjusted for teacher report of nonproductive coping were 20.8 for the control group, 18.6 ($p < 0.15$) for the coping group, 14.7 ($p < 0.001$) for the teacher feedback group and 17.8 ($p < 0.04$) for the group that received both interventions $F = 3.0$ ($df = 3,.45, p = 0.04$). With the exception of this latter result the data reported in the tables shows means moving in the expected directions but no contrasts were significant.

Both students and teachers reported a move toward increased use of productive coping for those students in the treatment groups. Parents, however, reported a small decrease in productive coping for the coping and coping/feedback group and a small increase for the feedback group. Adjusted mean scores for parent-report of productive coping were 16.8 for the control group, 16.5 ($p < 0.73$) for the coping group, 17.0 ($p < 0.79$) for the teacher feedback group and 17.2 ($p < 0.70$) for the group that received both interventions $F = 0.19$ ($df = 3,47, p = 0.90$). Again, with the exception of this latter result the data reported in the tables

Table 4.3. Results of Analysis of Covariance Post Program for Nonproductive Coping on the Adolescent Coping Scale (ACS)

	\multicolumn{5}{c}{Nonproductive Coping (ACS)}				
Group	Time 1 Mean	Time 2 Mean	Adjusted Means[a]	P-value	Estimate of Effect
Teacher report					
Control	19.2	21.0	20.2	—	—
Coping	18.4	18.2	18.5	0.18	1.8
Feedback	17.5	16.0	16.0	0.006*	4.3
Coping and feedback	18.4	17.7	17.6	0.05*	2.6
Parent report					
Control	18.7	19.9	19.8	—	—
Coping	19.5	18.4	18.3	0.27	1.5
Feedback	18.2	16.8	17.4	0.63	2.4
Coping and feedback	21.9	19.3	17.9	0.34	1.9
Student report					
Control	17.6	18.1	18.3	—	—
Coping	18.2	17.0	17.1	0.22	1.3
Feedback	19.0	18.2	17.8	0.63	0.5
Coping and feedback	18.7	17.2	17.1	0.32	1.2

[a]Mean scores at Time 2 adjusted for Time 1 scores on the ACS.
*$p < 0.05$.
Teacher report nonproductive coping ACS: F = 3.00 (df =3,45,p = 0.04).
Parent report nonproductive coping ACS: F =0.92 (df =3,46,p = 0.43).
Student report nonproductive coping ACS: F = 0.60 (df =3,66, p = 0.615).

shows means moving in the expected directions but no contrasts were significant.

Teachers implementing the feedback program indicated on the post-program response questionnaire that 24 of the 26 of the students they had worked with were putting more effort into their schoolwork, that 21 of the 26 made better use of strategies, that 17 of the 26 had increased their academic performance. Teachers also frequently commented during the program, that due to various demands both within the classes and within the schools, they had difficulty practicing the feedback techniques as frequently as they would have liked. Students' evaluations of the feedback program however indicated that 10 of the 23 felt their schoolwork had improved.

The three coping program teachers reported that some students in each class appeared to be more assertive, positive, and active in the face of difficulty, but that change and extent of change varied from individual to individual. These three teachers also expressed the view that, although the program was worthwhile and that they wanted to repeat the program, it was too short to allow necessary consolidation and revision for the students.

Twenty of the 36 coping program students indicated that they had learned something worthwhile in the program, 19 believed the program helped them to be more positive about difficult experiences, 17 believed the program helped them be more assertive, and 23 that it helped them to choose better responses to difficulties. In response to the question of what was "really useful" in the program, the assertion section was nominated most frequently by 11 of the 36 students. Other "really useful" responses included awareness of increased problem solving options, improved organizational skills, positive thinking, not self-blaming, thinking ahead, asking for help, and working hard. Three students indicated that there was nothing they had learned in the program that was really useful. Examples of students' statements for what was "really useful" were: "Learn how to control without a fight"; "Not to let things bottle up inside, to let them out"; "I learned that there is quite a lot of ways of solving a problem"; and "That if you think bad you feel bad."

> *Research Question 3:* Do the coping program and/or the teacher feedback intervention make positive changes to the level of stress experienced by teachers in this study who implement these programs?

Responses to the teacher stress questionnaire indicated that the programs assisted teachers with their own stress levels in regard to teaching students who had learning disabilities. The nine teachers who completed the questionnaire reported that they all intended to continue to use the teacher feedback program in the future. Eight out the 9 teachers also reported that, although they experienced initial stress in learning to use the program, in the long run they experienced stress relief.

The fact that it was a new technique meant that there was some initial stress involved in its implementation. One teacher noted, "It is more time consuming than giving a quick piece of help and moving on to the next person." One teacher who did not feel relief reported he was not under stress initially. Other teachers referred to positive effects on classroom climate and relationships with students. One teacher related the program to her own coping skills. She explained that she was thinking more about her own goals and remembering to think positively herself. Another teacher mentioned use of "a common language of coping" that became available for use between students and between students and teachers. All these teachers, except for the teacher who felt he was not initially stressed, seemed to be in no doubt that the programs had reduced their stress levels. Relief was due to improved relationships with students, to more time availability in class as dependent students no longer expected constant individual assistance, and to the fact that some students were more motivated and effective in regard to their academic work. Teachers also felt satisfaction seeing their students attaining increased independence.

DISCUSSION

Analysis of the results in regard to the coping and perceived control instruments varied according to the group, to who reported change, and in type of outcome. Specifically students who undertook only the coping program reported the greatest increase in sense of control and for this group the null hypothesis of no change in comparison to the control group was not supported. Surprisingly, although the group who received both programs reported change in the expected direction of increased control, this change was not statistically significant. It is possible therefore that combining both programs may have reduced the effect of increased personal control. Perhaps, contrary to expectations, the increased exposure to teachers' input increased dependency in the students. In regard to adaptive coping the feedback/coping group showed a teacher-reported decrease in nonproductive coping and a better but not significant increase in teacher- and parent-reported productive coping. Those who only undertook the feedback program also showed teacher- and parent-reported decreased nonproductive coping. Thus, the three conditions of coping program, feedback program, and coping/feedback program appeared to be beneficial. However, the parent and teacher ACS data was less reliable than the students' ACS data and some responses were missing. These findings therefore needed to be treated with caution.

The results also indicated that although the decrease in nonproductive coping was statistically significant the increase in productive coping was manifested only as trends that may or may not be meaningful. A decrease in nonproductive coping for both coping and feedback groups was reported by teachers and for the feedback group by parents. However, only teacher- and student-reported increase in productive coping for the coping/feedback group was close to significance. As this latter outcome also occurred in previous coping program research (Cotta, Frydenberg, & Poole, 2000; Frydenberg, 2004) it is suggested that these programs may have more effect in decreasing self-blame, worry, and other nonproductive strategies than in increasing use of productive strategies, such as positive thinking.

Another interesting outcome was that students' responses on the ACS and postprogram response questionnaires were more restrained than those of teachers' in regard to the efficacy of the programs in producing positive change. Results on the students' ACS were not statistically significant and some students did not record positive responses to the programs (e.g., only 23 out of 36 students felt the coping program helped them to choose better responses to difficulties). This is in spite of the positive change that the students in the coping group recorded on the Locus of Control scale. This response may be explained by Dweck's (2000) finding that low-achieving students who have a passive coping style tend to attribute change to luck rather than to their own efforts. Dweck (2000) has also shown that many low-achievers replace seeking alternative strategies with the activity of negative rumination. Such negative self-talk is likely to drain self-esteem and result in little energy for change. Additionally, as coping patterns have been established since early childhood (Prior, Sanson, Smart, & Oberklaid, 2001) they are likely to be resistant to change. Teachers indicated that the programs needed to be longer and more intensive for change to be well established. If the changes were just beginning as teachers suggested, it is even more likely that students who were not self-aware would fail to recognize and report them.

The majority of teachers involved in the both programs indicated in the postprogram response questionnaires or interviews that they believed there was a positive change in regard to student effort and student perceived control. One feedback teacher intended to implement the program for all students and to train students to use the same questioning techniques to help each other. In her interview, one coping program teacher commented, "I think it's incredibly worthwhile. I feel really excited about it." The majority of teachers also indicated that the program would assist them with stressful classes. Several teachers reported improved relationships with students. They all said they would use the programs in the future and that use of these programs enabled them to be successful in their work with students with learning disabilities.

Outcomes from interviews and questionnaires regarding effects on teacher stress levels indicated that although teachers experienced some initial stress as they implemented the programs for the first time, they experienced stress relief as students responded positively to the program. Additionally, one of the three coping program teachers discussed a definite connection for her between the program and her own coping skills. Another teacher mentioned use of 'a common language of coping' that became available for use between students and between students and teachers. Increase in coping language usage has also occurred in the coping program research involving general student populations (Frydenberg, 2004; Huxley, 2004).

A strength of this study was the range of data gathered in that it included views of students, parents, and teacher. Although many measures lacked statistical significance, all of the data sources showed trends in the expected direction of positive effects of the programs on teacher stress, student coping, and student perceived sense of control. Additionally, the interventions took place within the constraints of everyday school settings and were implemented by different teachers. While such a design lacks experimental control this "real world" research provides a contrast to interventions that show positive effects when implemented by highly committed researchers in ideal circumstances, but which fail to be reproduced in real school settings (Schumaker & Deschler, 2003). A further strength of the study lies in the careful pre-testing of the students according to an exact definition of learning disabilities. This is a feature that, due to the need for individual assessment, is difficult to achieve in research involving large numbers of this group of students (Schumaker & Deschler, 2003).

Limitations of the Study

The real life setting of the study, despite its inherent strengths, did however affect experimental control. Although use of the ANCOVA allowed for differences between the groups at the beginning of the study, there was variation in the interventions at each of the different schools, for example different teachers used their own individual teaching styles when implementing the programs. Additionally, due to school scheduling and teacher commitments, grouping was not random: one feedback teacher left the school during the implementation of the program, and some students' postprogram response questionnaires were not competed before the end of the year. Furthermore, although the individual testing for learning disabilities was an important aspect of the study, this intensive process limited the sample to a relatively small number of students. Also, the interventions were complex so that it is not clear which aspects of them were the most powerful in changing perceived control and coping choices. It is possible for example that the changes experienced by the students occurred due to improved relationships with teachers rather than because of the control-related aspects of the programs. Finally, although the inclusion of parent and teacher reports triangulated the results and reduced reliance on student self report, the reliability of some of the tests was low, especially the short form of the ACS for both parents and teachers. Additionally not all parents and teachers completed the scales.

FUTURE RESEARCH

Although it is challenging to access large numbers of students who are accurately assessed as having learning disabilities, a further study using larger numbers of students is required to reassess the above findings. Additionally, as teachers have suggested that programs be longer and more intensive, further research using longer, more intensive exposure to the programs would clarify the extent to which this element is crucial. Much of the previous research on coping programs has involved 10-weekly exposures to the programs (Frydenberg, 2004). It is becoming clear that programs that aim to change longstanding attitudinal patterns need to be at least this long (Gresham, 1998) and that the coping programs need on-going reinforcement (Frydenberg, 2004). This is especially likely to be the case in regard to children who have learning disabilities (Gresham, 1998). Studies are also needed to isolate the particular elements of interventions that facilitate increased sense of control and adaptive coping for adolescent students who have learning disabilities.

CONCLUSION

There is an urgent need to equip teachers to assist students who have learning difficulties to cope effectively with the emotional aspects of their learning challenges. Achieving this goal will avoid the negative relationship cycle that can develop when teachers are overwhelmed by the challenge of working with these students. Teachers need to feel they can adequately meet the needs of students who have learning disabilities as well as motivate and control the negative behavior of some of these students (Shoho, 2002). Teaching coping programs, such as the ones described in this chapter, have been shown to have promise in regard to addressing these issues.

The coping program intervention described in this chapter has provided preliminary evidence of it being possible to facilitate change in both sense of control and coping patterns in a positive direction for students who have learning disabilities. In their discussion of success predicting attributes, such as proactivity for people who have learning disabilities, Raskind et al. (1999) pointed to the need for research to discover ways to assist young people to develop these coping resources. Their 20-year study found that once patterns were established, they rarely changed in later life and Raskind et al. (1999) therefore emphasized the particular importance of early intervention.

In the current climate of accountability, and given the demand for schools to facilitate healthy emotional development in their curriculum, characteristics, such as sense of control and adaptive coping, need to be both taught, measured, and be given equal importance with academic outcomes. In the case of students who have learning disabilities these skills are known to be especially important for their future success. Equal status in the curriculum for social emotional aspects of development would open an added route for these students both to increased experience of success in a valued area of school life and to the positive self-esteem cycle that accompanies success. Additionally, teachers would have the satisfaction of acknowledgement that their work was producing much needed results.

Such an approach would be enhanced if it was implemented in tandem with environmental change, such as provision of appropriate professional development. It is also important that teachers understand the nature of the phenomenon of learning difficulties; in that it manifests differently for each individual, occurs across the spectrum of cognitive ability, and is a life-long situation. Teachers also need access to resources, such as the latest research-based teaching interventions (Louden, 2000), reduced class sizes, and extra time allocation if they are to be well equipped to work with students who have learning disabilities (Westwood & Graham, 2003).

The studies reported above indicated that coping programs designed to meet the particular needs of students who have learning disabilities are worth pursuing. Both teachers and students reap the benefits, one of these being less stress. In the words of one of the coping program teachers, "I think it's opened up some sensitive and fairly meaningful dialogue between the students. The way they're interacting with each other is more gentle and kind." Such comments from teachers are most encouraging. A gentler environment in and out of school for both teachers and students fosters lower stress levels in both teachers and students and is a goal worth pursuing.

REFERENCES

Australian Council of Educational Research. (2003). *Tests of reading comprehension (TORCH)*. Melbourne: Australian Council of Educational Research Press.

Bender, W. N. (1987). Secondary personality and behavioural problems in adolescents with learning disabilities. *Journal of Learning Disabilities, 20*(5), 280-285.

Brandon, C. M., & Cunningham, E. G. (1999). *Bright Ideas*. Melbourne, Australia: Ozchild.

Chan, L., & Dally, K. (2000). Review of literature. In W. Louden, K. S. Chan, J. Elkins, D. Greaves, H. House, M. Milton, S. Nichols, J. Rivalland, M. Rohl, & C. van Kraayenoord, *Mapping the territory: Primary students with learning difficulties in literacy and numeracy* (Vol. 2, pp. 161-331). Canberra, Australia: Department of Education, Training and Youth Affairs.

Cheshire, G., & Cambell, M. (1997). Adolescent coping: Differences in the styles and strategies used by learning disabled compared to non learning disabled adolescents. *Australian Journal of Guidance and Counselling, 5*(1), 65-73.

Cotta, A., Frydenberg, E., & Poole, C. (2000). Coping skills training for adolescents at school. *Australian Educational and Developmental Psychologist, 17*,103-116.

Cunningham, E. (2002). *Developing coping resources in early adolescence evaluation of control-related mechanisms in a universal health promotion intervention*. Unpublished doctoral thesis, University of Melbourne, Melbourne, Australia.

Dweck, C. (2000). *Self theories: Their role in motivation, personality, and development*. Philadelphia: Psychology Press.

Firth, N. (2000). *Taking charge*. Melbourne, Australia: Ozchild.

Friedman, I. A. (2004). Directions in teacher training for low-burnout teaching. In E. Frydenberg (Ed.), *Thriving, surviving or going under*. Greenwich, CT: Information Age.

Frydenberg, E. (2004). Teaching young people to cope. In E. Frydenberg (Ed.), *Thriving, surviving or going under: Coping with everyday lives*. Greenwich, CT: Information Age.

Frydenberg, E., & Brandon, C. (2002). *The best of coping*. Melbourne, Australia: Ozchild.

Frydenberg, E., & Lewis, R. (1993). *Adolescent coping scale*. Melbourne: Australian Council for Educational Research.

Frydenberg, E., & Lewis, R. (1996). A replication study of the structure of the adolescent coping scale: Multiple forms and applications of a self-report inventory in a counseling and research context. *European Journal of Psychological Assessment, 12*(3), 224-235.

Gomez, R. (1997). Locus of control and Type A pattern as predictors of coping styles among adolescents. *Personality and Individual Differences, 23*(3), 391-398.

Gresham, F. (1998). Social skills training: Should we raze, remodel or rebuild? *Behavioural Disorders, 24*(1), 19-25.
Huxley, L. (2004). *A study of teachers' coping strategies: The best of coping.* Unpublished master's thesis, The University of Melbourne, Australia.
Kauffman, A. S., & Kaufman, N. L. (1996). *Kaufman Brief Intelligence Test (Australian Adaptation).* Melbourne: Australian Council for Educational Research.
Kline, P. (1993). *The handbook of psychological testing.* London: Routledge.
Kyriacou, C. (2001). Teacher stress: Directions for future research. *Educational Review, 53*(1), 27-35.
Louden, W. (2000). Mapping the territory: Overview. In W. Louden, K. S. Chan, J. Elkins, D. Greaves, H. House, M. Milton, S. Nichols, J. Rivalland, M. Rohl, & C. van Kraayenoord, *Mapping the territory: Primary students with learning difficulties in literacy and numeracy* (Vol. 1). Canberra, Australia: Department of Education, Training and Youth Affairs.
Mamlin, N., Harris, K. R., & Case, L. P. (2001). A methodological analysis of research on locus of control and learning disabilities: Rethinking a common assumption. *Journal of Special Education, 34*(4), 214-225.
Neale, M. D. (1988). *Neale analysis of reading ability revised.* Melbourne: Australian Council for Educational Research.
Nowicki, S., & Strickland, B. R. (1973). A locus of control scale for children. *Journal of Consulting and Clinical Psychology, 40*, 148-154.
Otto, R. (1986). *Teachers under stress.* Melbourne, Australia: Hill of Content.
Peterson, C., Maier, S. F., & Seligman, M. E. P. (1993). *Learned helplessness: A theory for the age of personal control.* New York: Oxford.
Prifitera, A., & Saklofske, D. (Eds.). (1998). *WISC III clinical use and interpretation: Scientist practitioner perspectives.* San Diego, CA: Academic Press.
Prior, M. (1996). *Understanding specific learning difficulties.* Hove United Kingdom: Psychology Press.
Prior, M., Sanson, A., Smart, D., & Oberklaid, F. (2001). *Pathways from infancy to adolescence: Australian temperament project 1983-2000.* Melbourne: Australian Institute of Family Studies.
Raskind, M., H., Golberg, R. J., Higgins, E. L., & Herman, K. L. (1999). Patterns of change and predictors of success in individuals with learning disabilities: Results from a twenty year study. *Learning Disabilities Research and Practice, 14*(1), 35-49.
Reiff, H. B., Ginsberg, R., & Gerber, P. J. (1995). New perspectives on teaching from successful adults with learning disabilities. *Remedial and Special Education, 16*(1), 29-37.
Resnick, M. D., Bearman, P. S., Blum, R. W., Bauman, K. E., Harris, K. M., Jones, J., Tabor, J., Beuhring, T., Sieving, R., Shew, M., Ireland, M., Bearinger, L. H., & Udry, J. R. (1997). Protecting adolescents from harm: Findings from the National longitudinal study on adolescent health. *Journal of the American Medical Association, 278*(10), 823-832.
Schumaker, J. B., & Deschler, D. D. (2003). Designs for applied educational research. In H. L. Swanson, K. R. Harris, & S. Graham (Eds.), *Handbook of learning disabilities* (pp. 483-500). New York: The Guilford Press.

Shoho, A. R. (2002). A comparison of burnout between general and special education teachers. In G. S. Gates & M. Wolverton (Eds.), *Towards wellness: Prevention, coping, and stress* (pp. 143-158). Greenwich, Connecticut: Information Age.

Tabachnick, B. G., & Fidell, L. S. (1996). *Using multivariate statistics.* Boston: Allyn & Bacon.

Vaughan, S., Gersten, R., & Chard, D. (2000). The underlying message in LD intervention research: Findings from research syntheses. *Exceptional Children, 67*(1), 99-114.

Wehmeyer, M. L., & Kelchener, K. (1996). Perceptions of classroom environment, locus of control and academic attributions of adolescents with and without cognitive disabilities. *Career Development for Exceptional Individuals, 19*(1), 15-28.

Westwood, P. (1999). South Australian Spelling Test. In P. Westwood (Ed.), *Spelling: Approaches to teaching and assessment* (pp. 64-67). Melbourne: Australian Council of Educational Research.

Westwood, P., & Graham, L. (2003). Inclusion of students with special needs. *Australian Journal of Learning Disabilities, 8*(1), 3-15.

CHAPTER 5

MULTICULTURAL COMPETENCIES AND TEACHER STRESS

Implications for Teacher Preparation, Practice, and Retention

Sylvia C. Nassar-McMillan, Meagan Karvonen, and Cheryl Young

Multicultural diversity represents a potential area of stress for teachers in today's schools. In the context of contemporary society as more culturally diverse than ever, teachers are increasingly called on to develop multicultural competencies to best serve their respective student bodies. In this chapter, we describe a local inquiry into issues of diversity conducted by interviewing groups of teachers from two schools with relatively homogenous and heterogeneous populations, respectively. We identify the teacher challenges, external stressors, and coping strategies brought out through the interview discussions, and compare teachers perceptions across schools. Finally, we present implications for helping teachers develop effective strategies for developing multicultural sensitivity and competence.

Situational changes inherently pose stressors. The way in which individuals impacted by these stressors view them can influence both the cognitive and behavioral techniques they engage to cope with them (Folkman & Lazarus, 1988). In the wake of experiencing major demands seen as potentially taxing or damaging, either internal or external ones, individuals either intentionally or unintentionally determine the coping strategies they will use in handling their challenges.

Changes in the demographic landscape of school systems can cause similar situations for teachers and other school personnel, such as counselors and administrators. The appraisal by individual teachers of such challenges as potentially positive or negative can impact the ability of individuals to recognize and identify their available social and cultural resources as well as the coping strategies they subsequently employ (Lazarus & Cohen, 1977). In this chapter, we review background literature related to diversity in schools, as well as multicultural competence guidelines and practices. We explore teachers' appraisal of classroom and school diversity, preservice teacher preparation and other available resources in multicultural skill development, and coping strategies mobilized by teachers to address issues of diversity within the classroom and school environment. We support these findings by providing an overview of field-based research conducted in our local school system.

MULTICULTURAL DIVERSITY IN THE UNITED STATES

It is clear that the demographic landscape of the United States is rapidly becoming diversified. Population projections indicate that, by the year 2010, growth of African American and Latino populations will have accelerated while those of Caucasian Americans will increase only slightly (U.S. Census Bureau, 2001); and that by the year 2020, one in five children will have Hispanic backgrounds (Federal Interagency Forum on Child and Family Statistics, 2001). In addition, a U.S. Census Bureau language profile indicates that 3.5 million school-aged children, or approximately 5%, are linguistically challenged (Annie E. Casey Foundation, 2002). Finally, poverty afflicts nearly one child in four, most typically ethnic/racial minority populations, and has far reaching impacts in terms of issues, such as homelessness, family structure, and, not surprisingly, educational achievement and attainment (Flaxman, Schwartz, Weiler, & Lahey, 1998).

The vast majority of teachers and those in training represent a mainstream Caucasian European American population (Gay & Howard, 2000). At the same time, in response to the changing demographic landscape in the United States, teachers have increasingly been called on to deliver their respective services from a framework of multicultural competence.

Differences in the multicultural backgrounds between teachers in training and their future constituent populations may add challenges to ensuring effective teaching within a multicultural context. Thus, teacher preparation programs have been entrusted with the responsibility for providing adequate preparation for the multifaceted cultural arena that characterizes today's schools.

Multicultural development typically includes three general areas of self awareness, other awareness, and operationalizing the differences between the first two (Sue, Arredondo, & McDavis, 1992). Each of these three areas requires an in-depth self-analysis of attitudes and beliefs, knowledge, and skills. The responsibility of teachers to engage in this development process can seem overwhelming, particularly to those new to the profession. Because teachers' preparation in this area of competence varies, both their perceptions of readiness as well as their actual multicultural competence can vary. In addition, teachers often find themselves amidst perceived conflicting pressures of tangible outcome measures, such as high stakes test scores, on the one hand, and attending to culturally related crises within their classrooms, on the other. Without multicultural competencies, inexperienced teachers may not use the diverse classroom environment for instructional purposes, may not be equipped to interact in culturally appropriate ways with some students, and may simply feel overwhelmed by the exposure to cultural backgrounds or issues with which they are unfamiliar.

Several years ago, the local school system in our southeastern city was amidst an extensive, complex set of circumstances surrounding multicultural issues. These issues are detailed later in this chapter. In part, they prompted our inquiry into teacher's perceptions of multicultural aspects of their classrooms and schools. In an attempt to extend the cursory knowledge of these particular perceptions, which was gathered from an annually administered, system-wide, quantitative survey tool designed to measure many facets of school climate, we conducted focus groups of teachers from two different schools. We used a semistructured set of questions about cultural knowledge and cultural climate. We believed, going in, that those teachers who felt better prepared and more exposed to issues of diversity would perceive their impending challenges in that arena as positive, and potentially growth inducing. Outcomes of our inquiry are reported later in this chapter.

DIVERSITY IN SCHOOLS

Schools can be viewed as educational ecosystems within communities (Swartz & Martin, 1997). Within such a relational context, individual identities and the relationships between them interface in delicate balance, wherein even subtle changes in attitude or behavior can impact the entire system. Researchers have attempted to identify salient factors that play into this delicate balance by measuring ideas, labeled as school culture, school climate, and the like. In the assessment of these constructs, teachers, students, and parents serve as target audiences, often with the goals of better understanding the overall experience for the students as participants in the school system in an effort to enhance teacher preparation programs. Regardless of how the environmental and individual identities within the school are conceptualized or defined, we believe that among the ultimate criteria for healthy school communities is that school personnel embrace and respect students from diverse backgrounds. Ogbu (1988, 1994, 1995a) identified some of the challenges confronting contemporary educational systems involving differences in cultural frames of reference, or culturally accepted attitudes, beliefs, or behaviors, among other characteristics, between students and school environments. For example, an African American student might come from a cultural background in which Black Vernacular is used. If this behavior were employed by the student within a school culture where it were stigmatized, the resulting perception of his or her speech, or behavior, could have a potentially negative impact on the student's potential for upward mobility within the school culture.

As a result of many such cultural mismatches in perception, or cultural frames of references, systemic discrimination may impact some racial and ethnic groups differentially (Calabrese & Underwood, 1994; Ogbu, 1988). Students who are culturally and linguistically diverse (CLD) consistently achieve below their potential (National Assessment of Educational Progress, 2003). Alarmingly, national achievement test scores have not shown significant improvement among African American or Hispanic students in over thirty years (National Assessment of Educational Progress, 2000). During the same 30 years, African American students have been consistently overrepresented in diagnoses of mental retardation (U.S. Department of Education, 2002). Hispanic students often represent a higher drop out rate than their Anglo peers, and are disproportionately represented in special education programs (Trent & Artiles, 1998).

Those who are labeled as having social and emotional disorders are more likely to be absent, retained, experience overly severe punishments for lesser violations, and be placed in restrictive settings (Serwatka, Deering, & Grant, 1995). African American males are suspended from school at twice the rate of their White male counterparts; and African American females are suspended from school at a rate of three times more than theirs (Raffaele-Mendez & Knoff, 2003). Even within wealthier communities, African American students have been found more likely to be labeled with emotional and behavioral disorders (Oswald, Coutinho, Best, &

Singh, 1999). Indeed, it can be postulated that students with limited exposure to the mainstream curriculum continue downward into a spiral of lower levels of achievement, coupled with decreased likelihoods of postsecondary education and successful employment experiences (Patton, 1998). The obstacles confronting various multicultural groups also present immense challenges to teachers as they try to achieve increased end-of-testing scores. These seemingly conflicting circumstances can be perceived as either negatively stressful or as positive possibilities to enhance the growth of everyone involved in the classroom.

MULTICULTURAL COMPETENCE

The National Board for Professional Teaching Standards (NBPTS, 2003) includes several standards that speak to diversity and multicultural competence among early childhood and K-12 teachers. These standards emphasize the creation of a safe, caring, and inclusive learning environment, teacher modeling of appreciation for individual differences, and teaching that fosters student respect for diversity. In addition, the National Council for the Accreditation of Teacher Education Programs (NCATE, 2002) includes a standard on diversity for units responsible for providing teacher preparation programs:

> The unit designs, implements, and evaluates curriculum and experiences for candidates to acquire and apply the knowledge, skills, and dispositions necessary to help all students learn. These experiences include working with diverse higher education and school faculty, diverse candidates, and diverse students in P-12 schools. (p. 29)

Despite these mandates, a cursory on-line review of several teacher education programs yields coursework designated to prepare teachers in training for working with diverse learners that is limited to learning about differences in developmental level or cognitive abilities, rather than cultural or environmental uniquenesses. Scholars also note that, while present day preservice teachers' perceptions of their preparation in areas of multiculturalism indicate improvements over the last decade, they tend to reflect uncertainty about how to integrate multicultural issues into classroom and school environments (Milner, Flowers, Moore, Moore, & Flowers, 2003).

In response to some of the maladies of the educational system detailed earlier, multicultural education has historically played an important role in creating a more equality oriented environment (Flaxman et al., 1998). Banks (1995) described a typology of multicultural education as integration of diversity material into standard curricula and into both teaching and learning processes, educational strategies to foster tolerant and diversity-oriented attitudes, equitable assessment and evaluation strategies, and creating cultural empowerment within the school culture. It is our intent to revisit those strategies in this chapter. We believe that multicultural education may prove helpful to teachers struggling with diversity in their daily work as they attempt to maintain high academic performance levels in their classrooms and schools. In illustration, we provide an overview of the study we conducted in our local school system.

TEACHING REALITIES: ONE LOCAL INQUIRY

Teachers, through their academic preparation, are typically prepared to accommodate differences in developmental levels, cognitive abilities, and even learning styles. At the same time, students' personal profiles, which often include unique aspects of their individual culture, family, and community or other environmental issues, may interface or even interfere with their ability to learn in a standard classroom situation. Such are the realities of the challenges of present day teachers. These challenges, taken together with the history and environment of our urban school system, prompted us to engage in an inquiry of challenges and issues faced by our local teachers. In this examination, we were interested in both the common and distinctive experiences with multiculturalism of two contrasting schools.

Context of Our Inquiry

Charlotte-Mecklenburg Schools (CMS) has long been in the forefront of discussions on race relations and school desegregation. In 1971 the Supreme Court upheld the *Swann v Charlotte-Mecklenburg Board of Education* decision ordering the desegregation of schools. For many years desegregation was achieved primarily through bussing and the adjustment of attendance boundaries, although a few schools were designated as "choice" schools in the 1970s. In the 1990s, CMS began implementing magnet programs on a large scale in order to maintain the approximate 60% White and 40% Black/Other school enrollment required by the court order. A lawsuit brought by a White parent in 1997 resulted in a decision that the district was unitary and no longer required a court-ordered desegregation plan.

Three years after the parent lawsuit was filed and months before the appeals court declared CMS a unitary district, we conducted focus groups with faculty from two contrasting elementary schools. One of these was

Table 5.1. **Demographic Characteristics of Schools A and B***

	School A	School B	District
Total enrollment	1,013	503	102,013
Racial composition			
African American	5%	60%	42%
Asian	4%	3%	4%
Caucasian	87%	22%	46%
Latino	2%	12%	6%
Native American	0%	2%	1%
Multiracial	2%	1%	1%
Receive free/reduced lunch	4%	63%	36%
Limited English Proficiency	1%	12%	6%
Exceptional Children (excluding gifted and talented)	6%	13%	11%

*Enrollment data were not available for the year in which the study was conducted. These data are from the closest possible school year.

established as Charlotte's first choice school in the 1970s (School B). The other school (A) was in its fourth year of operation in an affluent, suburban location in the county. Demographic characteristics of the two schools and the district as a whole are included in Table 5.1.

School A served more than 1,000 students in grades K–5, 87% of which were European American. Very few students at School A were classified as English Language Learners (1%) or having low socioeconomic status (4%). In contrast, School B had an enrollment that was half the size of School A's. Sixty percent of students were African American, 22% were Caucasian, and 12% were of Latino origin. School B also had higher proportions of its students classified as English Language Learners (12%) and as having low socioeconomic status (63%). In addition, School B had more than twice as high a percentage of its students classified as exceptional children (>12%) as did School A (6%).

The school district collects annual survey data on a variety of topics from teachers, assistant teachers, parents, and students district wide. Available teacher survey data for the two schools highlight some contrasting opinions on school climate issues, depicted in Table 5.2.

There were considerable discrepancies in the percentages of teachers that perceived their school as fair, nonthreatening, and responsive to student needs. These survey responses, in conjunction with the demographic data, underscore the differences between the two schools selected for this study. We selected these contrasting schools to examine how teachers perceived the levels of diversity in terms of both challenge and opportunity.

Table 5.2. Teacher Survey Excerpt Endorsements
Reflecting Contrasting Climates in the Selected Schools

	% Agree/Strongly Agree	
Survey Item Excerpt	School A	School B
All students are treated fairly	93	62
All staff members are treated fairly	79	52
Needs of students with learning problems are addressed	71	28
Students are intimidated by other students	12	69

Participants and Procedures

Nine teachers and one counselor from School A and 11 teachers from School B participated in our focus groups. Our initial contact with these personnel was through the principals, who offered the opportunity and encouragement for participation to all their faculty members. Ethnic and gender composition in the School A group included nine females; two African Americans, and eight Euro Americans. School B's group included 11 females; one African American, eight Euro American, one Asian American, and one Latino American.

Groups were conducted by two faculty members from a nearby university, one in counselor education and another in teaching English as a second language. Both had interests in diversity and multicultural issues in school settings. Focus groups were conducted in a semistructured manner. A list of common guiding questions was developed for use with both groups, including questions, such as "Have you received any professional training in cultural competence?" "What problems have you encountered among students/parents/colleagues that you attribute to racial, ethnic, or cultural differences?" "What suggestions do you have for public school systems for improving the cross-cultural relationships among students/parents/school personnel?" and "How do you perceive your own cultural competencies?" Additional unscripted prompts were used to probe participants' ideas in greater depth.

All interviews were audio taped and transcribed verbatim. The transcripts were reviewed by one of the focus group facilitators (first author) for accuracy prior to analysis. A researcher who was familiar with the purpose of the study but who did not conduct the focus groups (second author) reviewed transcripts and wrote narrative summaries of the remarks, organized by major research questions. These summaries served as the foundation for discussions between the first and second authors about important themes related to the research questions. Transcripts were initially coded for teachers' descriptions of challenges related to diversity and how those challenges were addressed. Challenges were organized into domains based on the teacher's role (e.g., addressing academic and social needs), and categorized by their source (internal and external). Quotes provided in the sections below were chosen because they clearly illustrated common perceptions, or highlighted unique experiences, of the teachers.

Teachers' Challenges

Teachers from both schools identified a number of social stressors they faced related to multicultural education and diversity issues. Classroom-related stressors tended to fall into one of two categories: challenges about addressing multiculturalism from an instructional standpoint, and challenges related to social contexts. External pressures from parents and the public perception of the school also represented stressors for these teachers.

Academic Challenges

Teachers in both schools described the focus on cultural diversity incorporated into the formal curriculum as being limited to holidays, important figures, and contributions to society covered in grades K-2. This method is characterized by Banks (2001) as the contributions approach, an additive model that is relatively easy to add to curriculum but which can also lead to reinforcement of myths and stereotypes about the strangeness of other cultures. One teacher in School A also used children's literature from other countries as a way to incorporate cultural diversity into the set curriculum. Teachers in School B relied on students and parent volunteers to come to classes and talk about holidays, food, and other aspects of their native cultures. However, across 21 teachers, no other purposeful methods of incorporating multicultural themes into instruction were described. Teachers expressed concern about the lack of cultural elements in the standard curriculum beyond the first grade. One teacher at School A illustrated this point:

> Some of the kids will be talking about the whole religion thing. And they'll come to me—I said I don't really know, so I'll call a parent. I'll just bluntly come out and say, "I'm not being rude, but I need to ask you some questions ...", and they're more than willing to do it. But you're too afraid to ask to get to know, to talk about it. And then [the parent will] say, "Well they talked about it in kindergarten and first grade. How come you can't [in the upper grades]?" So I say, "Well, the kindergarten it's [holidays], in first grade it's the calendar." And that's what I've been told to say, is the excuse that it's talked about in kindergarten and first grade.

With the lack of opportunity to include multicultural elements in the formal curriculum, teachers also expressed confusion about how to take advantage of teachable moments:

> I have four Jewish kids in my class and they were talking about what they're allowed [in Passover]. And I'm sitting there going, "Oh no. Should I cover [that]?" Am I supposed to jump in and talk about that now, but they've learned about it in kindergarten and first grade and when they get older, it's like it comes to a stop.

In contrast, a teacher at School B described her approach to these unplanned, teachable moments:

> I use it as a teaching tool, when there's a situation or something that happens, as far as someone disrespecting another person because they don't understand their differences. Then I use that opportunity right then and there to put it back on and say "what if they did this? How would you feel about it?"

Teachers at School A received mixed messages about how to handle cultural elements in instruction. On one hand, their principal asked teachers to talk about diversity at times other than holidays. On the other hand, teachers had the impression they were not allowed to talk about cultures outside the standard curriculum:

> I got that list [of parents who would share about their cultural backgrounds] and I was like, "I thought we weren't supposed to talk about that," but then we get this list that we can call these people to come and ... so you just kind of back off. I don't, I do anyways. I don't want to get in trouble.

In contrast to the formalized efforts at School A, teachers at School B described informal methods they used to address their students' diversity. Two participants indicated that they used their knowledge of cultures and traditions in order to make sense of students' reactions to situations:

> I try to understand ... why they might have said something, or why they might [have] reacted that way. I try to think back, "Oh, ... their background is that, so that makes sense to me." So I try to have a better understanding of where they're coming from and why they're reacting the way they do.

A counselor at the same school indicated that she considered the child's background in planning individual student interventions.

Teachers also highlighted several barriers to working effectively with diverse students, especially in communicating with students and parents for whom English is a second language. Teachers at School A indicated they were often able to rely on strong bilingual students to help those with weaker English proficiency understand concepts in their native language. This approach was successful with commonly-spoken languages (i.e., Spanish), but more difficult when only one student with a different native language was in the class. Teachers at both schools also had difficulty communicating with non-English speaking parents about students' work.

Shifting away from racial and linguistic challenges, teachers at School B noted issues related to teaching students with very challenging life circumstances:

> If someone were to ask me what my job was … it's a teacher, but before anything else I'm a social worker … I cannot teach a child who's been at home all night long with somebody who's stalking his house with a gun. I can't teach that child, he's a mess—
>
> —Children are so tired they can't keep their eyes open and if you look you know they slept in their clothes and they come to your class and they can't function so you just lay out a mat and say "just sleep right here."

Additionally, some traditional stressors about teaching responsibilities were viewed as having implications for diversity. For example, large class enrollments were seen as a barrier to one teacher's ability to focus on individuals with different needs and talents.

Social Stressors

Besides the challenges of teaching diverse learners, teachers face stressors related to the social elements of the school environment. In School A, this challenge materialized in problems inherent in the disciplinary process. The following exchange by several teachers reveals one dilemma:

> You know, we're not going to punish him because, oh my goodness, look at his background! You know, I see that going on.
>
> Back in the office, they don't send him home because they know what's going to happen when he gets home and they just can't bear to subject that kid to that.
>
> When they send somebody home, then mama's boyfriend is gonna slam him up against the wall or lock him in his room. And so what are your choices as an administrator?
>
> What can you live with?

Teachers' decisions about how to address disciplinary problems in the classroom also have implications for how students view the teacher's fairness or prejudice:

> And then the kids ... turn around and say things like, "Well you're making me sit out because I'm Hispanic." And I'm like, "I wouldn't care if you're purple. You did something you weren't supposed to do, go sit down."

Other teachers validated students' concerns about preferential treatment:

> There have been times when it has been race, I've gone into classrooms and I've seen Black students who've been referred [to the office for disciplinary reasons] and then I've seen some White students who were doing that same thing, and have not been referred.

Teachers viewed a lack of guidelines for making disciplinary referrals, and teachers' inconsistencies in adhering to any guidelines, as a source of the problem. A teacher at School B expressed frustration with the lack of guidance about handling diversity challenges from a social perspective:

> [The social aspect is] the most important thing that you ever learn in any school setting.... To me it's all about how you interact with people and what you learn from the people who are around you. And that is what is very hard to teach, and that's what they don't teach us how to teach.

Likewise, tension was identified as a potential problem between teachers in the same school. In the focus group with teachers from School A, several remarked that they lacked the time to really talk with other teachers outside their immediate network based on grade level or subject. One teacher noted, "And if you don't talk, somebody might think that there is a problem or prejudice, but the fact is, it isn't."

External Stressors: Parent Interactions and Public Perceptions

Teachers at school A described stress related to interactions with parents in the school. Two African American teachers discussed a need to "prove" themselves to the Caucasian parents.

> I'm very comfortable with myself, so I don't always feel the need to necessarily prove myself because I figure that it will eventually show, but it is, it really is a stressor ...I 've been in schools all my life where parents come in ... it wasn't to come to help as much as was to observe.

These teachers described the subtle tension that occurred when Caucasian parents entered the classroom and approached a Caucasian assistant, mistakenly assuming she was the teacher and the African American was the assistant.

The high level of parent involvement in School A may have contributed to teachers' hesitancy to address cultural issues. One teacher indicated she was reluctant to talk about culture for fear that parents would confront her with school or district rules that prohibit talking about such things. Fear of parent complaints were not unfounded in this school; teachers described situations in which parents would "remind" teachers of the family's cultural values and "make sure" the teacher respected those values. Parental influence may seem especially strong to the novice teacher confronted on cultural issues:

> As a first-year teacher ... I'm very intimidated by parents, in the sense of, "You're picking on my child because he's Black."... I don't want to be, because I try not to be.... When I got an ear full of that, I was just like, "Ok. You know what, if you think I'm picking on your kid and you think that I'm racist, that's all I can do."

Coping with Challenges

How do teachers cope with the challenges of being culturally competent? One solution identified by a teacher in this study is to not talk about culture at all:

> A lot of us are a little shy about talking about it, because you do want to be careful to who's sensitive ... I wouldn't want to say anything to hurt somebody's feelings, so you say the wrong thing. So maybe I don't say anything, and that's not how I need to be.

Teachers from both schools had participated in some level of diversity training, yet this training did not thoroughly prepare them for dealing with the challenges of providing multicultural education and dealing with diverse student needs. Teachers from both schools shared their suggestions for supporting teachers' culturally competent practice:

- Consensus from administrators about behavioral expectations and enforcement;
- Permission from school leadership to have frank discussions about cultural differences;
- Use of specialized curriculum materials, such as *Teaching Tolerance*, a collection of educational materials and activities to address diversity and antibias projects (Southern Poverty Law Center, n.d.); and
- Prepare preservice teachers for the social aspects of school, including tolerance and behavior modification principles.

Summary of Findings

Initially we selected two demographically different schools in order to observe how those differences played out in teachers' perceptions of multicultural diversity issues as stressors. The district's own quantitative survey results reflect more dissatisfaction and concern in School B than in School A; our focus group results yield some possible explanation for that phenomenon. In the focus group interviews, it seemed apparent that teachers from both schools perceived issues of multicultural diversity as stressful. Essentially, teachers' perceived their internal, school based challenges as representing either academic or social domains. Key external stressors emerging from the interviews were identified as parental interactions and public perceptions. In School A, teachers expressed discomfort with diversity stemming from their uncertainty with how to handle such issues within their classrooms and curricula. In School B, although teachers expressed some similar discomfort, the nature of their diverse school and classroom demographics necessitated them handling the ongoing challenges related to diversity in a more direct manner. Thus, the challenges expressed by School A's teachers were more of an academic nature, while those expressed by School B's teachers were more representative of a social one. Further, because School B's teachers were more overtly confronted with issues of diversity, they seemed more likely to respond to those stressors and challenges more directly. It should be noted that many of the teachers in both groups indicated choosing to be at their assigned school. The teachers in School B, then, in particular, may have viewed their stressors as desirable ones, tended to view the diversity in their classrooms as a resource, and dealt with challenges related to diversity directly because they perceived the environment as a desirable one.

IMPLICATIONS

Given the seeming disconnect between professional teaching standards and teacher preparation programs in terms of multicultural issues, bridging this gap will ultimately involve multiple layers. Teacher preparation programs must be held accountable for assessing their individual course content to ensure adherence to national teaching standards, particularly in the realm of diversity. From individual teachers' perspectives, learning strategies can be developed to overcome the skill deficiency experienced by many teachers. Additionally, teacher reform must address not only disparities in developmental or economic levels of student learners, but must begin to examine the educational climate in more comprehensive and complex ways.

Finally, and perhaps most importantly, the way in which teachers perceive the concept of multicultural competence can impact their own appraisal of their challenges as well as inform their development of coping strategies. Teachers who view themselves as multiculturally competent may interpret the challenges before them as less stressful than those who do not. Those who value multicultural competence may, in turn, their impending diversity related demands as opportunities to further develop their own competence.

Teacher Strategies

Teachers are cognizant of their challenges in the arena of diversity. They realize that their lack of cultural competence may impede the growth and learning within their own classroom ecosystem. Like some of the teachers in our focus groups, many teachers recognize that student learners are unlikely to be able to learn on a given day if they are hungry, exhausted, bullied, or even disrespected.

The potentially different cultural backgrounds and experiences of teachers and their students underscores the need for additional multicultural development. The acquisition of such enhanced competencies can serve as a powerful resource for teachers confronting the stress of a diverse classroom and school environment for which they may be underprepared. Through engaging in the process of multicultural development, teachers will, ideally, become more equipped to develop effective and culturally competent teaching strategies.

School counselors typically have extensive training in areas of diversity and can serve as an excellent resource to teachers. Such counselors are charged with facilitating student development in educational, career, personal, and social arenas (Lee, 1995). Counselor and teacher collaboration is an ideal model through which to help students achieve their corresponding goals. By developing and implementing large-group classroom guidance interventions as well as creative curricula integration on diversity issues, counselors and teachers, collectively, can help students from culturally diverse backgrounds develop healthy self-concepts while working toward positive outcomes in both their curricular and non curricular endeavors. Thus, it may behoove teachers to seek out the collaboration and consultation of their school counselors.

Finally, teachers can ask for and encourage more staff discussions and training on community populations and resources, diversity, and culturally appropriate limit and expectation setting as well as disciplinary practices. Indeed, in order for comprehensive teacher reform efforts to be effective, they need to aggressively address these same issues. Included in these efforts must be recruitment of more teachers with culturally diverse perspectives and broadening the scope of school climate assessments to include multicultural issues within the educational ecosystem.

Perhaps one place to begin might be fostering better understanding and openness among school faculty and administrators. If teachers are going to successfully engage students in deep understanding of various cultural backgrounds, they must address diversity as it manifests in the school climate as well as through more formalized multicultural education. Teachers must be prepared to deal with diversity questions when they arise and provide safe spaces for students to raise such questions (Jervis, 1996). Rather than expecting students to assimilate to the mainstream culture (Sleeter & Grant, 1999), schools, and their personnel, should view acculturation as a two-way interaction between teachers and students (Banks, 2001).

ACKNOWLEDGMENT

The authors wish to acknowledge the Association for Counselor Education and Supervision and the University of North Carolina at Charlotte College of Education University-School Teaching Education Partnerships Program for providing partial funding for our study. Our thanks go to the school members who participated in our study as well as the two school principals who supported our efforts.

REFERENCES

Annie E. Casey Foundation. (2002). *Kids count 2002 data book online*. Baltimore, MD: Author. Retrieved January 7, 2005 from http://www.aecf.org/kidscount/kc2002/summary.htm

Banks, J. A. (1995). Multicultural education: Historical development, dimensions, and practice. In J. A. Banks & C. A. M. Banks (Eds.), *Handbook of research on multicultural education* (pp. 3-24). New York: Macmillan.

Banks, J. A. (2001). *Cultural diversity and education: Foundations, curriculum, and teaching* (4th ed.). Boston: Allyn & Bacon.

Calabrese, R. L., & Underwood, E. (1994). The effects of school-generated racism on students of color. *High School Journal, 77*(4), 267-273.

Federal Interagency Forum on Child and Family Statistics. (2001). *America's children: Key national indicators of well-being*. Washington, DC: U.S. Government Printing Office.

Flaxman, E., Schwartz, W., Weiler, J., & Lahey, M. (1998). *Trends and issues in urban education, 1998*. New York: Institute for Urban and Minority Education. (ERIC Document Reproduction Service No. ED425247)

Folkman, S., & Lazarus, R. S. (1988). Coping as a mediator of emotion. *Journal of Personality and Social Psychology, 54*, 466-475.
Gay, G., & Howard, T. C. (2000). Multicultural teacher education for the 21st century. *The Teacher Educator, 36*(1), 1-16.
Jervis, K. (1996). How come there are no brothers on that list?: Hearing the hard questions all children ask. *Harvard Educational Review, 66*, 546-577.
Lazarus, R. S., & Cohen, J. B. (1977). Environmental stress. In I. Altma and J. F. Wohlwill (Eds.), *Human Behavior and Environment* (Vol. 2). New York: Plenum.
Lee, C. C. (1995). School counseling and cultural diversity: A framework for effective practice. In C. C. Lee (Ed.), *Counseling for diversity: A guide for school counselors and related professionals* (pp. 3-17). Boston: Allyn & Bacon.
Milner, H. R., Flowers, L. A., Moore, E., Jr., Moore, J. L., III, & Flowers, T. A. (2003). Preservice teachers' awareness of multiculturalism and diversity. *The High School Journal, 87*, 63-70.
National Assessment of Educational Progress. (2000). *The nation's report card.* Washington, DC: National Center for Educational Statistics, US Department of Education. Retrieved July 10, 2003, from http://nces.ed.gov/nationsreportcard/reading/results2003/stateresults.asp
National Assessment of Educational Progress. (2003). *The nation's report card.* Washington, DC: National Center for Educational Statistics, US Department of Education. Retrieved October 18, 2004, from http://nces.ed.gov/nationsreportcard/reading/results2003/stateresults.asp
National Board for Professional Teaching Standards (2003, May 30). *Standards and national boards certification: Standards.* Retrieved January 10, 2005 from http://www.nbpts.org/standards/stds.cfm
National Council for Accreditation of Teacher Education (2002). Professional standards for the accreditation of schools, colleges, and departments of education. Washington, DC: Author. Retrieved January 9, 2005 from http://www.ncate.org/standard/m_stds.htm
Ogbu, J. (1988). Black education: A cultural-ecological perspective. In H. P. McAdoo (Ed.), *Black Families* (2nd ed., pp. 169-184). Thousand Oaks, CA: Sage Publications.
Ogbu, J. (1994). From cultural differences to differences in cultural frame of reference. In R. R. Cocking & P. M. Greenfield (Eds.), *Cross-cultural roots of minority child development* (pp.365-391). Hillsdale, NJ: Lawrence Erlbaum Associates.
Ogbu, J. (1995a). Origins of human competence: A cultural-ecological perspective. In J. B. Veroff & N. R. Goldberger (Eds.), *The culture and psychology reader* (pp.245-275). New York: New York University Press.
Ogbu, J. U. (1995b). Cultural problems in minority education: Their interpretations and consequences—Part one: Theoretical background. *Urban Review, 37*(3), 189-297.
Oswald, D. P., Coutinho, M. J., Best, A. M., & Singh, N. N. (1999). Ethnic representation in special education: The influence of school-related economic and demographic variables. *Journal of Special Education, 32*(4), 194-206.
Patton, J. M. (1998). The disproportionate representation of African Americans in special education: Looking behind the curtain for understanding and solutions. *The Journal of Special Education, 32*, 25-31.

Raffaele-Mendez, L. M., & Knoff, H. M. (2003). Who gets suspended from school and why: A demographic analysis of schools and disciplinary infractions in a large school district. *Education and Treatment of Children, 26*(1), 30-51.

Serwatka, T. S., Deering, S., & Grant, P. (1995). Disproportionate representation of African Americans in emotionally handicapped classes. *Journal of Black Studies, 25*(4), 492-506.

Sleeter, C. E., & Grant, C. A. (1999). *Making choices for multicultural education: Five approaches to race, class, and gender* (3rd ed.). Upper Saddle River, NJ: Prentice-Hall.

Southern Poverty Law Center. (n.d.). *Teaching tolerance*. Montgomery, AL: Author. Retrieved January 7, 2005 from http://www.tolerance.org/teach/

Sue, D. W., Arredondo, P., & McDavis, R. J. (1992). Multicultural counseling competencies and standards: A call to the profession. *Journal of Counseling and Development, 70*, 477-483.

Swann v. Charlotte-Mecklenburg Board of Educ., 402 U.S. 1 (1971).

Swartz, J. L., & Martin, W. E. (Eds.). (1997). Ecological psychology theory: Historical overview and application to educational ecosystem. In *Applied ecological psychology for schools within communities: Assessment and intervention* (pp. 3-27). Mahwah, NJ: Erlbaum.

Trent, S. C., & Artiles, A. J. (1998). Multicultural teacher education in special and bilingual education: Exploring multiple measurement strategies to assess teacher learning. *Remedial and Special Education, 19*(1), 2-6.

U.S. Census Bureau. (2001). *United States census 2000*. Washington, DC: U.S. Government Printing Office.

U.S. Department of Education. (2002). *Twenty-fourth annual report to Congress on the implementation of the Individuals with Disabilities Education Act, Section 618*. (No. HS97020001). Retrieved October 18, 2004, from http://www.ed.gov/offices/OSERS/OSEP

CHAPTER 6

TEACHER STRESS AND CLASSROOM STRUCTURAL CHARACTERISTICS IN PRESCHOOL SETTINGS

Richard G. Lambert, Megan O'Donnell, Jennifer Kusherman, and Christopher J. McCarthy

The Classroom Appraisal of Resources and Demands (CARD) was used to explore stress among preschool teachers ($N = 317$). The sample yielded reliable difference scores, which measured the gap between a teacher's appraisal of both classroom demands and the resources available to meet those demands. These scores were used to classify teachers according to risk of stress and were examined for associations with classroom structural characteristics. Teacher stress was related to the number of children with problem behaviors in the classroom.

Teaching has been recognized as an emotionally taxing and potentially frustrating occupation for centuries. For several decades, researchers in the social sciences have identified teaching as an occupation with a high risk of stress (Dunham & Varma, 1998; Kyriacou, 2000, 2001; Kyriacou & Sutcliffe, 1977; Travers & Cooper, 1996). The working conditions for

Understanding Teacher Stress in an Age of Accountability, 105–120
Copyright © 2006 by Information Age Publishing
All rights of reproduction in any form reserved.

teachers also present a high risk for burnout. In fact, teachers are the largest homogenous occupational group investigated in burnout research, comprising 22% of all samples (Schaufeli & Enzmann, 1998).

Researchers of stress in general and teacher stress in particular have used a variety of strategies to measure the construct of stress. Self-reports of negative life events (Sarason, Johnson, & Siegel, 1978) have been applied extensively. Another approach has been to ask respondents to identify the stress symptoms they experience (Green, Walkey, McCormick, & Taylor, 1988). The symptoms approach has included measures of physical and mental health; behavioral indicators, such as difficulties in relationships or on the job; and physiological changes during the stress response, such as heart rate and hormonal indicators (Kyriacou, 2001). Measures of coping strategies and resources have also been widely used (Hammer & Marting, 1988).

The most common strategy for measuring teacher stress has been self-report questionnaires that ask respondents to rate how stressful they find various aspects of their working conditions (Kyriacou & Sutcliffe, 1978). Another approach has been to combine perceptions of various sources of stress with the severity of manifestations of the stress response (Fimian, 1984, 1985, 1987, 1988). When multiple constructs have been included in teacher stress measurement tools, they often examine different aspects of the global domain of job demands, such as role strain, job satisfaction; specific sources of stress, such as the lack of parental or administrative support; and finally, the outcomes of excessive job demands, such as the symptoms of burnout and the stress response. Specifically, the measurement of teacher burnout has been a widely employed strategy to identify those teachers who may have experienced high levels of demand for extended periods of time (Maslach & Jackson, 1981; Maslach & Schaufeli, 1993; Maslach, Schaufeli, & Leiter, 2001).

All of these strategies, with the exception of those focused on coping resources, attempt to measure all or part of a single global construct: perceived demands. Stress researchers in general continue to treat stress as a single construct rather than the difference between two distinct constructs: resources and demands (McCarthy, Lambert, Beard, & Dematatis, 2002). Increased occupational demands do often lead to increased occupational stress for many teachers. However, stress theorists view stress as more than an increase in demands. Stress is defined as the result of an interaction, or imbalance, between two distinct constructs involving an internal psychological process of appraising both demands and resources. Furthermore, this appraisal process is regarded as integral to both optimal functioning and the stress response (Lazarus & Folkman, 1984).

Some measures have been generated by a conceptualization of teacher stress as a function of the compatibility of teachers and students, focusing on the demands of working with specific children with problem behaviors and the teacher's sense of efficacy about handling the demands of interactions with these children (Greene, Abidin, & Kmetz, 1997). Few, if any, instruments have attempted to measure simultaneously both the job demands and coping resources of teachers within the classroom setting, and rely on the relationship between the two as the indicator of risk for the stress response.

Recent theoretical developments suggest that both coping and the subjective experience of stress can be situationally specific (Sapolsky, 1998). Individuals may report perceived control in one situation while making a different appraisal of resources and demands under other circumstances. Such a distinction seems especially important to examine in an educational context, where both resources and demands can vary considerably depending on classroom characteristics, teacher background, and school environment (McCarthy et al., 2002). Furthermore, experts in the field of teacher stress research have called for measures that consider each teacher's unique occupational circumstances, particularly their perceptions of excessive administrative demands, teacher-child interactions, and classroom climate (Kyriacou, 2001).

The Classroom Appraisal of Resources and Demands (CARD, preschool version) (Lambert, Abbott-Shim, & McCarthy, 2001) was therefore developed to assess teacher stress by examining teachers' perceptions of both the demands that are specific to their classrooms and the resources their schools provide to address these demands. This approach is rooted in the transactional models of stress and coping, the most influential of which has been suggested by Lazarus and Folkman (1984). A central construct of this model is cognitive appraisal, which is essentially one's cognitive categorization of an event, its various features, and its significance for one's well-being. Stress theorists define resources broadly as both material resources (money, materials, technical support from others, etc.) and personal resources (coping strategies, interpersonal skills, etc.). The CARD focuses on the material resources available to teachers.

Two types of cognitive appraisals, according to Folkman and Lazarus (1988), are: (1) primary appraisal of whether a specific event represents a threat to the individual and (2) secondary appraisal of one's perceived capacity for handling the potential stressor. Events that are perceived as potentially threatening can result in the stress response, which is a set of physiological and psychological changes that occur reflexively whenever coping resources are seriously challenged. Any event perceived to be aversive triggers this response and while a hyper vigilant nervous system was extremely adaptive to our ancestors, modern stressors are mainly psychosocial (Matheny, Aycock, Pugh, Curlette, & Canella, 1986). As such, they can persist for extended periods of time and contribute to a large array of psychological and physical disorders.

The dominant models of stress and coping emphasize the importance of subjective evaluations of events in determining whether or not demands will be experienced as stressors (Cox, 1978; Hobfoll, 1988a, 1988b; Matheny et al., 1986). Such transactional models of stress assume that when a potentially threatening event is encountered, a reflexive, cognitive balancing act ensues in which the perceived demands of the event are weighed against one's perceived capabilities for dealing with it. Instances in which the estimated demands exceed one's resources are presumed to result in the stress response.

The few extant investigations of stress in teachers of young children have focused only on the demands side of this equation. Two clusters of occupational demands have been reported: children with problem behaviors in the classroom and external demands from outside the classroom, such as administrative and policy-related issues. Pratt (1978) found that teachers who serve young children view children with behavior problems as the most demanding aspect of their jobs. Subsequent efforts have revealed concerns with excessive paperwork requirements, workload and time constraints, and pressure from administrators, specifically those related to mandated curricula and instructional strategies (Moriarty, Edmonds, Blatchford, & Martin, 2001). This last issue is particularly relevant to Head Start teachers as the federal agency that governs the program has instituted a variety of performance standards that require specific curricular and assessment practices (Zill & Kim, 2005).

The purpose of this study was to examine teacher stress in preschool settings with particular attention to whether any structural features of the classroom were associated with high teacher stress. Structural characteristics are defined for the purpose of this study as the number of children in the classroom, both in total and in specific subgroups, as well as teacher qualifications. The researchers were also interested in comparing various aspects of classroom demands and resources to determine which components of the workplace were perceived by preschool teachers as most demanding and which resources were seen as most helpful in meeting those demands. In addition, this study extended the process of establishing reliability and validity evidence for the CARD.

METHOD

Participants

The participants were a sample of 317 preschool teachers from Alabama, Georgia, North Carolina, and South Carolina (see Table 6.1). The

Table 6.1. **Demographic Composition of the Sample (*N* = 317)**

Characteristic		Percent
Gender	Male	1.8
	Female	98.2
Ethnicity	European American	40.7
	African American	55.6
	Hispanic/Latino(a)	0.0
	Asian/Pacific Islander	1.9
	Other	1.9
Education level	High school	38.6
	Technical school	16.5
	AS	14.2
	BS	26.7
	MS/MEd	4.0
Child development associate credential	Yes	57.9
	No	42.1
Currently working on a degree	Yes	59.5
	No	39.9
Degree in education or related field	Yes	39.7
	No	60.3
Work setting	Head Start	92.5
	Public pre-K	5.0
	Private preschool	2.5

teachers had an average of 7.81 years of teaching experience, including 4.89 years experience at their current place of employment. The teachers reported an average class size of 17.74. The average age of the teachers in the sample was 37.81 and they reported their ethnicity as follows: African-American (55.6%), European-American (40.7%), and other (3.8%). Only 30.7% reported having a bachelor's or master's level college degree, 14.2% an associate's degree, and 59.5% were currently in school working toward a degree. The sample teachers reported their settings as follows: Head Start (92.5%), Public Prekindergarten (5.0%), and private preschool settings (2.5%), and all served low income populations.

Procedure

The CARD, preschool version, was administered to the sample of preschool teachers. Each teacher reported the demographic composition and unique or demanding features of his/her classroom, and whether personal and school-provided resources were sufficient to handle classroom demands. Teachers were contacted through the intraoffice mail system within the Head Start programs. A similar procedure was followed in the private and public school settings. Teachers returned surveys to an on-site data collection coordinator who worked for the researchers. This method insured anonymity, confidentiality, and separated ratings of the classroom from administrators. Three waves of data collection took place over two academic years. The first two waves were part of a larger study of classroom quality in Head Start programs, while the third wave was part of a larger study that evaluated a particular preschool curriculum model.

Results

The CARD has two scales, Classroom Demands and Classroom Resources. The Demands scale asks teachers to rate the extent to which various features of the classroom context are demanding and yielded a Cronbach's alpha reliability of .941. The Classroom Resources scale asks teachers to rate how helpful the school-provided resources are in assisting with the demands of the classroom and showed a similarly high value, .950. The two scales were not correlated ($r = -.080$). Subtracting standardized versions of the scales scores, Demands minus Resources, created a difference score. Application of the reliability of a difference score formula (Crocker & Algina, 1986) yielded a reliability estimate for this sample of .950. Since the difference score approach, using data from this sample, indicated acceptable reliability, the standard error of measurement for the difference score was calculated using this reliability estimate. A 95% confidence interval was constructed around zero and the upper and lower bounds of this interval were used to establish the cut scores for classifying teachers. Each teacher was classified into one of three groups: Resources greater than Demands (R > D) (34.7%), Resources equal to Demands (R = D) (30.9%), and Demands greater than Resources (D > R) (34.4%). This last group was hypothesized to be at risk for a stressful experience in the classroom. This method allowed the researchers to be 95% confident that the true score for the difference between Resources and Demands was not zero in either of the extreme groups. This three-group distinction would be useful in testing the transactional model of stress and coping.

Factor analysis was used to explore the underlying dimensions of both the resources and demands sections of the CARD. When principal components analysis with varimax rotation was applied to the data from the demands section, a four-factor solution emerged that accounted for 67.31% of the variance. The administrative demands subscale addressed about demands associated with meetings, paperwork, assessments, and various noninstructional duties. The classroom environmental demands subscale described demands associated with the physical classroom space,

Table 6.2. Measurement Properties of the CARD Scales and Subscales

Measure	Subscale	Mean	SD	Number of Items	Reliability
Demands	Administrative demands	2.769	0.978	10	0.920
	Classroom environmental demands	2.174	1.142	6	0.908
	Children with behavior problems	3.110	1.182	3	0.911
	Children with other special needs	2.522	0.812	7	0.808
	Total score (D)	2.602	0.795	26	0.941
Resources	Speacialized resources	3.728	0.900	11	0.944
	General program resources	4.205	0.684	9	0.891
	Parents	3.418	1.098	2	0.785
	Total score (R)	3.921	0.707	22	0.950
Stress	Difference score (D – R)	0.005	1.470	48	0.950

program facilities, and available materials. The children with problem behaviors subscale addressed the demands associated with behavior management and interactions with children who disrupt the learning environment. The children with other special needs subscale outlined demands involved with children who present other needs to the teacher, such as English language acquisition and physical disabilities.

The means, standard deviations, number of items, and Cronbach's alpha reliability coefficients for each of the subscales are presented in Table 6.2. The total score for Demands and each of its subscales yielded information from this sample with adequate reliability. The items in the Demands scale required teachers to rate the severity of the demands associated with various aspects of the classroom environment using a 5-point Likert scale that ranged from 1 (*not demanding*) to 5 (*extremely demanding*). The means of each of the Demands subscales ranged from 2.17 (*occasionally demanding*) for the classroom environmental demands subscale to 3.11 (*moderately demanding*) for the children with problem behaviors subscale.

When principal components analysis with varimax rotation was used with the Resources section, a three-factor solution emerged that accounted for 73.85% of the variance. The specialized resources subscale referred to resources designed to help teachers with children who have special needs. The general program resources subscale allowed the teachers to rate how helpful they find administrators, other teachers, general instructional materials, and staff development opportunities. The parents subscale referred to the help and support teachers receive from parents.

Two of the subscales and the total score for the Resources section yielded information from this sample with adequate reliability. The parents subscale offered information that approached adequate reliability (.79). The items in the Resources scale asked the teachers to rate the helpfulness of various resources using a 5-point Likert scale that ranged from 1 (*very unhelpful*) to 5 (*very helpful*). The means of each of the Resources subscales ranged from 3.42 (*occasionally helpful*) for the parents subscale to 4.21 (helpful) for the general program resources subscale.

A mixed factorial analysis of variance using the multivariate approach was used to test whether there were statistically significant differences in mean scores between the subscales and stress groups. Separate analyses were performed for the demands and resources sections. Subscale was entered as a within subjects term and stress group was entered in the model as a between subjects term. There was a statistically significant main effect for stress group in each analysis (Demands: $F_{(2, 310)} = 131.68$, $p < .001$; Resources: $F_{(2, 311)} = 79.06, p < .001$). A statistically significant main effect for subscale was also found in each analysis (Demands: $F_{(3, 308)} = 76.02, p < .001$; Resources: $F_{(2, 310)} = 151.26, p < .001$), as was a statistically significant stress group by subscale interaction (Demands: $F_{(6, 616)} = 5.50, p < .001$; Resources: $F_{(4, 620)} = 3.62, p = .006$).

Graphical displays and Tukey post hoc comparisons were used to enhance interpretation of the interaction effects. The cell means, standard deviations, and post hoc comparison results are reported in Table 6.3. Not surprisingly, the stress groups could be rank ordered in the predictable order given how they were formed. The only finding of note emerged from the Parents resources subscale scores where there was not a statistically significant difference between the D = R and D > R groups. For the entire sample, the subscales concerning Demands could be rank ordered as follows (most demanding to least demanding): children with behavior problems (B), administrative demands (A), children with other special needs (O), and classroom environmental demands (E). The interaction appeared to be related to differences between the stress groups with respect to this pattern. For example, there was no difference between the B, A, and O subscales for the R = D group while B and A subscales were both rated as more demanding than the O and E subscales for the D > R group. For entire sample on the Resources section of the measure, the subscales could be rank ordered as follows (most helpful to least helpful): general program resources (G), specialized resources (S), and parents (P). The interaction effect was related to a small difference in this pattern for the D > R group where there was no difference in the perceived helpfulness of the S and P subscales.

Only one statistically significant difference was found between teachers who rated Demands greater than Resources and those who rated Resources equal to or exceeding Demands with respect to classroom characteristics (see Table 6.4). Teachers who rated Demands greater than Resources had, on average (mean = 3.600, 84.7% with at least one problem behavior child), more children in their classrooms with behavior

Table 6.3. Differences in CARD Scores Between the Stress Level Groups

Measure	Subscale		Group 1 n = 110 R > D	Group 2 n = 98 R = D	Group 3 n = 109 D > R	Total n = 317	Post Hoc Comparisons
Demands	Administrative demands (A)	Mean SD	1.961 0.646	2.959 0.806	3.414 0.823	2.754 0.973	3 > 2 > 1
	Classroom environmental demands (E)	Mean SD	1.404 0.563	2.198 1.033	2.928 1.165	2.156 1.138	3 > 2 > 1
	Children with problem behaviors (B)	Mean SD	2.568 1.091	3.177 1.164	3.610 1.056	3.110 1.182	3 > 2 > 1
	Children with other special needs (O)	Mean SD	2.003 0.590	2.640 0.748	2.941 0.780	2.508 0.801	3 > 2 > 1
	Total score (D)	Mean SD	1.904 0.456	2.717 0.576	3.203 0.685	2.602 0.795	3 > 2 > 1
	Post hoc comparisons		B > A, O > E	B, A, O > E	B, A > O, E	B > A > O > E	
Resources	Specialized resources (S)	Mean SD	4.294 0.550	3.826 0.679	3.070 0.936	3.735 0.890	1 > 2 > 3
	General program resources (G)	Mean SD	4.655 0.307	4.316 0.444	3.651 0.756	4.204 0.684	1 > 2 > 3
	Parents (P)	Mean SD	3.800 0.838	3.378 1.156	3.061 1.161	3.417 1.100	1 > 2, 3
	Total score (R)	Mean SD	4.421 0.349	4.006 0.485	3.340 0.726	3.921 0.707	1 > 2 > 3
	Post hoc comparisons		G > S > P	G > S > P	G > S, P	G > S > P	
Stress	Difference score (D − R)	Mean SD	−1.580 0.672	0.030 0.334	1.583 0.831	0.005 1.470	3 > 2 > 1

Table 6.4. Differences in Teacher and Classroom Characteristics Between the Stress Level Groups

		Group 1 n = 110 R > D	Group 2 n = 98 R = D	Group 3 n = 109 D > R	N = 317 Total	F	Post Hoc
Teacher Characteristics							
Years of experience in teaching	Mean	7.154	7.867	8.411	7.809	0.936	
	SD	5.866	6.570	7.733	6.772		
	%[a]	13.9%	11.2%	18.5%	14.83%		
Years of experience at current program	Mean	4.598	5.739	4.410	4.887	2.040	
	SD	4.528	5.760	4.929	5.090		
	%[a]	22.9%	26.5%	26.6%	25.24%		
Age	Mean	37.200	40.810	36.190	37.810	1.063	
	SD	10.401	11.297	9.148	10.094		
Classroom Characteristics							
Class size	Mean	17.509	18.061	17.685	17.741	1.439	
	SD	2.333	2.402	2.406	2.383		
English language learners	Mean	4.673	4.163	3.252	4.032	2.155	
	SD	5.686	5.256	4.229	5.114		
	%[b]	26.2%	22.3%	18.4%	22.3%		
Children who are behind developmentally	Mean	2.229	2.755	2.870	2.613	2.525	
	SD	2.146	2.368	2.192	2.244		
	%[b]	12.5%	15.2%	16.7%	14.8%		
Children with poor attendance	Mean	1.287	1.449	1.713	1.484	2.377	
	SD	1.381	1.458	1.504	1.455		
	%[b]	7.3%	7.9%	9.8%	8.4%		
Children with problem behaviors	Mean	1.755	2.367	3.284	2.470	13.326***	3 > 1, 2
	SD	1.940	2.102	2.524	2.290		
	%[b]	10.2%	13.1%	19.1%	14.2%		

[a]Percentage of teachers with less than 2 years of experience in teaching or program.
[b]Mean percentage of the total class size. ***$p < .001$.

problems than did teachers in the other groups. In the classrooms in which Resources outweighed Demands, 69.0% of the teachers reported at least one problem behavior child (mean = 1.8736), while 71.9% of the teachers from the classrooms with Demands equal to Resources reported having at least one (mean = 2.2584). However, the three groups did not report significant differences in class size, number of non-English speaking children, children who were developmentally behind, special needs children, homeless or transient children, or those with poor attendance.

Mean years of teaching experience, years of experience in their current schools, educational level, and age of teachers were equivalent across the groups. Similarly, there was not a statistically significant difference between the three groups with respect to the percentage of each that is comprised of teachers who are within their first two of teaching: R > D—13.9%, R = D—11.2%, and D > R—18.5%. This same analysis can be reported in terms of the percentage of each experience level grouping who reported demands greater than resources: 43.5% of those within their first two years of teaching as compared to only 32.8% of more experienced teachers. Although not statistically significant ($\chi^2_{(2)}$ = 2.26, p = .32), these differences are in the expected direction and future research may need to focus on the appraisals of new teachers.

At the end of the instrument, the respondents were asked to rate directly whether the demands of their classroom were greater than they can handle given the resources available from their school or program. This was accomplished through the use of a graphic display of a scale with demands on one side of the scale and resources on the other. They were given three choices (demands greater than resources, demands equal to resources, and resources greater than demands) and asked to circle the picture that most accurately describes their working conditions. The appearance of the scale related to each of three choices by either tipping to one side or the other, or remaining level. A second question followed, using the same graphic display options, which asked them to reevaluate the relationship between resources and demands by considering both the personal resources they bring to the classroom and the resources provided by their school or program. For the first question, 35.5% of teachers selected the demands greater than resources option, while 25.3% indicated demands were greater than resources when asked to include personal resources.

DISCUSSION

The findings from this study suggest that teacher ratings of classroom demands can be identified according to the following themes, presented in order of their perceived severity (high to low): (a) children with problem behaviors, (b) administrative demands, (c) children with other special needs, and (d) classroom environmental demands. Teacher perceptions of resources fell into three themes, presented in order of perceived helpfulness (high to low): (a) general program resources, (b) specialized program resources, and (c) parents.

The relationship between perceived demands and resources appeared to be a viable strategy for classifying teachers. Over 30% of the present sample was identified as having a substantial risk for stress, confirming previous studies that have generally found around one quarter of teachers rate their working conditions as very stressful (Kyriacou, 2001). The classification strategy was validated by evidence for an association between teacher stress and the number of preschool children with problem behaviors in a given classroom. Specifically, the presence of just one or two more such children in the classroom was associated with a pattern of appraisals and perceptions that indicate classroom demands are greater than resources, and thereby place a teacher at for stress. These findings offer partial evidence for the applicability of the transactional model of stress and coping to educational settings (Lazarus & Folkman, 1984) and confirm previous studies that have found behavior management issues to be among the most significant stressors for teachers (Kyriacou, 2001; Kyriacou & Sutcliffe, 1978; Makimen & Kinnunen, 1986; Parkay, Greenwood, Olenjik, & Proller, 1988; Pratt, 1978; Turk, Meeks, & Turk, 1982). Administrative demands were rated as the next most demanding aspect of the preschool teacher's work life, confirming the findings of Moriarty et al. (2001).

These findings suggest that preschool administrators consider teacher stress as an important contextual variable when placing children with problem behaviors into classrooms, particularly as teachers perceive the classroom environment as more stressful when a critical threshold of disruptive children has been reached. Teachers may be sensitive to inequalities between classrooms with respect to the number of children with problem behaviors. Administrators may need to assess the classroom social environment early in the academic year and consider transferring some children with problem behaviors to different classrooms to establish a more positive balance between classrooms. In addition, teachers who experience stress themselves may be less able to enhance the social development of children, making their classrooms potentially inappropriate placements for the children who have the most to gain from a positive environment for social development. Administrators may also need to consider novel strategies for nurturing preschool teachers in the areas of behavior management and coping with the stresses associated with interactions with children with problem behaviors.

The results from the single item appraisals of the balance between resources and demands at the end of the measure must be taken with caution given the possibility for measurement error inherent in using single item indicators. However, it is interesting to note that number of respondents who selected demands greater than resources declined 10.2 percentage points when the respondents added their personal resources to the equation. This finding suggests that at least some of the teachers spend their own resources on classroom materials and find this a useful coping strategy for handling classroom demands. This figure represents 28.7% of those who indicated that demands exceeded resources when considering only program resources.

Limitations

This study had several limitations. The overwhelming majority (92.5%) of the teachers in the study worked in Head Start settings. Therefore, the findings may have limited generalizability outside the Head Start environment. The Head Start environment presents an interesting combination of contextual characteristics. Given the level of federal funding available to Head Start programs, and the opportunities for supplementing that funding with state and local sources, these classrooms were likely to be reasonably well equipped with materials. However, teacher salaries are likely to be well below, in many cases half, those available in public school settings in the same communities. In addition, all of the teachers in the sample served children from low income families.

All of the data for this study were collected using one self-report instrument. The findings are descriptive and correlational, and caution should be exercised in making any causal inferences based on the findings of this work. However, the transactional model of stress upon which this work is based emphasizes the role of the cognitive process by which *perceived* demands are weighed against *perceived* resources. Cognitive appraisals, categorizations of demands and resources rooted in one's idiosyncratic *perceptions* of events and circumstances, are presumed to be central to this process and ultimately related to one's risk of the stress response (Lazarus & Folkman, 1984). Therefore, self-report data is critical to an understanding of teacher stress and an appropriate data collection strategy given the nature of the research questions.

Future Research

Future research that makes use of mixed methods by adding some observational data to the self-report information from standard measures of teacher stress may help advance our understanding of the differences in classroom processes and interactions that are characteristic of teachers who experience stress and those who do not. Future research using the CARD will be most useful if it can extend the reliability and validity evidence for the use of the measure in various educational contexts. Specifically, the factor analysis results suggest the possibility of adding additional items to several of the subscales with relatively few items. It may be useful to test additional items for the general program resources subscale, paying particular attention to whether it can be separated into two subscales: physical materials and human resources (assistance and support from colleagues and administrators). Additional studies are needed to extend the evidence for the construct validity of the measure, particularly by using it along with existing measures of coping, burnout, and stress.

Conclusion

This study began the process of establishing reliability and validity evidence for the use of the CARD in preschool settings. The method of measuring teacher stress in a context-specific way by directly assessing and comparing teacher perceptions of classroom resources and demands offers promise as a strategy to further investigate and test the application of the transactional model of stress and coping in educational settings.

REFERENCES

Cox, T. (1978). *Stress*. Occupational stress in British educational setting: A review. *Education Psychology, 10* (2), 103–126.

Crocker, L., & Algina, J. (1986). *Introduction to classical & modern test theory*. Orlando, FL: Holt, Rinehart and Winston.

Dunham, J., & Varma, V. (Eds.). (1998). *Stress in teachers: Past, present, and future*. London: Whurr.

Fimian, M. J. (1984). The development of an instrument to measure occupational stress in teachers: The Teacher Stress Inventory. *The Journal of Occupational Psychology, 57,* 277-293.

Fimian, M. J. (1985). The development of an instrument to measure occupational stress in teachers of exceptional students. *Techniques: Journal for Remedial Education and Counseling, 1,* 270-285.

Fimian, M. J. (1987). Teacher stress: An expert appraisal. *Psychology in the Schools, 24,* 5-14.

Fimian, M. J. (1988). *Teacher Stress Inventory*. Brandon, VT: Clinical Psychology.

Folkman, S., & Lazarus, R. (1988). The relationship between coping and emotion: Implications for theory and research. *Social Science Medicine, 26,* 309-317.

Green, D. E., Walkey, F. H., McCormick, I. A., Taylor, A. J. W. (1988). Development and evaluation of a 21-item version of the Hopkins Symptom Checklist with

New Zealand and United States respondents. *Australian Journal of Psychology, 40,* 61-70.

Greene, R. W., Abidin, R. R., & Kmetz, C. (1997). The index of teaching stress: A measure of student-teacher compatibility. *Journal of School Psychology, 35,* 239-259.

Hammer, A. L., & Marting, M. S. (1988). *Coping Resources Inventory manual.* Palo Alto, CA: Consulting Psychologist Press.

Hobfoll, S. E. (1988a). Conservation of resources: A new attempt at conceptualizing stress. *American Psychologist, 44,* 513-524.

Hobfoll, S. E. (1988b). *The ecology of stress.* Washington, DC: Hemisphere.

Kyriacou, C. (2000). *Stress busting for teachers.* Cheltenham, United Kingdom: Stanley Thornes.

Kyriacou, C. (2001). Teacher stress: Directions for future research. *Educational Review, 53,* 27-35.

Kyriacou, C., & Sutcliffe, J. (1977). Teacher stress: A review. *Educational Review, 29,* 299-306.

Kyriacou, C., & Sutcliffe, J. (1978). Teacher stress: Prevalence, sources, and symptoms. *British Journal of Educational Psychology, 48,* 159-167.

Lambert, R. G., Abbott-Shim, M., & McCarthy, C. J. (2001). *Classroom appraisal of resources and demands, preschool version.* Atlanta, GA: Head Start Quality Research Center.

Lazarus, R. S., & Folkman, S. (1984). *Stress, appraisal, and coping.* New York: Springer.

Makinen, R., & Kinnunen, U. (1986). Teacher stress over a school year. *Scandinavian Journal of Educational Research, 30,* 55-70.

Maslach, C., & Jackson, S. E. (1981). The measurement of experienced burnout. *Journal of Occupational Behavior, 2,* 99-113.

Maslach, C., & Schaufeli, W. B. (1993). Historical and conceptual development of burnout. In W. B. Schaufeli, C. Maslach, & T. Marek (Eds.), *Professional burnout: Recent developments in theory and research* (pp. 1-18). Washington, DC: Taylor & Francis.

Maslach, C., Schaufeli, W. B., & Leiter, M. P. (2001). Job burnout. *Annual Review of Psychology, 52,* 397-422.

Matheny, K. B., Aycock, D. W., Pugh, J. L., Curlette, W. L., & Canella, K. A. (1986). Stress coping: A qualitative and quantitative synthesis with implications for treatment. *The Counseling Psychologist, 14,* 499-549.

McCarthy, C., Lambert, R., Beard, M., & Dematatis, A. (2002). Factor structure of the Preventive Resources Inventory and its relationship to existing measures of stress and coping. In G. S. Gates & M. Wolverton (Eds.), *Toward wellness: prevention, coping, and stress* (pp. 3-37). Greenwich, CT: Information Age.

Moriarty, V., Edmonds, S., Blatchford, P., & Martin, C. (2001). Teaching young children: Perceived satisfaction and stress. *Educational Research, 43,* 33-46.

Parkay, F. W., Greenwood, G., Olenjik, S., & Proller, N. (1988). A study of the relationships among teacher efficacy, locus of control, and stress. *Journal of Research and Development in Education, 21,* 13-22.

Pratt, J. (1978). Perceived stress among teachers: The effects of age and background of the children taught. *Educational Review, 30,* 3-14.

Sapolsky, R. M. (1998). *Why zebras don't get ulcers: An updated guide to stress, stress-related diseases, and coping.* New York: W. H. Freeman.

Sarason, I., Johnson, J., & Siegel, J. (1978). Assessing the impact of life changes: Development of the Life Experiences Survey. *Journal of Consulting and Clinical Psychology, 46,* 932-946.

Schaufeli, W. B., & Enzmann, D. (1998). *The burnout component to study and practice.* London: Taylor & Francis.

Travers, C. J., & Cooper, C. L. (1996). *Teachers under pressure: Stress in the teaching profession.* London: Routledge.

Turk, D. C., Meeks, S., & Turk, L. M. (1982). Factors contributing to teacher stress: Implications for research, prevention, and remediation. *Behavioral Counseling Quarterly, 2,* 3-25.

Zill, N., & Kim, K. (2005, April). The Head Start national reporting system: Reporting on first year implementation. In T. Schultz (chair), *The development of and findings from the National Head Start reporting system child assessment.* Symposium conducted at the meeting of the Society for Research in Child Development, Atlanta, Georgia.

CHAPTER 7

STRESS IN THE STUDENT-TEACHER RELATIONSHIP IN DUTCH SCHOOLS

A Replication Study of Greene, Abidin, and Kmetz's Index of Teaching Stress (ITS)

H. A. Everaert and J. C. van der Wolf

Teachers vary widely in their responses to children who present classroom difficulties. Consistent with goodness-of-fit theory challenging students might evoke different levels of subjectively experienced stress in different teachers. In the first replication study, Greene, Abidin, and Kmetz's Index of Teaching Stress (ITS) was used to measure perceived stress in Dutch classrooms ($N = 320$). Making use of Multiple Group Method (MGM), a number of general theoretical underpinnings of ITS are confirmed. At the same time some methodological problems showed up. We have drawn another, second sample ($N = 136$) to study in detail the relation between prevalence of student behavior and concomitant teacher stress. While we endorse ITS with respect to behaviorally challenging students, some suggestions are made to improve the general applicability of the instrument.

With the influx of exceptional students into regular classrooms, within the framework of worldwide inclusion and integration oriented policies, teachers in regular schools often incur new and additional duties for which they have either limited or no formal training (Brophy, 1996; Palmer Wilson, Gutkin, Hagen, & Oats, 1998). Due to the students' problematic behavior and lower abilities, the teachers also experience minimal and infrequent pupil progress (Coladarci, 1992). Continual exposure to challenging behavior, both from pupils and their parents, can seriously deplete the teacher's emotional and physical resources, leading to self-doubt, loss of satisfaction from teaching, impulsivity, rigidity, or feelings of anger and guilt (Coie & Koeppl, 1990; Van der Wolf & Defares, 1994). In an attempt to provide the required services, work overload and hence stress are almost inevitable. In this respect, considerable strain has been placed on the coping resources of teachers (Borg, 1990; Boyle, Borg, Falzon, & Baglioni, 1995; Van der Wolf & Everaert, 2003). As a result teachers may react negatively and irritated to problem children. Children then may not receive the human contact, attention, and support they need. This in turn can result in problem behavior (Baker, 1999). In other words, stress affects not only the teacher, but also ultimately the student. Teachers under stress are concerned with survival and these concerns take precedence over instructional and student-behavior oriented activities. Stressed teachers contribute little to the students' academic growth and many students may suffer a lower self-esteem and have feelings of anger or anxiety as a result of the teacher's uninterested, hypercritical, irritated, or uncaring behavior (Brouwers & Tomic, 1998; Lamude, Scudder, & Furno-Lamude, 1992). As Greene, Abidin, and Kmetz (1997) rightly suggest, the parent-child relationship is investigated far more often than the teacher-pupil interaction. Research has shown convincingly that children with behavior problems cause stress in their parents (Anastopoulos, Guevremont, Shelton, & DuPaul, 1992; Mash & Johnston, 1990; Webster-Stratton, 1990). Regarding the goodness-of-fit theory stress amongst parents is related to the child's characteristics and those of the parents (Thomas & Chess, 1980). Mention must be made of the fact that there are parental differences regarding the reaction to a child's behavior problems. The same behavior in a child has differing effects on parents. Teachers also manifest different attitudes toward pupil behavior.

In this study we interpret teacher stress as a process, rather than as a state. Stress occurs progressively in more virulent phases, not seldom ending in burn-out (Golembiewski, Bodreau, Sun, & Luo, 1998). Burnout is a condition that develops when an individual (i.e., a teacher) works too hard for too long in a high pressure environment. Frequent exposure to problem behavior of children (and their parents) often drives teachers into exhaustion. Based on goodness-of-fit theory, students might evoke different levels of experienced stress in different teachers. That is, student-teacher relations can be conceptualized as a product of the combined characteristics of both student and teacher.

METHODS

In line with the above-mentioned theoretical viewpoints Greene et al. (1997) introduced the Index of Teaching Stress (ITS) as an instrument to focus on stress experienced by a teacher in interaction with a specific student. Originally, they developed ITS as a parallel to the Parenting Stress Index (PSI), developed by Abidin (1986, 1995). ITS focuses on the teacher's perceptions and transactions in relation to a given pupil and quantifies the impact of the behavior of that pupil on the teacher's instruction and the teacher's perception of himself or herself. ITS is a 90-items questionnaire consisting of two parts. In Part A (Student Domain) teachers have to rate on a 5-point Likert scale the degree to which they found different problematic behaviors (i.e., ADHD, emotional lability, anxiety/withdrawal, low ability/learning disability, and aggressive/conduct disorder) to be stressful or frustrating as applied to each student being rated. In Part B (Teacher Domain) teachers were asked to rate statements, which explored the impact of the student and the parents upon the teacher and teaching process (i.e., self-doubt, loss of satisfaction from teaching, disruption of teaching process, and frustration working with parents). Teachers are supposed to fill in the questionnaire twice, the first time with respect to the most behaviorally challenging student in the class room and the second time with respect to the seventh student on their class roster (i.e., comparison student). From the very start of the Dutch replication study, we took a slightly different approach to one aspect of ITS. With respect to Part B, Dutch teachers had to rate the items on a scale ranging from 1 (*totally disagree*) to 5 (*totally agree*), where Greene et al. (1997) had asked American teachers to respond in terms degree they found a described situation stressful. That is, ranging from 1 (*never stressful*) to 5 (*very often stressful*). The reason for this is almost trivial in Dutch classrooms. The word stress has an extremely negative connotation in Dutch and if possible, should be avoided with respect to pupils. Dutch teachers will refer to the word stress with respect to colleagues, board of directors, or whatsoever, but not in describing their relation with pupils. The goal of our study changed slightly during the research process.

Inspired by Greene et al. (1997) we set out to study teacher stress in Dutch classrooms as a result of the interaction between teacher and student. One of the most attractive characteristics of ITS is the ability to show how specific aspects of student behavior may contribute to the well-being of the teacher. However, we also became more and more intrigued by assessing the psychometric quality and general applicability of ITS in the Netherlands.

RESULTS

We translated the Index Teacher Stress into Dutch and in October 2003 a sample of 320 teachers was drawn in the Dutch provinces Groningen, Noord-Holland, and Zuid-Holland. The degree to which teachers find 47 problematic behaviors (Part A of ITS) stressful or frustrating was rated on a 5-point Likert scale ranging from 1 to 5. In part B teachers were asked to rate 43 statements, which explored the impact of the student and the parents upon the teacher and teaching process. Teachers were asked to fill in the questionnaire twice, the first time with respect to the most behaviorally challenging student in the classroom and the second time with respect to the seventh student on their class roster (i.e., comparison student).

The sample chosen proved to be representative for the Netherlands with respect to sex, ethnic affiliation, urban/rural population density, and religious affiliation of the teachers.[1] On average, the 320 elementary teachers who participated in the study had 13.8 years of experience in elementary school. This is almost at the same level as reported in Greene's et al. (1997) study (14.2 years of experience). The frequency distribution of gender also was more or less the same. Of the teachers in the Dutch survey 85% was female as compared to 86% in the American study. With respect to type of school, there were several differences. In the American survey, teachers were primarily employed in public school settings (89%). In our study, no teachers worked in private schools. In the Netherlands, there was a distinction between public and religious schools, although both types of schools are fully financed by the Dutch government. The curricula of both types of schools, with the exception of religion class, were the same. In our sample, 39% of the teachers were employed in public schools, while 48% worked in religious schools. The other 13% ranged from schools based on the views of the Italian Montessori to the Dalton educational system. Of the so-called religious schools, 73% is Protestant. The religious affiliation of the remaining 27% is Catholic. In contrast with Greene et al. (1997), we did not include teachers employed in special educational schools.

We also gathered information with respect to the pupil age, sex, ethnic affiliation, and situation at home. The age difference between behaviorally challenging students ($M = 8.2$, $SD = 2.4$) and comparison students ($M = 8.0$, $SD = 2.3$) is negligible. Eighty-five percent of the behaviorally challenging students were male, compared to 48% of the comparison students. Official Dutch statistics do not measure ethnicity. Instead, the official Central Bureau of Statistics refers to the country where the parents were born and defines a person as migrant if at least one of his parents was not born in the Netherlands. According to this definition 24% of the behaviorally challenging students was migrant compared to the 21% of the comparison children. Another important demographic variable is the family situation at home. The family situation of 77% of the behaviorally challenging children can be described as a nuclear family. With respect to other forms of family-life, 15% were one-parent households headed by the mother, and 3% were headed by the father. For the comparison children these figures were different. In our sample, 88% lived in a nuclear family and 11% was a member of a one-parent household headed by the mother. We also asked the teachers to indicate whether the pupil was diagnosed by a psychiatrist or psychologist. Of the comparison children only 3% was diagnosed. This rate is much higher for the behaviorally challenging children (16%). Attention-deficit/hyperactivity disorder (16 out of 49 children) and PDDNOS (8 out of 49 children) were the two most frequently mentioned DSM-IV diagnoses. The characteristics of the teachers and the pupils they had in mind were to a great extent similar in the American and Dutch samples. Compared with the research study of Greene et al. (1997), the only major difference concerned Special Education Needs.

We used the Multiple Group Method (MGM) to examine whether our data support the factor structure found by Greene et al. (1997). MGM consists basically of three steps (Nunnally, 1978; Ten Berge & Sierro, 2000). First, we computed Pearson r product-moment correlations of all 47 items with the five factors belonging to Part A and the Pearson r product-moment correlations of all 43 items with the four factors belonging to Part B. Second, because high correlations between an item and the factor it is part of might be partly the result of the correlation of the item with itself, we used the corrected item-total correlation instead of the Pearson r product-moment correlation. The third and last step consisted of comparing the corrected item-total correlation of every item with the respective Pearson correlation coefficients of the other factors. If the corrected item-total correlation of an item is equal or higher than the Pearson r product-moment correlation of that item with the other factors belonging to the respective Part A or B, then our data confirm the factor analysis as presented by Greene et al. (1997).

Greene et al. (1997) published a full list of all 90 items in the *Journal of School Psychology*. With respect to Part A we conclude that the general quality of the five underlying scales is good. However, seven of the original 47 items deserve closer consideration: "When wants something, persists in getting it," "Difficulty adjusting to changes in class," "Usually in a bad mood," "Always clinging to me," "Does not socialize well with other children," "Exhibits strange behaviors," and "Hard to get used to new things."[2] MGM analysis also shows us that three ("Child prevents me from doing things I'd like to do," "Exhausted by energy it takes to monitor child," and "Handling student about as well as any other teacher") out of 43 items of Part B could be rejected. With the exception of scale Disrupts Teaching Process most of the items fit well in the scales of Part B. We also strongly recommend mirroring the item "Does things for me that make me feel good" before summing it up with other items belonging to that particular scale. Our computations showed this item correlates *negatively* with scale Loss of Satisfaction from Teaching.[3] Compared with the other items, closer inspection points out that item "Does things for me that make me feel good" is the only one that is positively formulated, and we think that it is difficult to argue that feeling good as a result of working with a particular child, is stressful.

Table 7.1 presents the mean scores of the Index of Teaching Stress for behaviorally challenging students. We compare our data with the results reported by Greene et al. (1997). Instead of copying the total score of the ITS as a summative measure of the distress induced in the teacher, we present the means of the different scales. The reason for the choice of this approach is threefold. First of all, adding up all scores of the items that make up a particular scale implies imputing missing data. At this stage of the development or validation of the Index of Teaching Stress we regard this solution as inappropriate. Also, we suppose that when teachers are asked to rate 90 items two times, there will be several missing values. It is not clear how Greene et al. dealt with missing values. Second, the level of stress is directly related to the number of items included in a particular scale. In Greene et al. (1997) aggressive/conduct disorder turns out to be a bigger stressor with a score of 13.5 than low ability/learning disabled with a score of 12.5 (p. 254). This stems partly from the fact that aggressive/conduct disorder contains six items whereas low ability/learning disabled consists only of five items. If we take the respective means, it turns out that low ability/learning disabled with a mean of 2.5 causes more stress than aggressive/conduct disorder with a mean of 2.3. We would like to add here that our focus is to outline a reliable and parsimoniously way to measure stress inducing behavior of students. In line with our theoretical approach as developed in the beginning of this chapter, our interest is the contribution of ADHD in proportion to aggressive/conduct disorder, or to give another example, emotional lability/low adaptability in proportion to anxiety/withdrawal as a minor or major part of the student domain score. This is equally true for scales of the teacher domain score of self-reported stress in relation to a particular student. Average standard scores instead of summative scores ought to be the norm to discuss stressors. Third, and in line with the above mentioned argument, we also compare our modified Index of Teaching Stress with the index as presented of Greene et al. (1997), leaving 10 items out of the calculations.

In the first columns of Table 7.1, we have listed the results of the analyses by Greene et al. (1997). The grand means found in their study are 12.9 (Part A) and 9.4 (Part B). Using the same ninety items, our scores are respectively 13.3 and 9.2. With respect to our modified scales the means of Part A (13.0) and Part B (9.4) are even more in line with the results found by Greene et al. (1997). Naturally by now, the mean sum score of the student and teacher domain are more or less identical (22.3 versus 22.4). Within the teacher domain we can conclude that our results are almost identical to the means found by Greene et al. (1997). Only with respect to aggressive/conduct disorder (2.3 versus 2.5) the difference is notable. The best way to look at this figure is to compare the relative contribution of each scale to its respective part. Dutch teachers experience more stress as a result of aggressive/conduct disorder (2.5) than low ability/learning disabled (2.4). In the United States, this proves to be the other way round. Stress as a result of low ability/learning disabled (2.5) is higher than stress related to low ability/learning disabled (2.3).

Within Part B the differences between the results as reported by Greene et al. (1997) and ours, are larger. Only the scale self-doubt/needs support has in both studies the same mean (2.0) and three out of four scales divert remarkable. While it is possible to argue that even the scale *Frustration working with Parents* is somewhere in accordance with results found by Greene et al. (2.1 versus 1.8), this is not the case for the scales measuring Loss of Satisfaction from Teaching and Disrupts Teaching Process. Although in both studies these scales are the major contributors to the *Teacher Domain, Disrupts Teaching Process* scores a mean of 2.7 in the original American study compares to 3.4 in the Dutch study. In the Netherlands, *Loss of Satisfaction from Teaching* (2.2) is substantially lower than its American counterpart (2.6).

A first clue to understand part of the reported difference of *Loss of Satisfaction from Teaching* has to do with the mirroring item "Does things for me that make me feel good." Although the contribution of one single item might be negligible if added up to or averaged out with 12 different items, we note that mirroring an item almost doubles its "small" effect if compared to the original scale. So, part of the difference is not substantial, but computational.

Table 7.1. Index of Teaching Stress Means, Standard Deviation, Alpha Reliabilities for Behaviorally Challenging Students—A Comparsion Between American and Dutch Results (First Sample; N = 320)

	American Results as Presented by Greene, Abidin, and Kmetz (1997)			Dutch Results, Original Scales (90 items)[a]			Dutch Results, Modified Scales (80 items)[a]		
	M	SD	Alpha Reliabilities	M	SD	Alpha Reliabilities[c]	M	SD	Alpha Reliabilities[c]
Total stress of Part A and Part B[b]	22.3	2.8	.97	22.5	2.4	.87	22.4	2.6	.85
Student Domain (Part A)	12.9	2.3	.96	13.3	1.9	.84	13.0	2.1	.79
ADHD	3.1	1.1	.96	3.2	0.8	.92	3.2	0.9	.92
ADHD									
ELLA	2.8	1.1	.94	2.7	0.8	.84	2.8	0.8	.83
Emotional ability/low adaptability									
ANWI	2.2	0.8	.86	2.4	0.7	.83	2.1	0.8	.83
Anxiety/withdrawal									
LOLD	2.5	1.1	.89	2.5	0.9	.81	2.4	1.0	.83
Low ability/learning disabled									
AGCO	2.3	1.0	.87	2.5	1.1	.85	2.5	1.1	.85
Aggressive/conduct disorder									
Teacher Domain (Part B)	9.4	1.7	.96	9.2	1.5	.80	9.4	1.5	.78
GSDNS	2.0	0.8	.95	2.0	0.6	.91	2.0	0.6	.91
Self-doubt/needs support									
LOST	2.6	1.0	.94	2.2	0.7	.88	2.2	0.7	.88
Loss of satisfaction from teaching									
DIST	2.7	0.7	.46	3.2	0.8	.72	3.4	0.9	.71
Disrupts teaching process									
FRPA	2.1	0.8	.78	1.8	0.8	.79	1.8	0.8	.79
Frustration working with parents									

Note: The figures for the individual scales are divided by the number of items. Summation scores are computed on the basis of the respective scales. [a]Item "Does things for me that make me feel good" of Part B is mirrored. [b]The mean of total stress is computed by summing up Part A and Part B. [c]Cronbach alphas for Part A and Part B are computed on basis of scale values instead of item values.

Another clue to understanding the differences between the respective results starts with highlighting their respective alpha reliabilities. We already underlined the somewhat problematic quality of the scale *Disrupts Teaching Process* in the study of Greene et al. (1997). Their alpha reliability is only .46. In our replicated study the internal consistency is better, but still relatively low (.71). Nunnally (1978) proposed a value of .70 as a criterion for a satisfactory internal consistency. Although in general our internal consistency is lower than in the study reported by Greene et al. (1997), this can not be taken as a difference of quality in itself. In comparing these alpha reliabilities, we should not disregard the influence of the larger number of teachers surveyed in the United States ($N = 532$). Also the number of items in the American study is a bit higher as compared to our modified scales. The same holds for scales contributing to Part A. The number of respondents as well as the number of items contribute positively to higher alpha reliabilities as a measure for internal consistency (Mellenbergh & Van den Brink, 1998).

At this point only one difference between the respective studies needs to be addressed: the alpha reliabilities of Greene et al. (1997) reported in Table 7.1 of Total Stress (.97), Part A (.96) and Part B (.96) are much higher than ours (respectively .85, .79, and .78). This is due to the fact that in line with our theoretical approach of the relation between domains and their respective scales, we computed the internal consistency of scales within the domain. If we compute the internal consistency of the (numerous) items within a domain, our results are in line with Greene et al. (1997). For the original Parts A and B as well as our modified Parts A and B reported in Table 7.1 the data show—just to underline the above mentioned relationship between number of items and alpha—alphas ranging from .94 to .96.

To summarize, the similarity of the American and Dutch results is striking. This is certainly true for scales making up Part A. For Part B the differences between the two countries are greater, although parts of these differences are not substantial, but computational.

With respect to the results of the Comparison Students as presented in Table 7.2, the differences between the American and Dutch results are more notable. Before we deal with these differences, we first address the high alpha reliabilities in both studies. For Part A of the modified scales alpha fluctuates between .89 and .96. For Part B this is remarkably lower, but still sufficient. Inspecting the reasons for the high internal consistency and looking at the stress-means for comparison students in Table 7.2, it turns out that the Dutch means for the Student Domain (between 1.5 and 1.7) are low, and for the Teacher Domain (between 1.2 and 1.6) even lower. Probably it is not adequate to compare our scores with the means reported by Greene et al. (1997). In comparison with American school

Table 7.2. Index of Teaching Stress Means, Standard Deviation, Alpha Reliabilities for Comparison Students— A Comparsion Between American and Dutch Results (First Sample; N = 320)

	American Results as Presented by Greene, Abidin, and Kmetz (1997)			Dutch Results, Original Scales (90 items)[a]			Dutch Results, Modified Scales (80 items)[a]		
	M	SD	Alpha Reliabilities	M	SD	Alpha Reliabilities[c]	M	SD	Alpha Reliabilities[c]
Total stress of Part A and Part B[b]	17.5	2.7	.96	13.5	2.1	.89	13.4	2.2	.88
Student Domain (Part A)	9.9	2.2	.97	8.1	1.9	.92	8.1	1.9	.90
ADHD	2.2	1.1	.97	1.7	0.8	.96	1.7	0.8	.95
Emotional lability/low adaptability	2.1	1.1	.96	1.6	0.8	.94	1.6	0.8	.94
Anxiety/withdrawal	1.8	0.8	.88	1.6	0.8	.92	1.6	0.8	.89
Low ability/ learning disabled	2.1	1.0	.90	1.7	0.9	.90	1.7	0.9	.92
Aggressive/conduct disorder	1.7	1.0	.90	1.5	1.0	.96	1.5	1.0	.96
Teacher Domain (Part B)	7.6	1.6	.96	5.4	0.9	.76	5.3	1.0	.74
Self-doubt/needs support	1.6	0.7	.95	1.2	0.3	.88	1.2	0.3	.88
Loss of satisfaction from teaching	2.0	0.9	.95	1.3	0.3	.75	1.3	0.3	.73
Disrupts teaching process	2.3	0.7	.44	1.7	0.6	.66	1.6	0.7	.75
Frustration working with parents	1.7	0.8	.83	1.2	0.5	.71	1.2	0.5	.71

Note: The figures for the individual scales are divided by the number of items. Summation scores are computed on the basis of the respective scales.
[a] Item "Does things for me that make me feel good" of Part B is mirrored. [b] The mean of total stress is computed by summing up Part A and Part B. [c] Cronbach alphas for Part A and Part B are computed on basis of scale values instead of item values.

teachers working in both elementary and in Special Educational Needs-Schools (15%), many Dutch elementary school teachers scored 1 on the 5-point Likert scale ranging from 1 to 5. Although it is obvious that alpha scores are high if items scores are extremely positively skewed, hardly any information is gathered by asking teachers to rate the 90 items again with a comparison student in mind. This became also clear by reading the different comments numerous teachers have written down on the questionnaire. These remarks dealt with two related problems. First of all, some of them argued that although the items are valid for behaviorally challenging students, they are at the same time, too extreme to capture the behavior of the comparison students. The second and partly related complaint had to do with the frequency versus stress of the response set of Part A. Comparison students often do not behave as described in the response set. So how can a teacher rate distress if the student does not display the behavior? Taking into account this comment as well as the time a respondent needs to score the questionnaire completely, we suggest leaving out the comparison student in future research.

We encountered unsuspected support for this way of reasoning. In a study concerning teacher's referral judgments of students with challenging behaviors, one of the cofounders of ITS presents standard scores of teachers for students who rarely or never display challenging behavior (Abidin & Robinson, 2002). The item scores they present for teachers dealing with these students seem to be positively skewed.

What is really at stake here, is the relation between frequency and distress as a consequence of displayed behavior. Greene et al. (1997) state:

> [t]he ITS was developed under the assumption that the level of a teacher's distress regarding the specific behaviors of a given student is not merely a reflection of the frequency of the behaviors. This assumption emanates from the extensive cognitive/social learning literature ... positing that an individual's response to an event is a function of his or her affective and perceptual appraisal of the event and not merely the frequency of the event" (p. 241).
> They also "present preliminary empirical evidence in this paper regarding the frequency versus perception issue as related to the ITS, however the issue will clearly require further research." (p. 242)

The question of whether or not teachers' responses to a child's behavior are merely a reflection of the frequency of the behavior versus a reflection of stress following the teacher's cognitive processing of the child's behavior is examined by Greene et al. (1997) in a randomly selected sample of 76 teachers using correlation analyses. They ran Pearson r product-moment correlation coefficients between the teacher scale scores on the Student Domain for the frequency versus stress response set. "As expected, moderate correlations were obtained: ADHD, .70; emotional lability/low adaptability, .62; anxiety/withdrawal, .54; aggressive/conduct disorder, .45. Unexplained variance for the five subscales ranged from .49 to .80" (p.252-253).

The expected moderate correlation coefficients and concomitant high figures of unexplained variance only indicate that the relation between frequency and stress is not adequately described by a linear function. Any other (continuous) monotonous climbing function—for instance an S-shaped, polynomial or exponential equation—might be more in harmony with theoretical assumptions to describe the relation between frequency and perceived stress.

Also, there is no reason to expect that the relation between frequency and distress is the same for every scale. Greene et al. (1997) conclude:

> Simply put, if a teacher's subjective experience of distress is not distinct from an estimate of the frequency of a child's behavior, then the ITS would make little meaningful contribution to an understanding of the teacher-effect relationship. It will be important for further research to replicate these findings and explore the relative predictive utility of frequency scores of child behavior rating scales versus the ITS Child Domain score in predicting the quality and nature of student-teacher relationships and interactions. (p. 255)

This is exactly the reason why we started the second study.

In February 2004, 136 teachers who work with behaviorally challenging students in elementary schools filled out a questionnaire. Measured teacher characteristics in the second sample were almost the same as in the first sample. In the first sample 85% were female; in the second sample 84% were female. Years of teaching experience also hardly differed across groups. In the first sample the mean was 13.8 years. In the second sample the mean years of experience were 14.5 years. Apart from a number of ITS-items, two general questions about behaviorally challenging students were asked. It turned out that 86% of the behaviorally challenging students were male and they were on average one year older than the children teachers had in mind when they filled out the first questionnaire. Their mean age was 9.3 years compared to 8.2 years in the first replication study.

The number of items in Part A in the second study was limited to 15 items. Every scale was represented by three items and each item had to be rated twice on a 5-point Likert scale. First, the teacher had to score the frequency of the behavior of a problem-student. Next to frequency scores, they had to rate the perceived stress. So teachers had the direct opportunity to compare the different scores on frequency and stress with each other. The selection of these 15 items was based on principal components analysis (*PCA*) after Varimax rotation with Kaiser Normalization of all 47 items in the just described replication study of Greene et al. (1997). Only high loading (>0.60) items on the scale of which they were theoretically a part were selected. Items that loaded high on more than one factor were omitted. We also omitted items rejected on the basis of the MGM analysis of the first sample. After the initial selection a second Varimax rotated matrix with Kaiser Normalization was produced to check that all 15 items loaded on the right factor or scale. This proved to be the case for just three scales. Items of the scales emotional lability/low adaptability and anxiety/withdrawal loaded on the same factor. In total, the explained variance was 66%.

For the selection of the items in Part B the same approach was followed. The selection of 12 items was based on the analysis of the PCA-output after Varimax rotation with Kaiser Normalization of all 43 items. So every scale is made up of three different items. Only high loading (>0.50) items on the scale of which they were theoretically a part were selected. Again, after the initial selection a second Varimax rotated matrix with Kaiser Normalization was produced to check that all 12 items loaded on the right factor or scale. This was confirmed by further analysis and total explained variance was 70%.

Compared to the questionnaire we used in the first study, the scoring dimension was also changed. The scoring dimension ranges on a 5-point Likert scale from 0 to 4 instead of 1 to 5. Compared to range 1 to 5, the inclusion of a 0 in the scoring dimension scale turned out to be better understood by the respondents. Before discussing the correlations between the different scales, an assessment had to be made of the quality of the different scales of the second sample. In Table 7.3 means, standard deviations, and alpha reliabilities were compared to each other.

With the exception of scales aggressive/conduct disorder and disrupts teaching process the internal consistency is satisfactory. The very low Cronbachs' alpha of scale disrupts teaching process (.52), even after selecting high correlating items on the basis of former results, underscores our need to reconsider these items and scale. Although it is difficult to give a satisfactory explanation for the low internal consistencies for aggressive/conduct disorder (.42 for the level of incidence and .45 with respect to experienced stress), it is the high frequency mean of item "Lewd or obscene gestures or inappropriate behavior" (2.5) with respect to the means of "Steals and lies" (1.3) and "Can be very destructive" (1.8), which draws our attention. With respect to the stress response set, the same structure exists. The last two items have much to do with real and physic aggression while "Lewd or obscene gestures or inappropriate behavior" point to inappropriate conduct in general.

On the Student Domain teachers in the second sample experience more stress with respect to externalizing behavior (ADHD, emotional

Table 7.3. Index of Teaching Stress Means, Standard Deviation, Alpha Reliabilities for Behaviorally Challenging Students—A Comparsion between two Dutch Replication Studies ($N = 320$ and $N = 136$)

	Student Domain (Part A)	First sample ($N = 320$) Stress M	SD	Alpha Reliabilities	Second sample ($N = 136$) Frequency M	SD	Alpha Reliabilities	Stress M	SD	Alpha Reliabilities
ADHD	ADHD	2.2	1.1	.77	3.0	0.9	.74	2.4	1.0	.76
a02a12	Much harder to keep on a routine than others	2.6	1.2		3.4	0.9		2.8	1.1	
a06a16	So active it exhausts me	1.8	1.4		2.5	1.3		2.1	1.4	
a13a23	Squirms and fidgets a great deal	2.1	1.3		3.1	1.2		2.4	1.2	
ELLA	Emotional Lability/Low Adaptability	1.5	1.0	.74	2.6	1.0	.66	1.9	1.1	.71
e02a07	Seems to cry or fuss more than most others	1.4	1.3		2.3	1.5		1.6	1.4	
e04a09	Very moody and easily upset	1.7	1.3		2.8	1.2		2.1	1.2	
e07a30	When upset, difficult to calm	1.4	1.3		2.6	1.3		2.1	1.4	
ANWI	Anxiety/Withdrawal	1.0	0.9	.80	1.3	1.1	.79	0.9	0.9	.72
w01a02	When playing, does not often giggle or laugh	0.9	1.0		1.5	1.4		1.0	1.2	
w02a03	Does not smile as much as most other children	1.1	1.1		1.5	1.5		1.0	1.2	
w05a33	Very withdrawn	0.9	1.1		0.7	1.2		0.8	1.2	
LOLD	Low Ability/Learning Disabled	1.4	1.1	.82	1.8	1.1	.67	1.2	1.0	.79
l01a04	Not able to do as much as most other children	1.4	1.3		2.1	1.5		1.2	1.2	
l03a24	Has significant learning disabilities	1.5	1.3		2.0	1.5		1.3	1.2	
l05a26	Does not seem to learn as quickly as most others	1.2	1.1		1.4	1.1		1.3	1.2	
AGCO	Aggressive/Conduct Disorder	1.5	1.2	.80	1.9	1.0	.42	1.6	1.0	.45
c02a40	Steals and lies	1.4	1.5		1.3	1.2		1.1	1.3	
c03a43	Can be very destructive	1.6	1.4		1.8	1.4		1.6	1.3	
c06a46	Lewd or obscene gestures or inappropriate behavior	1.5	1.4		2.5	1.5		2.2	1.5	

Teacher Domain (Part B)

GSDNS	Self-Doubt/Needs Support	1.3	1.0	.79	1.9	1.1		.80
s17b31	Wish I had someone to turn for the guidance	1.4	1.3		1.9	1.4		
s18b33	Have received much less support or help then I expected	1.0	1.1		1.7	1.3		
s6b16	I feel I need more help then I am being provided	1.5	1.3		2.0	1.3		
LOST	Loss of Satisfaction from Teaching	1.1	0.9	.76	1.5	1.2		.85
l12b36	I do not enjoy teaching this child	0.8	1.0		1.4	1.3		
l5b08	I do not feel as close to or warmly about child	0.9	1.1		1.2	1.3		
l6b09	Child does things that bother me a great deal	1.4	1.2		1.8	1.3		
DIST	Disrupts Teaching Process	2.6	0.9	.69	3.1	0.7		.52
d2b25	Give up more of my time to meet child needs	3.0	1.0		3.2	0.9		
d5b35	Frustrated that student is not successful	2.7	1.1		3.2	1.0		
d6b43	Takes my attention away from other children	2.2	1.3		3.0	1.1		
FRPA	Frustration working with Parents	0.9	0.9	.80	1.2	1.2		.84
f01b13	Interacting with parents is frustrating	1.3	1.3		1.3	1.5		
f03b39	I feel harassed by parents of child	0.4	0.8		0.9	1.2		
f06b42	Unable to agree with parents re: handling child	0.9	1.1		1.4	1.4		

Note: Scale figures are based upon three respective items. The scoring dimension in the second sample ranges on a 5-point Likert scale from 0 to 4 instead of 1 to 5, so one is subtracted from the means in the first sample.

lability/low adaptability, and aggressive/conduct disorder) than their counterparts in the first sample. Teachers in the first sample scored higher on internalizing behavior (anxiety/withdrawal and low ability/learning disabled). About a month before the second replication study took place, a student at a high school shot to death a teacher in The Hague. Just a week after this incident took place, a teacher while at work in school in Amsterdam was stabbed by an alumnus. Methodologically speaking, they are both classical examples of bias caused by history and also may have contributed to the low internal consistency of scale aggressive/conduct disorder (see discussion above). In any case, teachers who took part in the conference where the second replication study was held were probably more focused on aggressive or externalizing behavior. Apart from the fact that teachers taking part in a conference differ from teachers sampled at random, we also think that these incidents may have biased the results in Part B. For all scales the experienced level of stress of the Teacher Domain in the second study is higher.

In Table 7.4 the Pearson r product-moment correlation on both the item and scale levels is presented. Compared to the results of Greene et al. (1997), the correlation coefficients found in our second Dutch sample are somewhat higher. Explained variance for the five subscales ranges from .31 (Anxiety/Withdrawal) to .64 (Aggressive/Conduct Disorder). Also shown in Table 7.4 are the results of modeling the relation between frequency and stress.

The model, which suggests that all three items are part of one scale, can be simultaneously described by one regression equation (H_0: $\beta_{01} = \beta_{02} = \beta_{03}$ (= β_0) and $\beta_{11} = \beta_{12} = \beta_{13}$ (= β_1)) and tested against a model in which the regression coefficients of the separate items may differ from each other (H_1: $\beta_{01} \neq \beta_{02} \neq \beta_{03}$ and $\beta_{11} \neq \beta_{12} \neq \beta_{13}$). For separate items and scales, the relationship between frequency (IV) and stress (DV) can be adequately described with regression models. An alpha level of .05 was used for[4] the statistical tests and with respect to scales ADHD, anxiety withdrawal, and aggressive/conduct disorder the null hypotheses were not rejected. For the scales emotional lability/low adaptability ($F(4,118) = 3.23, p < .01$) and low ability/learning disabled ($F(4,119) = 3.93, p < .00$) the null hypotheses were rejected. So it is troublesome to treat perceived stress simply as additive, independently of the frequency of the behavior under study.

At this point, two conclusions can be drawn. First of all, although we accept the idea that stress is additive—we even have taken the assumption of linearity between frequency and stress for granted—it might be inadequate to measure the distress perceived by teachers without explicitly taking into account the frequency response set. So instead of just measuring stress, the results of our analysis advocate also measuring the perceived

Table 7.4. Response Set—Frequency Versus Stress; Relative and Absolute Differences Between Means; Pearson Correlation Coefficients for Behaviorally Challenging Students (Second sample; *N* = 136)

		American Results as Presented by Greene, Abidin, and Kmetz (1997) PM Correlation Coefficient	Second Dutch Sample (*N* = 136)					
			PM Correlation Coefficient*	Linear models				
				Regression Coefficients				
	Student Domain (Part A)			B_0	B_1	F	df	p
ADHD	**ADHD**	.70	.70	.25	.73	.75	[4, 119]	.5599
a02a12	Much harder to keep on a routine than others		.63	.24	.75			
a06a16	So active it exhausts me		.71	.27	.73			
a13a23	Squirms and fidgets a great deal		.69	.22	.71			
ELLA	**Emotional lability/low adaptability**	.62	.71	.07	.70	3.23	[4, 118]	.0148
e02a07	Seems to cry or fuss more than most others		.74	-.09	.71			
e04a09	Very moody and easily upset		.53	.55	.54			
e07a30	When upset, difficult to calm		.78	-.04	.80			
ANWI	**Anxiety/withdrawal**	.54	.56	.36	.44	.45	[4, 118]	.7722
w01a02	When playing, does not often giggle or laugh		.52	.34	.42			
w02a03	Does not smile as much as most other children		.56	.34	.44			
w05a33	Very withdrawn		.51	.38	.51			

(Table continues)

Table 7.4. (Continued)

	Student Domain (Part A)	American Results as Presented by Greene, Abidin, and Kmetz (1997) PM Correlation Coefficient	Second Dutch Sample ($N = 136$)					
			PM Correlation Coefficient*	Linear models				
				Regression Coefficients				
				B_0	B_1	F	df	p
LOLD	**Low ability/learning disabled**	a				3.93	[4, 119]	.0049
l01a04	Not able to do as much as most other children		.65	.31	.50			
l03a24	Has significant learning disabilities		.62	.09	.50			
l05a26	Does not seem to learn as quickly as most others		.67	.14	.57			
			.45	.58	.49			
AGCO	**Aggressive/conduct disorder**	.45				.84	[4, 116]	.5024
c02a40	Steals and lies		.80	.10	.81			
c03a43	Can be very destructive		.80	.00	.86			
c06a46	Lewd or obscene gestures or inappropriate behavior		.76	.28	.73			
			.82	.05	.83			

[a]The figure for low ability/learning disabled is not presented in Greene, Abidin, and Kmetz (1997).
*All p-values < .001.

frequency of problem behavior. Second, in the Index of Teaching Stress as developed by Greene et al. (1997), the discussion of the relation between frequency and stress is limited to the Student Domain. A closer inspection of some items, which are part of the Teacher Domain (Part B), for instance "Have this feeling I cannot handle student very well," "Child does things that bother me a great deal," "Makes my school day less enjoyable," "Exhausted by energy it takes to monitor child," or "Unable to agree with parents re: handling child," do at least at face value suggest a relation between the frequency of student behavior (Part A) and the distress perceived by the teacher with respect to the behavior (Part B). To put it the other way around, it is even hard to imagine how tension is rising because of "Takes my attention away from other children" or "Does not like me and does not want to be close" without dealing with the number of times a student (mis)behaves in a certain way.

The future challenge of ITS is to focus on the relation of the frequency response set of Part A with the stress response set of Part B. This approach is potentially more fruitful than just adding up 90 items to get a measure of the Total Stress. This approach also gives us a deeper understanding of the daily job-related stress elementary school teachers experience in a common classroom of thirty students.

DISCUSSION

In general, we may conclude that our analyses reaffirm the Varimax factor solution presented by Greene et al. (1997). The Multiple Group Method demonstrated that of 90 items in total, ten items should be reconsidered. This may be due to translating the items into Dutch as well as reflecting genuine differences between American and Dutch elementary schools. Special attention should also be paid to item "Child comes from very poor home situation." Only with respect to scale disrupts teaching process can it be argued that completely new items should be incorporated in the ITS.

A second conclusion deals with the computation of the total stress. Mean scores per scale are more meaningful in understanding the distress a teacher perceives than just adding up any number of items to estimate the contribution of a particular scale to the total stress. So, perhaps it is useful to select, for instance, the six items per scale with the highest internal consistency for use in a future research project. This would also reduce the number of items of 90 to 54 per student. Another way to reduce the number of items is to skip the questionnaire for the comparison student. The scoring dimension in the second sample ranged on a 5-point Likert scale from 0 to 4 instead of 1 to 5. It is also advisable if not obligatory to include in the questionnaire items explicitly measuring the incidence of challenging student behavior. A direct link between frequency and stress in the Student Domain needs further research and can no longer be taken for granted or assumed to be the same for every item within a particular scale.

We are fully aware that at this time some uncertainties with the ITS itself and the selection and translation of the items hamper the drawing of some general conclusions about comparisons of the level of stress of American and Dutch elementary teachers. We acknowledge that differences between American and Dutch scores on Part B might in theory be the result of using different answering scales. At the same time, using the original stress answering categories as proposed by Greene et al. (1997) would have probably resulted in even lower average scores than the ones actually measured in Dutch classrooms.

Although there is evidence to suggest cross-cultural validity in the kinds of measures employed in this study (e.g., Part A in this study), it is often difficult to interpret results across cultures in studies such as this for many reasons, we highlight one here. It is very difficult to understand patterns of teacher functioning without understanding the specific educational and community practices, values, and norms out of which such patterns emerge. By focusing only on outcomes and not the ecological correlates of such outcomes in this study, we are not in a strong position to understand the social sources and consequences of the kinds of differences we found. Understanding the overall organization of teacher behavior necessitates, ultimately, a situating of such behavior in the unique life-spaces that comprise their development. These findings suggest that, phenomenologically at least, American teachers are under more stress than their colleagues in other industrialized nations, such as the Netherlands, and such stress may engender educational consequences.

However, some interesting final comments are to be made. We paid special attention to the sample characteristics of teachers in the first sample and the pupils they had in mind when filling out the questionnaire. Only with respect to Special Educational Needs did we find some differences between the American and the Dutch sample reported. This may explain why we hardly found any differences between the Dutch and the American results with respect to Part A of the behaviorally challenging children, while at the same time the differences are quite large between Dutch and American comparison children. Given the fact that in our sample we have fewer children with Special Educational Needs in comparison to Greene et al., we simply expect the seventh child on the class roster to cause more behavioral problems in the special educational needs than in common elementary school. Apart from that, we also found evidence that that the formulation of some items is too extreme for the seventh child on the class roster in the mind of a common elementary school teacher. The mere fact that the differences with respect to the Student Domain between the United States and the Netherlands are negligible, strengthens our view that ITS can be a very valuable instrument in measuring teacher-student compatibility. This view is further substantiated by differences we found between the two countries with respect to the Teacher Domain. It is noteworthy to state that Part B reflects stress reactions of teachers that are culturally or nationally colored and further research into this topic is required.

NOTES

1. The source of information comes from the Central Bureau of Statistics, Kerncijfers Wijken en Buurten 1999. We also would like to thank students H. Blom, A. Dekkers, D. Kooistra, T. Geerts—de Leeuw van Weenen, and G. van der Zwaag of the University of Professional Education of Utrecht for collecting the data in the first sample.
2. As a matter of fact, we endorse the American Psychological Association (APA) guideline "the essence of the scientific method involves observations that can be repeated and verified by others" (APA, 2001, p.3 48). This is also the reason we cite the items here at length.
3. For behaviorally challenging children, the corrected item-total correlation between item "Does things for me that make me feel good" and loss of satisfaction from teaching was –.43. The three Pearson correlation coefficients between this item and the other scales also were negative (i.e., –.30, –.23, and –.11).
4. There is no reason to assume that the signs of the slopes in the regression equations within one factor are differently influenced by the reported incidents. And even if this happens to be the case in very exceptional circumstances, it merely strengthens our case that the relation between incidence and stress needs to be incorporated in the measurement of experienced stress.

REFERENCES

Abidin, R. R. (1986). *Parenting Stress Index* (2nd ed.). Charlottesville, VA: Pediatric Psychology Press.

Abidin, R. R. (1995). *Parenting Stress Index: Test manual* (3rd ed.). Osessa, FL: Psychological Assessment Resources.

Abidin, R. R., & Robinson, L. L. (2002). Stress, biases, or professionalism: What drives teachers' referral judgments of students with challenging behaviors. *Journal of Emotional and Behavioral Disorders, 10*(4), 204-212.

American Psychological Association. (2001). *Publication manual of the American Psychological Association* (5th ed.). Washington, DC: Author.

Anastopoulos, A. D., Guevremont, D. C., Shelton, T. L., & DuPaul, G. J. (1992). Parenting stress among families of children with Attention Deficit Hyperactivity Disorder. *Journal of Abnormal Child Psychology, 20*, 503-520.

Baker, J. A. (1999). Teacher student interaction in urban at-risk classrooms: Differential behavior, relationship quality, and student satisfaction with school. *Elementary School Journal, 100*(1), 57-70.

Borg, M. G. (1990). Occupational stress in British educational settings: A review. *Educational Psychology, 10*, 103-126.

Boyle, G. J., Borg, M. G., Falzon, J. M., & Baglioni, A. J. (1995). A structural model of the dimensions of teacher stress. *British Journal of Educational Psychology, 65*(1), 49-67.

Brophy, J. (1996). *Teaching problem students*. New York: The Guilford Press.

Brouwers, A., & Tomic, W. (1998). *Student disruptive behaviour, perceived self-efficacy in classroom management and teacher burnout*. Paper presented at the Ninth European Conference on Personality, University of Surrey.

Coie, J. D., & Koeppl, G. K. (1990). Adapting intervention to the problems of aggressive and disruptive children. In S. R. Asher & J. D. Coie (Eds.), *Peer rejection in childhood* (pp. 309-337). New York: Cambridge University Press.

Coladarci, T. (1992). Teachers' sense of efficacy and commitment to teaching. *Journal of Experimental Education, 60*, 323-337.

Central Bureau of Statistics. (2002). *Kerncijfers Wijken en Buurten 1999* [Statistics of districts and neighborhoods 1999]. Voorburg: Heerlen.

Golembiewski, R. T., Bodreau, R. A., Sun, B., & Luo, H. (1998). Estimates of burnout in public agencies: Worldwide, how many employees have which degree of burnout, and with what consequences? *Public Administration Review, 58*(1), 59-65.

Greene, R. W., Abidin, R. R., & Kmetz, C. (1997). The Index of Teaching Stress: A measure of student-teacher compatibility. *Journal of School Psychology, 35*(3), 239-259.

Lamude, K. G., Scudder, J., & Furno-Lamude, D. (1992). The relationship of student resistance strategies in the classroom to teacher burnout and teacher Type-A behavior. *Journal of Social Behavior and Personality, 7*, 597-610.

Mash, E. J., & Johnston, C. (1990). Determinants of parenting stress: Illustrations from families of hyperactive children and families of physically abused children. *Journal of Clinical Child Psychology, 19*, 313-338.

Mellenbergh, G. J., & Van den Brink, W. P. (1998). The measurement of individual change. *Psychological Methods, 3*, 470-485.

Nunnally, J. C. (1978). *Psychometric Theory*. New York: McGraw-Hill.

Palmer Wilson, C., Gutkin, T. B., Hagen, K. M., & Oats, R. G. (1998). General education teachers' knowledge and self-reported use of classroom interventions for working with difficult-to-teach student: Implications for consultation, preferral intervention and inclusive services. *School Psychology Quarterly, 13*(1), 45-62.

Ten Berge, J. M. F., & Siero, F. W. (2000). Factoranalyse. In A. Van Knippenberg & F. W. Siero (Eds.), *Multivariate analyse: Beknopte inleiding en toepassingen* (3^c druk, pp. 53-82) [Multivariate analyses: Introduction and applications]. Houten/Zaventem: Bohn, Stafleu Van Loghem.

Thomas. A., & Chess, S. (1980). *The dynamics of psychological development.* New York: Brunner/Mazel.

Webster-Stratton, C. (1990). Stress: A potential disruptor of parent perceptions and family interactions. *Journal of Clinical Child Psychology, 19*, 302-312.

Van der Wolf, J. C., & Defares P. B. (1994). Stress bij leraren in het basisonderwijs [Stress in primary school teachers]. In N. Ph Geelkerken, G. J. J. Goetheer, F. H. J. G. Brekelmans, & F. A. J. van Moorsel (Eds.), *Praktijkboek bedrijfsgezondheidszorg in het onderwijs. Deel C: Instrumenten, hulpmiddelen en methoden* (pp. 45-53). Den Haag: VUGA.

Van der Wolf, K., & Everaert, H. (2003). Teacher stress, challenging parents and problem students. In S. Castelli, M. Mendel, & B. Ravn (Eds.), *School, family, and community partnership in a world of differences and changes* (pp. 135-146). Gdánsk: Wydawnictwo Uniwersytetu Gdanskiego.

CHAPTER 8

SOURCES OF TEACHER DEMOTIVATION

Zeynep Kiziltepe

This study focuses on teacher demotivation, which is defined as the specific external causes that reduce the motivational basis of a behavioral intention or an ongoing action. High school teachers ($N = 340$) were asked to rank order the 3 factors that demotivated them most as a teacher. Using content analysis, participants' answers were categorized under 6 categories: Students (S), Economics (E), Administration (A), Parents (P), Structural and Physical Characteristics (SPC), I (Ideals), and Social Status (SS). The results showed that A, SPC, and S were the most frequently cited demotivating factors for the high school teachers.

Herzberg, Mausner, and Snyderman (1959), in their influential work on industrial motivation, defined various factors in the work setting as satisfiers, and dissatisfiers. They hypothesized that satisfiers, when present, led to increased worker satisfaction, but did not necessarily lead to worker dissatisfaction if absent. Conversely, dissatisfiers could decrease motivation when present, but necessarily increase motivation if eliminated.

Evans (1997) suggested that an individual's job satisfaction is determined by whether her/his job related needs are met. When needs go unmet, the result is dissatisfaction. Evans (1998) claimed that Herzberg's theory (1968) emphasized that dissatisfaction is not the same as no satisfaction. She furthermore thinks that what Herzberg means by "dissatisfaction" is "unsatisfactory" and by "no satisfaction "lacking the capacity to be satisfying." In a study done by Holdaway (1978), 50% of the respondents (teachers) were dissatisfied on 10 items: practices involving consultation, decision making, and collective bargaining, preparation time and methods used in making staffing decisions. In the same study, 31% of the subjects stated that attitudes of society and parents to education were the cause of their overall dissatisfaction and 30% stated administration and politics were the cause. Moreover, it was pointed out that it is not clear whether depression causes job dissatisfaction or vice versa; but they may both be caused by another factor, such as poor working conditions (Maslach, Schaufeli, & Leiter, 2001).

TEACHER MORALE

Evans (2000) refered to morale as a state of mind determined by the individual's expectation of how far her/his needs are satisfied and how far those needs significantly affect that individual's total work situation. She further claimed that low morale within the teaching profession results from low salaries and low status. Similarly, Halsey (1995), after examining life styles of university and polytechnic school teachers, asserted that the low morale of academicians is linked to loss of status and deterioration of working conditions. The vast majority of polytechnic staff in his study reported that over the past decade they had lost the public respect and the appreciation of politicians and civil servants.

Young (2000) claimed that teacher morale is related to job satisfaction. In a study conducted in Hawaii, he found seven factors that negatively impacted teacher morale, including lack of administrative support and management skills, overcrowded classes, teacher overload and poor physical working conditions. These results provided evidence that when teachers are distressed and the educational system is perceived as letting them down, consequences such as teacher burnout, absenteeism, and attrition can result.

TEACHER BURNOUT

Although there is no standard definition of burnout, Maslach (1982, 1998) claimed that it has three dimensions: exhaustion, cynicism (depersonalisation) and inefficacy (reduced personal accomplishment).

Although exhaustion is found to be the central quality of burnout, a strong relationship between exhaustion and cynicism is also found consistently in burnout research. According to Maslach, Schaufeli and Leiter (2001), in an extensive study of burnout, the relationship of inefficacy to the other aspects of burnout is somewhat more complex. In some instances, it appears to be a function of either exhaustion, cynicism, or a combination of the two (Byrne, 1994; Lee & Ashforth, 1996). In the establishment of the multidimensional theory of burnout, one of the primary concerns was whether burnout was a distinctly different phenomenon from other established constructs, specifically from depression and job satisfaction. Research conducted with the Maslach burnout inventory (MBI) by Maslach and Jackson, (1981) suggested that burnout and depression were distinct phenomena, , although it has been found that individuals who are more depression-prone are also more vulnerable to burnout (Bakker, Schaufeli, Demerouti, Janssen, Van der Hulst, & Brouwer, 2000; Glass & McKnight 1996; Leiter & Durup, 1994).

In another study, it was proposed that teacher burnout is associated with student misbehavior (Hastings & Bham, 2003). The literature generally supports the hypothesis that occupational stress and teacher burnout are associated with poor health in teachers affecting the learning environment and interfering with the achievement of educational goals because they lead to teacher's detachment, alienation, cynicism, apathy, absenteeism and ultimately the decision to leave the field (Guglielmi & Tatrow, 1998). Rivera-Batiz and Marti (1995) conducted a survey of opinion with 599 students and 200 teachers in New York public schools and found that overcrowding in classrooms also had significant negative effects on instruction and learning in the system. Futher, only 50% of the teachers looked forward to each working day in their school. In addition, Day (1999) further reported that in England it has become more difficult to retire early due to the changes in government pension rules, leading to a decline in the morale of teachers.

TEACHER STRESS

Hans Selye (1956, 1993), a pioneer researcher on stress, has defined it as the nonspecific result of any demand on the body, be the effect mental or somatic. His research investigated the effects of stress on the release of adrenal gland hormones. These hormones usually lead to useful adaptation to the stress producing stimulus. However, in the cases of the failure of the adaptation process, individuals can become susceptible to one or more diseases of maladaptation. Other stress researchers (Aldwin, 1994; Lazarus, 1966, 2000; Spielberger & Sarason, 1991; Toch, 2002) moving from a biological understanding to one that emphasizes perception and psychological resources, have described it as the conflict between demands of the environment and needs of the individual.

Relating stress to educational settings, Carlyle and Woods (2003) defined it as the interaction between the stresses that originate at the school, such as poor leadership and communication systems, autocratic decision making, and bullying management styles, and those which originate at home, such as bereavement and illness, children's problems, and marital status. Stress is also claimed by Kyriacou (1997) to be the experience by a teacher of unpleasant emotions, such as tension, frustration, anxiety, anger, and depression. He further suggests that the teaching profession is one of the most stressful occupations. Moreover, stress in teachers is considered serious by experts and needs to be kept at a minimum (Czubaj, 1996) because it is a negative influence on teacher motivation (Dörnyei, 2001).

TEACHER DEMOTIVATION

Dörnyei (2001) argued that demotivation stems from specific external causes that reduce the motivational basis of a behavioral intention or an ongoing action. Thus, demotives are the negative counterparts of motives: While a motive increases an action tendency, a demotive decreases it, and a motivated person who was once motivated but for some reason has lost it, is considered to be demotivated. Therefore, a demotivated teacher is assumed to be a person who once had motivation but has lost it due to some specific causes in the teaching environment. Young (2002) pointed out that teacher motivation is so poor in developing countries that it may threaten the aim of providing primary education for all children by 2015. Young further claimed that the tendency among policymakers to neglect teachers' needs and to fail to consult them when considering new policies results in demotivation among teachers. Substantiating this perspective, the Organization for Economic Cooperation and Development (OECD, 1989) reported that an uncommitted and poorly motivated teaching body will have disastrous effects for even the best of intentions for change. This view is echoed by Tedesco (1997), who believed that there is a decline in expenditure and significant deterioration in the working conditions of teachers in many developing countries, producing demoralisation, abandonment of the profession, absenteeism, the search for other occupations, and finally, a negative impact on the quality of education offered.

GENDER, AGE AND SCHOOL TYPE DIFFERENCES

Relatively few studies have examined the relationship between teachers' demographic characteristics, such as gender, age, or the types of school they work in and their job satisfaction/dissatisfaction or stress. Results are mixed in the studies that do exist. In Lacy and Sheehan study (1997), where job satisfaction across eight nations (Australia, Germany, Hong Kong, Israel, Mexico, Sweden, United Kingdom, United States) was studied, it was found that with the exception of Israel and Mexico, males in comparison to females showed a tendency toward higher overall satisfaction. However, according to the courses they teach, little difference in satisfaction levels was apparent between male and female academics from most nations. Furthermore, with this aspect of their job, females were significantly more satisfied than males in both Australia and Israel. Likewise, females from Israel and Hong Kong were slightly more satisfied with their relationships with colleagues, while in Sweden and the United States the opposite was true.

Sünbül (2003) reports that male teachers exhibited more emotional exhaustion than female counterparts but that age did not have significant effect. In contrast, Claxton and Catalan (1998) report that burnout is related to age, with younger workers obtaining higher burnout and anxiety scores than older ones.

THE TURKISH CONTEXT

Atatürk (1881-1938), the founder of the Turkish Republic in 1923, put special emphasis on teaching, teachers, and teacher education. In fact, in one of his speeches to teachers, he said that if he were not the president, he would like to be a teacher (Sarpkaya, 2002). Teachers' economical conditions at that time were much more satisfying than today's and therefore their socioeconomic situation was much better (Necati, 1928). According to the results of the questionnaire Necati applied in those early years of the republic, the teachers of that time were happy with their jobs and environment. However, they complained about lack of technical equipment, not having the opportunity and means to follow professional publications, and the shabbiness of the school buildings.

Unfortunately, during the 80 years of the republic, teacher salaries have drastically decreased in relation to the increased costs of living. According to Baykal (1997), the share of the national budget given to the Ministry of Education and the universities diminishes every year. Teachers are one of the lowest income groups in the country. Due to these conditions, the profession has lost its value in the Turkish society and teachers have started to work second jobs to make a living.

Happy, motivated teachers of Atatürk's time have been replaced by unhappy, demotivated, and burned-out teachers (Gök & Okçabol, 1998). The situation of the academic staff is no different: Their positions are not high paying jobs (Turgut, 1997). Salaries may increase by promotion or they may get a share from the revenues of the university operated units but the wages are much lower than corresponding private sector salaries.

Due to these socioeconomic factors, Turkey has been losing some of its most highly trained manpower during the last 3 decades. Some students studying abroad to be teachers do not return after graduation, or successful academicians leave the country for better research and teaching positions. In a recent extensive study of teachers, Egitim-Sen (Union of Education, 2005), found that teachers have become dramatically more impoverished during the period from 1931 to 2005. For example, although teachers could buy 170 liters of olive oil or 164 kilograms of meat in 1931 with one salary, they now can buy only 87 liters of milk and 62 kilograms of meat. Furthermore, although a teacher in 1995 could buy 2,898 loaves of bread with one salary, s/he now can buy only 1,845 loaves in 2005. According to the same study, in the years between 1920 and 1950, the living standards of teachers were satisfying. The period between 1950 and 1965 were years of severe struggle for them, but from 1965 to 1970 they again improved. However, after the year 1970, the living standards of teachers worsened every year until they are now one of the lowest income groups in the country.

There have been no studies on teacher demotivation in Turkey. Therefore information about it is derived from studies conducted on work satisfaction and burnout. For example, Özday (1990) found support for Herzberg's two-factor theory (1968), concluding that intrinsic elements of the job are related to the actual content of work, such as recognition, achievement and responsibility. Having researched demographic characteristics, Varlik (2000), Basalp (2001) and Agan (2002) reported that teachers in private schools, no matter what their subject fields are, have more job satisfaction than their colleagues in the state schools. Other research from Günboyu (2001) presented a similar picture apart from the finding that male teachers were more satisfied than female teachers with management and supervision, salary, and working conditions. Kemaloglu (2001) investigated job satisfaction of the instructors of English at the English department of a university and has found that married instructors have more job satisfaction than single ones and so do the ones with children compared to the teachers with no children. Finally, there are two studies incorporating teachers' burnout level with job satisfaction: One of them found that there is a significant correlation between job satisfaction of teachers and burnout level, namely the more job satisfaction they have, the lower their burnout level (Gençer, 2002). Finally, in another study done by Sünbül (2003), job satisfaction was found to be a negative significant predictor of the depersonalization dimension of burnout. Burnout is claimed to be directly affecting teachers' professional lives in their work, particularly through its affect on their emotional well-being. According to this study, high school teachers' burnout is related to different aspects of locus of control, job satisfaction, and demographic characteristics such as age and gender.

Teacher Accountability Programs in Turkey

The Ministry of Education in Turkey has a subunit called the Board of Inspection, which oversees headmasters, department heads, and teachers in primary and secondary schools. The members of this committee visit schools unannounced and check the management notebooks, enter and observe classes, and write a report on the teaching methods, the teachers, the administrative group, and the school. However, concerns about the qualifications and competence and unpleasantness of the behavior of the inspectors have been frequently reported. This suggestion has empirical support: According to a study (Bakioglu & Hesapçioglu, 1997), 92.5% of all the inspectors are not specialized in education and 31% of them have not had any in-service training. It can, therefore, be stated that the inspectors are not aware of the latest teaching methods or devices and they have little understanding of modern assessment and evaluation techniques.

In a seminar the author attended in Antalya (personal communication, October 25, 2003), teachers complained about the behavior of inspectors, how poorly they treated teachers when they did not see the traditional teaching methods applied in classes, and how they could not grasp the idea of student-centered education. As a consequence, they tried to punish the teachers. In response, the ministry took steps to improve the system of inspection and has recently established new approaches to teacher accountability for quality programs (*Milli Egitim Bakanligi, Genel Yeterlik*, 2005). According to this new approach (683, 24100, July 5, 2000), to improve evaluation of the schools, a model based on quality education was developed. Moreover, a new understanding of the concept of inspection has also been developed in the near future: The members of the Board of Inspection will serve as mediators between educational institutions and the Ministry and provide teachers with new insights to the educational system.

Among the improvement studies of the Ministry of Education, the following criteria for an ideal teacher have been developed:

1. Establishing personal and professional values (appreciating national and global values).
2. Getting to know the students (appreciating, understanding and respecting the students).
3. Elaborating the teaching and learning process (lesson planning, material preparation, setting the learning environments, arranging activities outside the class).
4. Observing learning and development of students and evaluating them accordingly (assessment and evaluation according to the goals of the lesson, feedback formation, arranging the teaching-learning process according to the results of the evaluation).
5. Establishing a healthy relationship among the school, the family and the society (awareness of the environment and school as the cultural center, objectivity with the relationships with parents, cooperation with parents).
6. Being aware of the knowledge of the educational program with its contents (knowledge on the goals of the national program, management of the sources and their development).

What happens to teachers who are not found to be successful? There is a growing demand among parents for teachers who are not performing adequately to either receive in-service training or be dismissed to ensure the success of students. However, this demand cannot be realized for public school teachers because in-service training is rarely applied in state schools. Furthermore, they are civil servants and according to law, their jobs are permanent; they cannot be dismissed. The worst punishment that a public school teacher can receive is to be assigned to a remote and unpopular part of the country. The situation in the private schools, however, is not the same. Having no permanent jobs, the teachers usually have yearly contracts. They also get regular mentoring or training, or other forms of effective assistance.

METHOD

The present study took place in several high schools in the city of Istanbul in the winter of 2003. The main purpose was to identify factors that demotivate teachers. By convenience sampling, 340 high-school teachers, 180 female and 160 male, between the ages of 24 and 50 from both the state and private high schools were chosen. Of the 340 teachers, 270 were from the state schools and 70 from the private sector. Without explaining the idea of demotivation, they were asked to answer in writing to one open-ended question: "What demotivates you as a teacher?" In addition to that, they were asked to rank three of the factors they identified from the most to the least demotivating. To analyze the answers, content analysis was applied, which is a widely used method in social sciences (Weber 1990; Roberts 1995). It consists of screening any kind of oral or written document and counting the frequency of occurrence of key words or concepts, which can be categorized according to similarity in meaning. In this study, the concepts that are mentioned as the most demotivating were categorized according to their content and coded under some general headings. For example, if the concepts were about students, the general heading was Students (S), or about the administration, they were listed under the heading Administration (A). Later their second choices were scanned in the same manner and similarly their third. In sum, seven factors emerged. After the categories were set, the Statistical Package for Social Sciences 12.1 for Windows (SPSS) was used to compute the frequencies and the differences between the independent variables namely gender, school type (whether state or private), and teacher age (the first group aged between 24 and 37 and the second between 38 and 50).

Meanwhile, to make sure the data was as reliable as possible, two colleagues were asked independently to review the data and come up with a set of categorizations. When the notes were compared, it was observed that the categories were 90% the same. For the disputed 10%, revisions were made, and the categories were tightened up to the point that maximized mutual exclusivity. As for the validity of the study, classifications were studied with the above mentioned colleagues. In this way, coding errors were minimized. Finally, it should be mentioned that all factors mentioned by the subjects were coded under one of the categories.

RESULTS

Eighty-six different ways of expressing the demotivating aspects/factors were found, which were compressed and categorized under seven different categories. These categories are Administration (A), Students (S), Economics (E), Parents (P), Structural and Physical Characteristics (SPC), Ideals (I), and Social Status (SS). Examples of quotes from the teachers underlining the above groupings are as follows:

1. Administration
   - Conflicts or disputes with administration.

- Lack of communication with administration.
- Too much bureaucratic processes and control imposed on teachers.
2. Students
    - Improper behavior by students in class.
    - Poor communication with students.
3. Economics
    - Low income.
    - Economic difficulties.
4. Students' Parents
    - Poor relationships with parents.
    - Disputes with parents.
    - Irresponsible behavior by parents.
5. Structural and Physical Characteristics
    - Lack of technological materials in class.
    - Inadequate physical conditions of classrooms.
    - Overcrowded classes.
6. Ideals
    - Teachers feeling unsuccessful.
    - Teachers believing they are not useful to their students.
    - Teachers finding the education system insufficient and inefficient to prepare students to be citizens.
7. Social Status
    - The low value placed on the job of teaching by society.
    - Evaluation of the society that what teachers do is not important, or they chose this particular profession because they cannot do anything else.

Since this study had a non-parametric design, chi-square analyses with SPSS were conducted to examine frequencies of and the relationships between the demographic variables, namely gender, school type, and age and teachers' demotivation (see Tables 8.1, 8.2, 8.3 and 8.4). The most frequently and highly rated demotivation factor was Administration (29.4%). Administration (20.6%) with Structural and Physical Characteristics (20.6%) were suggested as the second most demotivating factor, and Students (35.3%) the third (see Table 8.1).

There were significant relationships between the dependent variables, demotivating factors, and the independent variables, gender (see Table 8.2), school type (see Table 8.3) and age groups (see Table 8.4).

Females stated that Administration (38.9%) was the most demotivating as their first choice. In contrast, Students (31.2%) was rated as the most demotivating factor by males $[\chi^2 (5, N = 340) = 40.073, p < .05)]$. For

Table 8.1. Frequency of Demotivating Factors

	A	S	E	P	SPC	I	SS
1st choice	29.4%	26.5%	14.7%	2.9%	14.7%	11.8%	—
2nd choice	20.6%	17.6%	17.6%	14.7%	20.6%	8.8%	—
3rd choice	17.6%	35.3%	8.8%	2.9%	23.5%	5.9%	5.9%

Note: N = 340, A = Administration, S = Students, E = Economics, P = Parents, SPC = Structural and Physical Characteristics, I = Ideals, SS = Social Status.

Table 8.2. Frequency of Demotivating Factors According to Gender

Choices	Gender	A	S	E	P	SPC	I	SS
1st choice	Female	38.9%	22.2%	11.1%	0	11.1%	16.7%	0
	Male	18.8%	31.2%	18.8%	6.2%	18.8%	6.2%	0
2nd choice	Female	27.7%	16.7%	16.7%	11.1%	16.7%	11.1%	0
	Male	12.5%	18.8%	18.8%	18.8%	25%	6.2%	0
3rd choice	Female	33.3%	44.4%	0	0	11.1%	5.5%	5.5%
	Male	0	25%	18.7%	6.2%	37.5%	6.2%	6.2%

Note: N = 340: Female, n = 180; Male, n = 160.

Table 8.3. Frequency of Demotivating Factors According to School Type

Choices	School Type	A	S	E	P	SPC	I	SS
1st choice	State	33.3%	25.9%	18.5%	3.7%	11.1%	7.4%	0
	Private	14.2%	28.6%	0	0	28.6%	28.6%	0
2nd choice	State	22.2%	14.8%	18.5%	18.5%	18.5%	7.4%	0
	Private	14.3%	28.5%	14.3%	0	28.5%	14.3%	0
3rd choice	State	14.8%	37%	11.1%	0	25.9%	3.7%	7.4%
	Private	28.5%	28.5%	0	14.3%	14.3%	14.3%	0

Note: N = 340: State, n = 270; Private, n = 70

their second choice, while it was again Administration (27.7%) for females, it was Structural and Physical Characteristics (25%) for males [χ^2 (5, N = 340) = 18.507, p < .05)]. As their third choice, however, while females chose Students (44.4%), males chose Structural and Physical Characteristics (37.5%) [χ^2 (5, N = 340) = 132.616, p < .05)] (see Table 8.2).

As for the school-type, although state school teachers stated Administration (33.3%) as their most demotivating factor, private school teachers identified Students, Structural and Physical Characteristics, and Ideals

Table 8.4. Frequency of Demotivating Factors According to Age Groups

Choices	School Type	A	S	E	P	SPC	I	SS
1st choice	Age group I	23.8%	32.1%	10.7%	3.6%	11.9%	17.9%	0
	Age group II	34.9%	20.9%	18.6%	2.3%	17.4%	5.8%	0
2nd choice	Age group I	33.3%	14.3%	22.6%	0	23.8%	6%	0
	Age group II	8.1%	20.9%	12.8%	29%	17.4%	11.6%	0
3rd Choice	Age group I	27.3%	19%	15.5%	6%	26.2%	0	6%
	Age group II	8.1%	51.2%	2.3%	0	20.9%	11.6%	5.8%

Note: $N = 340$ and age group I = 24-37 ($N = 168$) and age group II = 38-55 ($N = 172$).

(28.6% each) [χ^2 (5, $N = 340$) = 55.248, $p < .05$)]. The second most demotivating factor for state school teachers was Administration (22.2%) while again it was Students and Structural and Physical Characteristics (28.5% each) for the private school teachers [χ^2 (5, $N = 340$) = 26.898, $p < .05$)]. For their third choice, state school teachers identified Students (37%) as their demotivating factor, and for private school teachers it was Administration and Students (28.5% each) [χ^2 (6, $N = 340$) = 72.407, $p < .05$)] (see Table 8.3).

Finally, the significant differences between the two age groups were as follows: Although the younger group reported that it was Students (32.1%) which demotivated them most, the older group identified Administration (34.9%) [χ^2 (5, $N = 340$) = 23.876, $p < .05$)]. The second most demotivating factor was Administration (33.3%) for the younger group, while it was Parents for the older group (29%) [χ^2 (5, $N = 340$) = 86.593, $p < .05$)]. For the third choice, the younger group reported Administration (27.3%) as their demotivating factor while for the older group it was Students (51.2%) [χ^2 (6, $N = 340$) = 90.099, $p < .05$)] (see Table 8.4).

DISCUSSION

The primary aim of this study was to examine sources of high-school teachers' demotivation. The results showed that Administration was the most important demotivational factor, with Students and Structural and Physical Characteristics following. The findings support a study done by Almahboob (1987) who found that relationships with colleagues and management contributes most to job dissatisfaction. Similarly, Tye and O'Brien (2002) claimed that lack of administrative support is among the most important factors for those who have left the profession and by those who are still teaching. Likewise Slivar (2004), in a study on school climate and its effects on teachers, reported that among a range of school stressors, the principle's restrictive attitude had by far the most negative effect. Furthermore, Ross (1995) claimed that what makes the teaching profession so stressful and demanding is not leading of clubs, societies, coaching sports teams, or directing music and drama rehearsals, but the burden of administration and paperwork requirements.

Differences were found in the frequency of demotivating factors reported by male and female participants. For example, although female teachers and public schools ranked Administration as most demotivating, for males and private schools it was Students. In most schools the administrative staff is made up of males and the teachers of females. It is possible that relationships between the female teachers and the administration in state schools are problematic, which makes them unhappy in their working environment. The situation in private schools is different. Most of the staff, both administrative and teachers, are female. Therefore, it may be that the relationship between them is based on more equal and democratic terms. Another reason could be that state schools are too bureaucratic and dependent upon the state, which leaves them little room for freedom to act. In contrast the private schools, cooperating with teachers, are more free and independent, setting their own goals and rules within limits, which make these teachers more content than the ones in public schools.

The finding that Students and Administration were the major determinant factors of teacher demotivation may help substantiate Herzberg's (1968) two-factor theory because he included interpersonal relations with subordinates, superiors, or peers as factors contributing to the dissatisfaction of the worker. The findings of this study also support the extensive research done by Holdaway (1978), who revealed that working with students was among the most common sources of overall teacher satisfaction. Moreover, in a project by Calderhead and Shorrock (1997), it was observed that for the majority of the student teachers the most important factors drawing them into teaching were personal and intrinsic to the nature of teaching itself; namely, the satisfaction of working with children, of helping them to learn, of doing a job that was perceived to be useful and important. Therefore, when problems of any kind arose with students, dissatisfaction was highest.

Structural and Physical Characteristics were described as among the demotivating factors with private schools and male teachers. The reason for this may be the fact that private schools are charging their students considerable amounts of money unlike the free public schools. Therefore, the teachers may feel that they should be provided with better physical conditions and adequate technical materials in classrooms and less crowded classes.

What was most surprising in the results of the study was that Economics was not an outstanding demotivating factor for teachers although it was claimed that they were among the lowest income groups in absolute terms (Baykal, 1997). Either they have lost hope all together in gaining better salaries and working/living conditions, or the hopelessness of their economic situation is so obvious that they no more want to put emphasis on it and try to draw attention to other failing areas in their profession. It is believed that this aspect needs further investigation. Another explanation might be that many teachers who choose to remain in the profession can afford to do so because they are not the primary financial supporters of their families.

GENERALIZABILITY AND LIMITATIONS

How representative is the city of Istanbul of the rest of Turkey? Istanbul is the largest city in Turkey with a population of around 10 million. People from all over Turkey migrate to Istanbul every year to find better working and living conditions. The first migration wave took place between 1950 and 1960 from villages in Anatolia to the three big cities, Istanbul, Zimir and Ankara. Most of the migrants were single men who came to the big cities to find better working conditions (Tümertekin, 1971). The second wave started in the middle of 1960s and this time only Istanbul was targeted. From then on, migration to Istanbul has not abated (Özbay, 1999). Therefore, the population of stanbul may be said to be representative of the whole country.

Among the limitations, one can conclude that content analysis has some disadvantages (Babbie, 1995). The most important one is that it is limited to the examination of recorded communications whether oral, written or graphic within the study. That is, nothing else can be included for analysis leaving people with limited information to consider, analyze, and arrive at conclusions. Another limitation is that the word "administration" is not very clear within the statements of the teachers. We do not know what level of administration they mean: Do they mean the headmasters only, or their assistants, department heads, and inspectors who are also involved in the management of schools, or all of them?

In spite of the limitations stated above, it is believed that the findings presented and analyzed in this article make a significant contribution to the study of teacher demotivation by presenting a different perspective from the Turkish culture.

REFERENCES

Agan, F. (2002). *Özel okullarda, devlet okullarinda ve dershanelerde çalisan lise ögretmenlerinin is tatminlerinin karslastirilmasi* [Comparison of job satisfaction of high school teachers working in private schools, state schools, and private courses]. Unpublished master's dissertation, Marmara University, Istanbul.

Aldwin, C. (1994). *Stress coping and development.* New York: Guilford Press.

Almahboob, A. E. (1987). *An investigation of the degree of job satisfaction among university faculty in Saudi Arabian universities.* Unpublished doctoral dissertation, University of Pittsburg, Pennsylvania.

Babbie, E. (1995). *The practice of social research.* Belmont, TN: Wadsworth.

Bakioglu, A., & Hesapçioglu, M. (1997). Düsünmeyi ögretmekte ögretmen ve okul yöneticisinin rolü: Düsünmek! [The role of teachers and administration in teaching thinking: Thinking]. *Atatürk Egitim Fakültesi Egitim Bilimleri Dergisi, 9,* 49-78.

Bakker, A. B., Schaufeli, W. B., Demerouti, E., Janssen, P. M. P., Van der Hulst, R., & Brouwer, J. (2000). Using equity theory to examine the difference between burnout and depression. *Anxiety Stress Coping, 13,* 247-268.

Basalp, N. (2001). *Ilkögretim okullarndaki ögretmenlerin is tatmin düzeylerinin karsilastrilimasi* [Comparison of job satisfaction level of primary school teachers]. Unpublished master's dissertation, Sakarya University, Sakarya.

Baykal, A. (1997). Turkish educational system at the instructional level. In G. Yldran & J. Durnin (Eds.), *Recent perspectives on Turkish education: An inside view* (pp. 169-180). Indiana: Indiana University Turkish Studies and Turkish Ministry of Culture Joint Series XVI.

Byrne, B. M. (1994). Burnout: testing for the validity, replication, and invariance of causal structure across elementary, intermediate, and secondary teachers. *American Educational Research Journal, 31,* 645-673.

Calderhead, J., & Shorrock, S. B. (1997). *Understanding teacher education.* London: Falmer Press.

Carlyle, D., & Woods, P. (2003). *The emotions of teacher stress.* London: Trentham Books.

Claxton, R., & Catalan, J. (1998). Psychological distress and burnout among buddies: Demographic situational and motivational factors. *AIDS Care, 10*(2), 175-189.

Czubaj, C. A. (1996). Maintaining teacher motivation. *Education, 116*(3), 372-379.

Day, C. (1999). *Developing teachers: The challenges of lifelong learning.* London: Routledge Falmer.

Dörnyei, Z. (2001). *Teaching and researching motivation.* Essex, England: Pearson Education.

Egitim-Sen. (2005, January 20). *Radikal.*

Evans, L. (1997). Understanding teacher morale and job satisfaction. *Teaching and Teacher Education, 13,* 831-845.
Evans, L. (1998). *Teacher morale, job satisfaction and motivation.* London: Paul Chapman.
Evans, L. (2000). The effects of educational change on morale, job satisfaction and motivation. *Journal of Educational Change, 1,* 173-192.
Gençer, A. (2002). *Ögretmenlerin is doyumu ile mesleki tükenmislik düzeylei arasindaki iliskiler* [The relationship between teacher job satisfaction and their job burnout level]. Unpublished master's dissertation, Osmangazi University, Eskiehir.
Glass, D. C., & McKnight, J. D. (1996). Perceived control, depressive symptomatology, and professional burnout: A review of the evidence. *Psychology and Health, 11,* 23-48.
Gök, F., & Okçabol, R. (1998). *Ögretmen profili arastirma raporu* [A research report on teacher profile]. Ankara, Turkey: Eitim-Sen Yay.
Guglielmi, R. S., & Tatrow, K. (1998). Occupational stress, burnout, and health in teachers: A methodological and theoretical analysis. *Review of Educational Research, 68*(1), 61-100.
Günboyu, I. (2001). Primary and junior high school teachers' job satisfaction. *Kuram ve Uygulamada Egitim Bilimleri, 1*(2), 337-356.
Halsey, A. H. (1995). *Decline of Donnish dominion.* Oxford, England: Clarendon Press.
Hastings, R. P., & Bham, M. S. (2003). The relationship between student behavior patterns and teacher burnout. *School Psychology International, 24*(1),115-128.
Herzberg, F. (1968). *Work and the nature of man.* London: Staples Press.
Herzberg, F., Mausner, B., & Snyderman, B. (1959). *The motivation to work.* New York: Wiley.
Holdaway, E. A. (1978). Facet and overall satisfaction of teachers. *Educational Administration Quarterly, 14*(1), 30-47.
Kemaloglu, E. (2001). *A research on the job satisfaction of the instructors of English at Yldz Technical University Basic English Department.* Unpublished master's dissertation, Marmara University, Istanbul.
Kyriacou, C. (1997). *Effective teaching in schools.* Cheltenham, England: Stanley Thorne.
Lacy, F. J., & Sheehan, B. A. (1997). Job satisfaction among academic staff: An international perspective. *Higher Education, 34*(3), 305-322.
Lazarus, R. S. (1966). *Psychological stress and the coping process.* New York: McGraw-Hill.
Lazarus, R. S. (2000). Toward better research on stress and coping. *American Psychologist, 55,* 665-673.
Lee, R. T., & Ashforth, B. E. (1996). A meta-analytic examination of the correlates of the three dimensions of job burnout. *Journal of Applied Psychology, 81,* 123-133.
Leiter, M. P., & Durup, J. (1994). The discriminant validity of burnout and depression: A confirmatory factor analytic study. *Anxiety, Stress and Coping, 7,* 357-373.
Maslach, C. (1982). *Burnout: The cost of caring.* Englewood Cliffs, NJ: Prentice-Hall.

Maslach, C. (1998). A multidimensional theory of burnout. In C. L. Cooper (Ed.), *Theories of organizational stress,* (pp. 68-85). Oxford, England: Oxford University Press.

Maslach, C., & Jackson, S. E. (1981). The measurement of experienced burnout. *Journal of Occupational Behavior, 2,* 99-113.

Maslach, C., Schaufeli, W. B., & Leiter, M. P. (2001). Job burnout. *Annual Review of Psychology, 52,* 397-422.

Milli Egitim Bakanligi, Genel Yeterlik. (2005). Retrieved January 12, 2005, from http: //oyegm.meb.gov.tr/yet/index.htm

Necati, M. (1928). *Ilk mektep muallimleriyle mesleki bir hasbihal* [Conversations with primary school teachers about their jobs]. Ankara, Turkey.

Organization for Economic Cooperation and Development. (1989). The condition of teaching: General report. In M. Fullan & A. Hargreaves (Eds.), *Teacher development and educational change.* London: The Falmer Press.

Özbay, F. (1999). Istanbul'da göç ve il içi nüfus hareketleri (1985-1990) [Within-city and migration movements in Istanbul]. In O. Baydar (Ed.), *75 ylda köylerden ehirlere.* Istanbul, Turkey: Tarih Vakf.

Özday, N. (1990). *Resmi ve özel liselerde çalisan ögretmenlerin is tatmini ve is streslerinin karslastirmali analizi* [Job satisfaction of teachers working in state and private high schools, and the competative analysis of their job stress]. Unpublished master's dissertation, stanbul University, stanbul.

Rivera-Batiz, F. L., & Marti, L. (1995). *A school system at risk: A study of the consequences of overcrowding in New York City Schools* (Report No. 95-1). New York: IUME Research Report.

Roberts, C. (Ed.). (1995). *Text analysis for the social sciences: Methods for drawing statistical inferences from texts and transcripts.* Hillsdale, NJ: Erlbaum.

Ross, J. (1995). From middle to senior management. In J. Bell (Ed.), *Teachers talk about teaching* (pp. 50-60). Buckingham, United Kingdom: Open University Press.

Sarpkaya, R. (2002). Atatürk'ün egitim politikasinin kaynaklari ve temel ilkeleri [Sources and basic principles of Atatürk' education policy]. *Eitim ve Bilim, 27*(126), 3-10.

Selye, H. (1956). *The stress of life.* New York: McGraw-Hill.

Selye, H. (1993). History and the present status of the stress concept. In L. Goldberger & S. Breznits (Eds.), *Handbook of stress* (pp. 7-21). New York: Free Press.

Slivar, B. (2004). *The effect of competence and the school climate on the primary appraisal of stress situations and ways of coping in teachers.* Paper presented at the 25th Stress and Anxiety Research Society Conference, Amsterdam, Holland.

Spielberger, C., & Sarason, I. G. (1991). *Stress and anxiety.* Washington, DC: Francis & Taylor.

Sünbül, A.M. (2003). An analysis of relations among locus of control, burnout and job satisfaction in Turkish high school teachers. *Australian Journal of Education 47*(1), 58-73.

Tedesco, J. C. (1997). Enhancing the role of teachers. In C. Day, D. Van Veen, & S. Wong-Kooi (Eds.), *Teachers and teaching: International perspectives on school reform and teacher education* (pp. 68-79). Leuven/Apeldoorn, Belgium: Garant.

Toch, H. (2002). *Stress in policing*. Washington DC: American Psychological Association.
Turgut, M. F. (1997). Higher education. In G. Yldran & J. Durnin (Eds.), *Recent perspectives on Turkish education: An inside view* (pp. 59-83). IN: Indiana University Turkish Studies and Turkish ministry of Culture Joint Series XVI.
Tümertekin, E. (1971). Gradual internal migration in Turkey: A test of Ravenstein's Hypothesis. *Review of the Geographical Institute of the University of Istanbul, 7*(13), 157-179.
Tye, B. B., & O'Brien, L. (2002). Why are experienced teachers leaving the profession? *Phi Delta Kappan, 84*, 24-35.
Varlik, T. (2000). *Devlet ve özel ilkögretim okullarinda çalisan ögretmenlerin is doyumu* [Job satisfaction of teachers working in state and private primary schools]. Unpublished master's dissertation, Hacettepe University, Ankara.
Weber, R. (1990). *Basic content analysis*. Newbury Park, CA: Sage.
Young, D. J. (2000). Teacher morale in Western Australia: A multilevel model. *Learning Environments Research, 3*, 159-177.
Young, S. (2002, October 4). Low staff morale damages pupils. *The Times Educational Supplement*, pp. 20.

CHAPTER 9

TEACHERS' JOB STRESS AND HUMAN RESOURCE DEVELOPMENT

The Malaysian Experience

Reynaldo Gacho Segumpan and Fazli B. Bahari

The main purpose of this study was to determine the overall level of work stress among 1,209 secondary school teachers in the State of Malacca, Malaysia. Correlates of their work stress levels and subgroup differences were also investigated. Teachers in this study rated their work stress level as moderate overall. The following subgroups reported relatively higher stress levels: those between 31 and 40 years old, teachers who had been teaching for 15 years or less, arts teachers, those earning RM2,000 (1 U.S.$ = RM3.80) or less, and those possessing master's degrees.

Malaysia, formerly known as Malaya, gained its independence from the British on August 31, 1957. It is generally divided into Peninsular Malaysia (East Malaysia) and West Malaysia (Sabah and Sarawak) on the island of Borneo. It has a population of about 23 million, with Malays, Chinese, and Indians as the majority ethnic backgrounds. As of 2003, Malaysia had a total of 1,881 government secondary schools (regular, fully residential, religious, vocational, technical, special model, and special schools) and 126,544 secondary school teachers distributed across 15 states, one third (46,213 or 36.52%) of whom are males. Of this number, 4,156 secondary school teachers are from the centrally located State of Malacca (Ministry of Education, 2003), the locale of this study.

In Malaysia, as in other countries, concerns about teachers' stress levels have gained increased attention. Teachers' workloads are one source of stress (Siti, 1991) because the job is characterized historically by role conflict, ambiguity, and overload (Liebermann & Miller, 1984). Tan (1996) noted in his study on work stress among Malaysian teachers of *Sekolah Rendah Jenis Kebangsaan Cina* (National Chinese Elementary School) specific factors that caused work stress, namely, teaching too many students in a single classroom, inadequate income, students' negative attitudes toward their studies, few chances for promotion, dealing with students with different abilities and interests, dealing with students' misbehavior, replacing other teachers, too much administrative work, uncooperative parents, and shortage of time to rest because of packed teaching schedules.

Smylie (1999) suggested that the perceptions and consequences of stress depend on an individual's real and perceived capacity to deal with demanding situations, reactively or proactively, which may have as much to do with whether the consequences of stress are positive or negative as does the type or intensity of the stress itself. Generally, the most negative consequences are expected to occur under conditions in which stress exceeds individuals' capabilities to mediate it. In these circumstances, work-related stress could lead to varying levels of psychological tension and frustration. The literature suggests that in its most excessive forms, stress can lead to "job burnout," a psychological state of failure and exhaustion (Freudenberger, 1974).

Teachers also face new and complex challenges arising from changing student populations (Pallas, Natriello, & McDill, 1995) as well as heightened expectations for performance and accountability (Firestone, Bader, Massel, & Rosenblum, 1992). Teachers must also navigate the ambiguities of "postmodern" shifts in social, political, economic, and cultural relations. And, they must contend with concurrent challenges to long standing, taken-for-granted knowledge, assumptions, and values concerning teaching and schools as institutions. When taken together, these general conditions and current challenges present potentially stressful situations for teachers that may have deleterious consequences for them and for their work with students (Hargreaves, 1994).

This study was anchored in a theory of work stress proposed by Boyle, Borg, Falzon, and Baglioni (1995), who explicitly delineated five factors that may influence teachers' stress level: students' misbehavior, workload, time and resource difficulties, interpersonal relationships, and professional recognition. This same set of factors was explored with teachers in Malaysia by Mokhtar (1998), who devised the work stress questionnaire that was used in the present study.

In the present research, certain demographic variables, like age, gender, marital status, working experience, subject taught, monthly income, academic preparation, and school grade, were also assumed to be related to teachers' level of work stress. This assumption is supported by a number of researchers, such as Borg and Falzon (1989), who reported that teachers' work stress levels were constituted differently based on some of these demographics characteristics. Dobson (1982) reported that female teachers found several items regarding students' misbehavior to be greater sources of stress than did their male colleagues. It was also found that in terms of teaching experience, younger and less experienced teachers were more stressed than their colleagues on a number of items: students' misbehavior, workload, and professional recognition. In the present study, the researchers were interested in looking at how work stress could be related to the factors mentioned by Boyle et al. (1995) and Mokhtar (1998).

STUDENTS' MISBEHAVIOR

Mokhtar (1998) and Merret and Wheldall (1993) suggested that teachers often find it necessary to devote considerable attention to students' misbehavior and the need to control and organize the classroom. Dealing with trouble may be a source of stress for many teachers, especially those undergoing their probationary period (Dobson, 1982).

Students' disciplinary problems, in particular, have frequently been identified as important sources of stress for teachers (Trendall, 1989), and any teacher knows that disruptive and badly behaved students are particularly demanding and stressful to deal with (Tuettemann & Punch, 1992). Research carried out by Kyriacou and Sutcliffe (1978) found that the major stressors for teachers were students' poor attitude, poorly motivated pupils, individual pupils who continually misbehave, and pupils who show lack of interest. Therefore, disruptive behavior of students is an important area of potential stress for many teachers.

Among Malaysian secondary school teachers, specifically in the state of Malacca, how does students' misbehavior relate to work stress? This question needed further investigation, hence, an inclusion of the construct "students' misbehavior" in the present research, which was construed to include inattentiveness during instruction, boisterous behavior in the classroom, and unwillingness to perform certain assigned tasks, among others.

WORKLOAD

Mokhtar (1998) also hypothesized that workload has a significant bearing on teachers' work stress. Borg and Riding (1993) defined stressful workloads as involving excessive levels of work and too much responsibility. Having too many tasks can create stress for a person in two ways. First, the person becomes fatigued and thus less able to tolerate annoyances and irritations; second, a person subjected to unreasonable work demands may feel perpetually behind schedule, a situation that itself is a powerful stressor (Dubrin, 1994). From a teacher's perspective, workload refers to the tasks that have to be performed, such as preparation before teaching, responsibility for the student, checking files and student's exercises, and other administrative work (Abdul, 1996).

Cooper and Payne (1988) in their research involving 2,368 respondents (including the head masters, officers, and directors from several education institutions in England) found that the main factor that influenced work stress was heavy work requirements. Trendall (1989) also found that the most apparent stressor is teaching workload. Teachers have too many responsibilities and are playing too many roles. Indeed, the burden of attending to too many responsibilities, if sustained too long, can wear a person out (Yoe, 1985). Other researchers have also found workload to be a major source of stress for teachers (Cox, 1978; Tuettenmann & Punch, 1992).

TIME AND RESOURCE DEMANDS

The present study, anchored on Mokhtar's (1998) research, also attempted to determine how work stress levels of teachers are impacted by "time and resource demands," which were defined operationally in terms of limited time and resources teachers have for their personal leisure and relaxation as well as inadequacy of teaching-learning resources. Time and resource demands were found to cause stress by Mokhtar (1998). Not having enough time for preparation and lack of resources for teaching students were identified by Manthei and Gilmore (1996) as difficulties faced by most teachers. Most teachers do not have enough time to finish up their tasks at school, and continue working at home. At the same time, they must prepare for their teaching class the next day (Kelly, 1988).

Moreover, lack of resources during the teaching process was found by Dewe (1986) to increase teacher work stress level. The author also found that teaching equipment and education aids, such as an overhead projector or desktop computer, are the teaching equipment that can help teachers to teach more effectively. Teachers feel stressful when there are too many students in one classroom and when teaching equipment is lacking (Siti, 1991).

PROFESSIONAL RECOGNITION

The construct "professional recognition" was also explored by Mokhtar (1998) in the Malaysian context, and the present research attempted to identify how it would be associated with work stress. In this study, "professional recognition" is related to the type and amount of appreciation and sense of approval teachers derive from their superiors, among others.

The need for adequate salaries, professional status, involvement in decision making, and support from administrators are considered professional recognition needs. Poor career structure and lack of recognition for good teaching, and poor working conditions, including inadequate salary and inadequate rest periods, are the potential professional recognition need elements that can contribute to teachers work stress (Barbara & Lisa, 2000). The failure to recognize teaching as one of societies' most important occupations may well be part of the reason that today's teachers feel so unhappy and stressed (Margaret & Anthony, 1991).

In addition, Dewe (1986) suggested that teachers need to be involved in any decision making process because it gives them the opportunity to raise issues and suggestions that can benefit them. Minimum autonomy (Hall & Savery, 1986) and less involvement in making decisions that impact their work can significantly add to teachers' stress (Dewe, 1986).

INTERPERSONAL RELATIONSHIPS

Finally, Mokhtar (1998) suggested that work stress can result from interpersonal relationships. Janice (2000) found that junior colleges with a healthy social environment tend to have teachers who are less tense and uptight and report higher job satisfaction levels, suggesting that social environment plays an important part in teachers' well-being. A healthy social environment, which fosters good relations among colleagues, contributed positively to schools' performance in terms of students' grade point average. Some plausible explanations for this outcome are that teachers are not stressed and are most effective operating in an environment that is supportive, harmonious, has low conflict, has a sense of perceived helpfulness, and is conducive to relationship-building (Janice, 2000). Kelly (1988) conducted research among pre-school teachers in Queensland, Australia and found that poor interpersonal relationships and lack of communication are among the factors that caused work stress among teachers. Cooper and Kelly (1993) in their research of 2,368 respondents in England (including headmasters, officers, and directors from several education institutions) also found that interpersonal relationships influenced work stress among teachers.

Due to the seriousness and extent of stress-related problems, a concerted effort should be made to provide help for teachers. Thus, the primary interest of the present research was to determine teachers' level of work stress and the factors that could influence stress on the job.

Objectives of the Current Study

The main purpose of this study was to determine the overall level of work stress among secondary school teachers in the State of Malacca, Malaysia, and across the sub-dimensions of students' misbehavior, workload, time and resource demands, professional recognition, and interpersonal relationships. The study also investigated differences in work stress levels, and relationships between levels of work stress and the following demographic variables: age, gender, marital status, working experience, subject taught, monthly income, academic preparation, and school grade.

METHODS

Participants

This was a descriptive study involving 1,209 (30.53% of 3,960) teachers in Malacca, a state located in the central part of Peninsular Malaysia (or West Malaysia) consisting of three (3) major districts, Alor Gajah, Jasin, and Melaka Tengah. The state has a total of 64 secondary schools with 4,156 teachers (3,960 teachers, 196 administration teachers) (State of Malacca Education Department, 2002). The sample consists of all responding teachers within a random sample of schools. With the directive from the state education department and the cooperation and support from school principals and teachers, the study sampled 14 secondary schools in the districts of Alor Gajah ($n = 5$ schools, with 445 teachers),

Melaka Tengah ($n = 5$ schools, with 403 teachers), and Jasin ($n = 4$ schools, with 361 teachers).

The respondents' mean age was 38 years, the majority (60.7%) of whom were female, and married (90.0%). One third (34.9%) of them have been in the teaching profession for more than 15 years. One half (52.9%) taught Arts (e.g. languages, history, and geography) and the rest (47.1%) taught Sciences (e.g. mathematics, chemistry, and biology). Two thirds (65.5%) had a monthly income below RM2,500 (1US$ = RM3.80). In terms of academic preparation, almost three fourths (73.9%) of respondents held degrees (bachelor's and/or master's). The majority (78.6%) were from Grade A secondary schools (categorized by the Ministry of Education, Malaysia, as schools with student populations of at least 1,000).

Instrumentation

A questionnaire developed by Mokhtar (1998) to assess work stress was used. This instrument was based on the published work of Boyle et al. (1995). The first section of the questionnaire requested sociodemographic information on the respondents' age, gender, marital status, teaching experience, subject taught, monthly income, academic preparation, and school grade. Information on ethnicity was not requested because a large majority of the respondents were Malays. The second part of the questionnaire comprised the final version of the stress instrument with 34 five-point, Likert-type items (1 = *very low stress*; 2 = *low stress*; 3 = *Moderate stress*; 4 = *high stress*; 5 = *very high stress*) distributed across five subdimensions of work stress: students' misbehavior (8 items), workload (7 items), time and resource difficulties (7 items), professional recognition (3 items), and interpersonal relationships (9 items).

The questionnaire was pilot-tested on January 8, 2003 among 40 secondary school teachers from *Sekolah Menengah Kebangsaan Naning* (Naning National Secondary School), Alor Gajah, Malacca to determine further its reliability. Originally in English, the work stress questionnaire was translated into Bahasa Malaysia, the local language, to facilitate better understanding and ease in responding during the trial and final administration phases. Care, though, was taken so that the meaning of the original items was maintained. Experts on psychometrics and language translation were consulted prior to the trial and final administration of the questionnaire. Results of the pilot testing for the current study showed that the work stress questionnaire used has an overall Cronbach alpha of 0.957, which is relatively high. Across subdimensions, Cronbach alpha coefficients were: Students' misbehavior 0.918; workload 0.863;

time and resource difficulties 0.852; professional recognition 0.724; and, interpersonal relationships 0.846.

Since the objective of the study was to determine the level (as in "high" or "low") of teachers' work stress, the researchers summed up the respondents' ratings in the final version of the questionnaire with 34 items. The scores were assigned a high or a low work stress for qualitative descriptions and ease in interpretation for the purpose of this paper. The higher the sum, the higher is the work stress level.

Procedures

In compliance with university regulations and to facilitate cooperation and support from the target schools and respondents, an approval letter was first obtained from the Executive Development Center (formerly Graduate School) of Universiti Utara Malaysia prior to data collection. The letter of approval to conduct research in the schools had to be obtained from the Educational Planning and Research Division, Ministry of Education Malaysia. After initial approval was sought, the researchers wrote a letter to the Director of Malacca Education Department to obtain the approval needed to conduct the study in the randomly sampled secondary schools. After approval, the researchers personally approached the principals of the sample schools and explained the purpose of the survey and the importance of the teachers' participation and feedback as well as the confidentiality of the research data. A set of questionnaires was given to each principal, whose help was sought in distributing them to the respondents.

The visits to the sampled secondary schools were done on January 13, 14 and 15, 2003. The respondents were given approximately a week to complete the questionnaires. The researchers personally collected the questionnaires from the principals on January 20, 21, and 22, 2003.

Statistical Analyses

To determine whether there were statistically significant mean differences between overall work stress level and its sub-dimensions based on gender, marital status, subject taught, and school grade, t-test analyses were used, while one-way ANOVA was used to determine whether there were statistically significant differences between overall work stress level and its subdimensions and age, teaching experience, monthly income, and academic preparation.

RESULTS

Work Stress Levels

In terms of overall work stress level, the study found that almost one-half (539 or 44.6%) of the respondents experienced "moderate" levels of work stress. About one fourth (284 or 23.5%) of the respondents demonstrated "low to very low" levels of stress, while nearly one third (386 or 31.9%) of them showed "high to very high" levels of work stress.

Examination of the subscales revealed that 702 (57.2%) of the respondents had high stress levels with respect to students' misbehavior. The respondents' stress levels were moderate in terms of workload (416 or 34.4%), time and resource demands (509 or 42.1%), professional recognition (441 or 36.5%), and interpersonal relationships (460 or 38%). However, a sizeable proportion (19 to 27%) of the respondents also expressed "high" stress levels in workload, time and resource demands, professional recognition, or interpersonal relationships. See Table 9.1 for a summary of the data.

Differences in Overall Work Stress Levels

For tests of differences, the sums (that were used to assess levels of work stress) were converted into mean scores. ANOVA was used to compare the subscale mean scores to each other, which facilitated the direct determina-

Table 9.1. Frequency and Percentage Distribution of Respondents According to Overall Work Stress Level and Its Subscales

Level of Work Stress	Overall Work Stress	Students' Misbehavior	Workload	Time and Resource Difficulties	Professional Recognition	Interpersonal Relationships
Very low	50 (4.1%)	29 (2.4%)	83 (6.9%)	48 (4.0%)	114 (9.4%)	119 (9.8%)
Low	234 (19.4%)	129 (10.7%)	322 (26.6%)	292 (24.2%)	297 (24.6%)	347 (28.7%)
Moderate	539 (44.6%)	360 (29.8%)	416 (34.4%)	509 (42.1%)	441 (36.5%)	460 (38.0%)
High	341 (28.2%)	465 (38.5%)	321 (26.6%)	322 (26.6%)	228 (18.9%)	238 (19.7%)
Very high	45 (3.7%)	226 (18.7%)	67 (5.5%)	38 (3.1%)	129 (10.7%)	45 (3.7%)
Whole group	Moderate stress	High stress	Moderate stress	Moderate stress	Moderate stress	Moderate stress

tion of which areas were most stressful for the respondents. Results revealed that statistically significant differences existed in the overall work stress level among the respondents grouped according to age ($F = 5.249$, $p = 0.005$). The research rejected the null hypothesis that there are no statistically significant differences in the overall work stress level of the respondents when grouped by age. To identify where the significant differences lay, the posthoc Scheffe test was employed. The Scheffe analysis revealed that in terms of overall work stress level, the statistically significant differences were found between the age group of 30 years old and below and those 31 and 40 years old ($p = 0.005$). The study suggests that those respondents between 31 and 40 years old experienced more stress compared to those 30 years old and younger.

In terms of teaching experience, ANOVA results showed that statistically significant differences existed in the overall work stress level among the respondents grouped according to teaching experience ($F = 5.639$, $p = 0.004$). The research rejected the null hypothesis that there are no statistically significant differences in the overall work stress level of the respondents when grouped by teaching experience. The Scheffe test indicates that a statistically significant difference is found between those respondents who had teaching experience of 15 years and below and those who had teaching experience between 16 and 25 years ($p = 0.036$). In other words, respondents who had teaching experience of 15 years and below experienced higher stress compared to those who had teaching experience between 16 and 25 years.

With regard to monthly income, the findings showed that there were statistically significant differences in the overall work stress level among the respondents grouped according to monthly income ($F = 2.710$, $p = 0.044$). The research rejected the null hypothesis that there are no statistically significant differences in the overall work stress level of the respondents when grouped by monthly income. The Scheffe test indicates that the statistically significant difference lies between those respondents who earned monthly salary between RM2,001 and RM2,500 (1US\$ = RM3.80) and those whose salary was more than RM3,001. Respondents who earned monthly salary between RM2,001 and RM2,500 tend to experience higher stress compared to those who earned a monthly salary more than RM3,001.

In terms of academic preparation, results showed that there were statistically significant differences in the overall work stress level among the respondents grouped according to academic preparation ($F = 9.099$, $p = 0.001$). The study rejected the null hypothesis that there are no statistically significant differences in the overall work stress level of the respondents when grouped by academic preparation. After employing the Scheffe test, a statistically significant difference was found between those who were nondegree holders and bachelor's degree holders ($p = 0.005$). The results showed that the non-degree holders experienced statistically significantly less stress compared to the bachelor's degree holders. Another statistically significant difference was found between the nondegree holders and master's degree holders ($p = 0.004$). The study showed that respondents with no degrees were substantially less stressed compared to those who were master's degrees holders. Moreover, there was a statistically significant difference between respondents who were bachelor's degree holders and master's degree holders ($p = 0.039$), with the bachelor's degree holders experiencing higher stress compared to those who were master's degree holders.

Results of the t-test analyses also disclosed that statistically significant differences existed in overall work stress level among the respondents grouped according to subject taught (t-value = 8.979; $p = 0.003$). The study rejected the null hypothesis that there are no statistically significant differences in the overall work stress level of the respondents when grouped by subject taught. The findings indicate that the level of overall work stress was statistically significantly different among those respondents teaching the arts (e.g., languages, history) and those teaching science (e.g., mathematics, chemistry). The result suggests that respondents teaching arts tend to be more stressed than those teaching science.

Finally, it was found that there were no statistically significant differences in the work stress of respondents when grouped by gender ($t = 0.791; p = 0.374$), marital status ($t = 0.022; p = 0.882$), and school grade ($t = 0.950; p = 0.330$).

DISCUSSION

The secondary school teachers in this study reported moderate stress levels with respect to workload, time and resource demands, professional recognition, and interpersonal relationships. This finding concurs with Siti's (1991) research, whose earlier results showed that most Malaysian secondary school teachers experienced a moderate stress levels. In contrast to the finding of Trendall's (1989) that 74% of secondary school teachers in the United States experienced very high stress levels, the present study may be not be as alarming. Our findings do, however, reaffirm Liebermann and Miller's (1984) conclusion that teaching is a stress-prone occupation. Results also supported the literature reviewed (Barbara & Lisa, 2000; Cooper & Kelly, 1993; Dewe, 1986; Dobson, 1982; Dubrin, 1994; Manthei & Gilmore, 1996; Merret & Wheldall, 1993; Mokhtar, 1998; Trendall, 1989), citing workload, time and resource difficulties, professional recognition, and interpersonal relationships as work stressors.

Students' misbehavior, such as bullying in the classroom, was perceived to be a source work stress among teachers. This finding lends support to Tuettemann and Punch's (1992) suggestion that when students misbehave in the classroom, it produces demanding and stressful conditions. Students who misbehave (e.g., they make unreasonable noise) will require more effort from teachers to exert control in the classroom, which may lead to physical exhaustion and related health problems, like hypertension, for the teacher.

Work stress was also found to differ according to the teachers' age. Study participants whose age was less than 30 years old reported significantly lower stress than those aged between 31 and 40 years old. The finding contradicts conclusions drawn by Kyriacou and Sutcliffe (1978), Mohd (1995), and Siti (1991), who found that younger teachers reported higher stress levels. Younger teachers in this study may be physically more agile than their older colleagues and thus are more tolerant of physical strain associated with teaching-related work demands, such as field work or long hours of attending to paperwork and off-classroom activities.

Work stress was also found in this study to statistically vary significantly with respect to teaching experience. This study found that that respondents who had 15 years and less teaching experience had higher stress compared to those respondents with 16 or more years of teaching experience. This suggests that the longer the teachers' length of service in teaching, the lower is their level of work stress. Teachers who have stayed longer in teaching may have better stress-coping mechanisms than the younger ones. Payne and Furnham (1987) in their research on the dimension of teacher's work stress in one of the secondary schools in West Indies, Barbados, also found significant differences in the level of work stress to teachers' working experience. They found that teachers with less teaching experience tended to have higher stress compared to the experienced teachers. The finding that arts teachers demonstrated more stress compared to science teachers seems to be unexpected. This is because teachers in the sciences seem to have more challenging roles and responsibilities, such as guiding students on experiments and field work, exploring scientific problems, and relating theories with real-life situations. Some studies (Chei, 1996; Mokhtar, 1998) do indicate that there are statistically significant differences between stress level and subject taught, but they are not specific about which subjects impact teachers' work stress level.

In terms of monthly income, results suggest that the lower income respondents have higher levels of stress compared to those respondents who had higher income. This might imply that if workers are motivated by money (e.g., salary and other financial incentives), teachers who earned more may be more satisfied with their job, have better dispositions in life, and thus may be able to minimize, or cope effectively with work stress.

Nondegree holders reported lower stress levels than bachelor's degree holders. The study also indicated that teachers having master's degrees had higher stress level compared to the nondegree holders. These findings imply that academic preparation has a strong influence on the level of work stress. Teachers who have higher qualifications may have more responsibilities and tasks in their job. Demanding responsibilities can drive people to high uncertainty in their job, which in turn can influence their mood, and thus increase stress in the workplace. It should be noted that these study findings contradict Payne and Furnham's (1987) study, which found that teachers with predegrees (nondegree holders) have higher level of stress compared to those with degrees (bachelor's and master's degrees). According to Siti (1991), teachers with "lower" qualification (like *Sijil Pelajaran Malaysia* or Malaysian Certificate of Education) and those who received training from teacher training institutions are bound to have more stress compared to those with other higher qualifications. Abdul (1996) found that there are no statistically significant differences between the teachers' work stress and academic preparation, while Mohd (1995) disclosed that there were no statistically significant differences in the level of stress between graduate teachers and non-graduate teachers.

The statistically significant and positive relationships between age and overall work stress level implies that respondents tend to experience more stress when they become older. It may suggest that as teachers become older, their responsibilities increase due to their expertise and experience in teaching-related routines. As a result, they face more demands from peers, superiors, and community, and this may influence the rising of their level of stress.

Implications and Recommendations

The evidence from the study with regard to the relatively substantial number of teachers in Malacca having high to very high ($n = 386$ or 31.9%) levels of work stress requires considerable attention, and needs sustained commitment among school administrators and policymakers in terms of continuous programs and activities as well as administrative support and services that attempt to reduce work-related stress in the teaching-learning context. Although it is not possible to comment confidently on whether stress among teachers has been increasing over the years, it is important that educational managers and key decision makers be aware of the adverse and prolonged effects of work stress on job performance, absenteeism, job satisfaction, attrition, and employee's health (Cooper & Payne, 1988). This situation is further aggravated by the fact that most of the factors rated as most stressful by study participants were concerned with responsibility for "people" (in this case, the students' misbehavior).

School principals may wish to increase noncontact time and reduce after-hours work, provide more needs-based recreational facilities, and improve the social environment. Teachers who operate in an environment that is supportive, harmonious, has low conflict, has sense of perceived helpfulness, and is conducive to relationship building, may exhibit higher levels of performance. The teachers involved in the study also need some kind of training, mentoring, or coaching related to developing skills in reducing stress in schools. Mentoring activities may be implemented by selecting experienced senior teachers to help develop a plan of action for less experienced teachers. Peer collaboration approaches in work might also help ease conditions that contribute to stress.

The authors of this study also recommend that goverment officials and administrators periodically review policies on student discipline and school conduct, especially those that relate to the management of students' misbehavior in schools. Since the findings of this study revealed that misbehavior of students is a major source for teachers' stress, it may also be appropriate for relevant authorities to organize regular sessions and workshops on behavior modification or classroom psychology so that teachers can become more knowledgeable and skillful in dealing with misbehavior in the classroom and on school premises. In addition, workload distribution needs to be examined to ensure equitable allocation among across school teachers.

Future Research and Limitations of the Study

Future research should consider other stress-related factors, such as community involvement in schoolwork, stress-coping behaviors, and school leadership. Comparing Malaysian and non-Malaysian teachers' stress levels and coping behaviors would also be an interesting future agendum.

The researchers acknowledge limitations of the use of work stress questionnaire, and thus strongly recommend further reliability and validity analyses. Since the measure of teacher stress was arbitrary, it is impossible to infer causality. Addressing this in future research undertakings is suggested.

REFERENCES

Abdul, W. N. (1996). *Stress pekerjaan di kalangan guru* [Work stress among teachers]. Unpublished master's thesis, Universiti Utara Malaysia, Sintok, Kedah, Malaysia.

Barbara, T. B., & Lisa, O. (2000). *Hard truths: Uncovering the deep structure of schooling.* New York: Teachers' College.

Borg, M. G., & Falzon, J. M. (1989). Stress and job satisfaction among primary school teachers in Malta. *Educational Research, 41*(4), 271–276.

Borg, M. G., & Riding, R. J. (1993). Teacher stress and cognitive style. *British Journal of Educational Psychology, 63*(20), 271–286.

Boyle, G. J., Borg, M. G., Falzon, J. M., & Baglioni, A. J., Jr. (1995). A structural model of the dimensions of teacher stress. *British Journal of Educational Psychology, 63*(12), 271–286.

Chei, C. L. (1996). *Tekanan kerja di kalangan guru-guru di sebuah sekolah menengah kerajaan dan sebuah sekolah menengah swasta* [Teacher's work stress in public and private secondary schools]. Unpublished master's thesis, Universiti Putra Malaysia, Serdang, Selangor, Malaysia.

Cooper, C. L., & Kelly, M. (1993). Occupational stress in head teachers: A national UK study. *British Journal of Educational Psychology, 63*(5), 130-143.

Cooper, C. L., & Payne, R. (1988). *Causes, coping, and consequences of stress at work.* Chichester, England: Wiley.

Cox, T. (1978). Stress. In Borg, M. G. (1990). Occupational stress in British educational setting: A review. *Education Psychology, 10*(2), 103–126.

Dewe, P. J. (1986). An investigation into the causes and consequences of teacher stress. *New Zealand Journal of Educational Studies, 21*(2), 145-157.

Dobson, C. B. (1982). *Stress: The hidden adversary.* London: MTF Press.

Dubrin, A. J. (1994). *Applying psychology: Individual and organizational effectiveness* (4th ed.). Upper Saddle River, NJ: Prentice Hall.

Firestone, W. A., Bader, B. D., Massel, D., & Rosenblum, S. (1992). Recent trends in state educational reform: Assessing the prospect. *Teachers' College Record, 94,* 254–277.

Freudenberger, H. J. (1974). Staff burnout. *Journal of Social Issues, 30*(5), 159–165.

Hall, K. H., & Savery, L. K. (1986, Jan.–Feb.). Tight reign, more stress. *Harvard Business Review,* 160- 164.

Hargreaves, A. (1994). *Changing teachers, changing times: Teachers' work and culture in the postmodern age.* London: Cassell.

Janice, T. S. H. (2000). Managing organizational health and performance in junior colleges. *International Journal of Educational Management, 14*(2), 62-73.

Kelly, M. J. (1988). *The Manchester survey of occupational stress among head teachers and principals in the United Kingdom.* Manchester, England: Manchester Polytechnic.

Kyriacou, C., & Sutcliffe, J. (1978). A model of teacher stress. *Educational Studies, 4*(1), 1–6.

Lieberman, A., & Miller, L. (1984). *Teachers: Their world and their work.* VA: Association for Supervision & Curriculum Development.

Manthei, R., & Gilmore, A. (1996). Teacher stress in intermediate schools. *Educational Research, 38*, 3-19.

Margaret, D. L., & Anthony G. D. (1991). *Giving up on school: Student dropouts and teacher burnouts.* Thousand Oaks, CA: Corwin.

Merret, F., & Wheldall, K. (1993). How do teachers learn to manage classroom behavior: A study of teachers' opinions about their initial training with special reference to classroom behavior management. *Educational Studies, 19*(1), 91-106.

Ministry of Education, Malaysia. (2003). *Educational statistics.* Retrieved March 28, 2004 from http://www.moe.gov.my/statistik/frinstat/htm

Mohd, H. Z. (1995). *Faktor ciri-ciri kerja yang mempengaruhi stres guru: Kajian di kalangan kakitangan sumber Kemahiran Hidup sekolah menengah negeri Johor* [Work-related factors influence teachers' stress: A study among staff of vocational schools in Johor]. Unpublished master's thesis, Universiti Teknologi Malaysia, Skudai, Johor, Malaysia.

Mokhtar, A. (1998). *Tekanan kerja di kalangan guru sekolah menengah: Satu kajian di Daerah Kulim Bandar Baharu* [Work stress among secondary school teachers: A tudy at Kulim Bandar Baharu]. Unpublished Master's Thesis, Universiti Malaysia Sarawak, Kuching, Sarawak.

Pallas, A. M., Natriello, G., & McDill, E. L. (1995). Changing students, changing needs. *94th Yearbook of the National Society for the Study of Education (Part II).* IL: University of Chicago Press.

Payne, M. A., & Furnham, A. (1987). Dimensions of occupational stress in West Indian secondary school teachers. *British Journal of Educational Psychology, 57*(2), 141-150.

Siti, M. S. (1991). *Pengaruh faktor sekolah ke atas tekanan guru* [Factors affecting school treachers' stress]. Unpublished master's thesis, University of Malaya, Kuala Lumpur, Malaysia.

Smylie, M. A. (1999). *Teacher stress in a time of reform and understanding and preventing teacher burnout.* United Kingdom: Cambridge University Press.

State of Malacca Education Department. (2002). *Statistics report.* Malacca: Department of Education, Malaysia.

Tan, H. C. (1996). *Tekanan kerja di kalangan guru sekolah rendah jenis kebangsaan cina dalam Daerah Gombak* [Teachers' work stress in a national primary Chinese school in Gombak District]. Unpublished master's thesis, University of Malaya, Kuala Lumpur, Malaysia.

Trendall, C. (1989). Stress in teaching and teacher effectiveness: A study of teachers across mainstream and special education. *Educational Research, 31*(1), 52-58.

Tuettemann, E., & Punch, K. F. (1992). Psychological distress in secondary teachers: Research findings and their implications. *Journal of Educational Administration, 30*(1), 42-52.

Yoe, A. (1985). *Living with stress.* Singapore: Times Books International.

CHAPTER 10

RELATIONSHIP OF TEACHERS' PREVENTIVE COPING RESOURCES TO BURNOUT SYMPTOMS

Christopher McCarthy, Debra Kissen, Lauren Yadley, Teri Wood, and Richard G. Lambert

Many teachers find the demands of being a professional educator in today's schools difficult and at times stressful. Current models of stress assume that when a potentially threatening event is encountered, a reflexive, cognitive balancing act ensues, weighing the perceived demands of the event against one's perceived ability to deal with them. Accordingly, teacher stress may be seen as the perception of an imbalance between demands at school and the resources teachers have for coping with them. The purpose of this study was to examine the relationship between preventive coping resources and burnout in elementary and preschool teachers. Results indicated that preventive coping resources are related to symptoms of burnout in teachers, and implications for burnout prevention are discussed.

Teaching can be considered a profession with a high risk for burnout. This is reflected in the fact that teachers are the largest homogenous occupational group investigated in burnout research, and comprise 22% of all samples used in burnout research (Schaufeli & Enzmann, 1998). Early studies indicated that teachers at risk for burnout came to see their work as futile and inconsistent with the ideals or goals they had set as beginning teachers (Bullough & Baughman, 1997), while other early studies cited role conflict and role ambiguity as significantly related to burnout (Dworkin, 1986). Such results are not surprising, given that teachers must negotiate many demands every work day. These include facing a classroom full of students and negotiating potentially stressful interactions with parents, administrators, counselors, and other teachers. At the same time, teachers must also contend with relatively low pay, shrinking school budgets, and recently enacted standards of accountability, such as the No Child Left Behind legislation.

Although it is clear that teachers are at risk for burnout, what is less clear is how to best help them prevent burnout in order to remain happy and productive workers. Although research into job burnout has been underway for the past 30 years (Zellars, Hochwarter, & Perrewé, 2004), job burnout studies have predominantly focused on workplace conditions (e.g., poor communication, lack of job roles specification, layoffs) as the cause of burnout. Despite ongoing recognition of the need to explore individual differences that serve as antecedents to burnout, research in this area is limited. Zellars and colleagues (2004) noted in their review of the burnout literature that the role of personality differences has been largely ignored in favor of exploration into the systemic issues that occur at an organizational level. The question still remains as to why some teachers flourish and prosper in similar work settings while others will experience stress, exhaustion, and burnout. Further exploration into the impact of individual differences in reported burnout seems warranted, particularly with regard to the relationship between stress and burnout (Cocco, Gotti, de Mendonca, & Carles, 2003).

Efforts at primary prevention of burnout, in which teachers are given greater control over their environment and more resources for coping with the demands of being an educator, seem preferable over secondary or tertiary interventions that occur after burnout symptoms have surfaced (Wood & McCarthy, 2002). Therefore, the purpose of this chapter is to examine the relationship between preventive coping resources and burnout symptoms among preschool and elementary school teachers. In order to provide a context for this study, the phenomena of burnout will be explored, including its applicability to various work settings and with persons from different backgrounds. The potential benefits of developing and using preventive coping resources are then reviewed before introducing the current study.

The Process and Assessment of Burnout

Early research into symptoms of stress in the workplace described burnout as a loss of idealism and enthusiasm for work (Matheny, Gfroerer, & Harris, 2000). However, Freudenberger (1974), a psychiatrist who noticed that his once idealistic and motivated clinical staff suffered from a gradual loss of energy, motivation, and commitment, is largely credited with first using the term burnout. Maslach and Jackson refined the meaning and measurement of the burnout construct in the 1980s (Maslach & Jackson, 1981; Maslach & Schaufeli, 1993) to include three subdomains: depersonalization, in which one distances oneself from others and views others impersonally; reduced personal accomplishment, in which one devalues one's work with others; and emotional exhaustion, in which one feels emptied of personal emotional resources and becomes highly vulnerable to stressors.

The Maslach Burnout Inventory (MBI) (Maslach & Jackson, 1986; Maslach, Jackson, & Leiter, 1996) is the most well-established measure of burnout and has been used in over 90% of empirical research to measure burnout (Hastings, Horne, & Mitchell, 2004; Schaufeli & Enzmann, 1998). The MBI is the burnout scale with the strongest psychometric properties and is the only measure that assesses all three of the core dimensions of burnout (Maslach, Schaufeli, & Leiter, 2001).

Emotional exhaustion (EE) is the central quality of and the most obvious manifestation of the complex syndrome of burnout (Maslach et al., 2001). It follows that EE is the most widely reported and thoroughly analyzed of the three dimensions of the MBI. High scorers on EE report feelings of being exhausted and overextended by contact with other people at work. They report a loss of positive attitudes toward others, a lack of personal emotional resources, and a sense of becoming highly vulnerable to stressors. Maslach and colleagues (2001) noted that EE is a necessary but insufficient criterion for burnout. Although this component reflects the stress dimension of burnout, it fails to capture the critical aspects of the relationship people have with their work. The EE dimension has even been suggested as a coping mechanism in that it prompts actions to distance oneself emotionally and cognitively from her or his work (Maslach et al., 2001).

In effect, emotional exhaustion is a way to cope with work overload, leading to depersonalization (DP). Emotional exhaustion is therefore thought to lead sequentially to the feelings of cynicism associated with DP, and this link has been well established by empirical research (Maslach et al., 2001).

Depersonalization is an attempt to put distance between oneself and service recipients by treating them impersonally, actively ignoring the qualities that make them unique. DP involves development of negative, unfeeling, callous, and cynical attitudes towards clients. In particular, depersonalization may be expressed through poor attitudes toward students and the work environment. In general, people use cognitive distancing by developing an indifferent or cynical attitude when they are exhausted and discouraged (Maslach et al., 2001). If applied to burnout and the DP dimension of the MBI as a coping strategy, work demands become more manageable when they are considered impersonal objects of one's work. As mentioned previously, distancing is such an immediate reaction to exhaustion that a strong directional relationship from EE to DP is consistently found in empirical research, across a wide range of organizational and occupational settings (Maslach et al., 2001).

The third construct assessed by the MBI involves a lack of personal accomplishment (PA), which entails a more complex relationship with the other two dimensions. When experiencing burnout, one's feeling of personal accomplishment is reduced and work with others is devalued. The lack of PA includes a decline in feelings of competence and personal achievement in one's work. Whereas EE and DP emerge from the presence of work overload and social conflict, the sense of diminished efficacy involved in lack of PA seems to arise more clearly from insufficient relevant resources (Maslach et al, 2001). In contrast to the sequential development of DP from EE, the current data supports the simultaneous development of lack of PA with the other dimensions.

Burnout in Educators and Other Professions

Teacher burnout. The risk of teachers developing a burnout symptom, such as depersonalization, looms large because much of their daily work life typically includes large doses of professional isolation. Teachers spend a great deal of time with students, of course, but in many cases these interactions can add to their daily stress levels. Even the physical layout of most campuses, with teachers working alone in their classrooms, and scheduling constraints that make finding time to meet with peers or administrators to discuss stressful events virtually impossible, can cause teachers to feel disconnected (Bennett & LeCompte, 1990). Thus, developing a symptom of burnout, such as depersonalization, could be seen as a type of protective mechanism that allows the teacher to remain in the field, even in a diminished capacity (Farber, 1998). Unfortunately, the use of such a mechanism over time could exacerbate isolation and put the teacher at greater risk for increased symptoms of burnout.

Interestingly, LeCompte and Dworkin (1991) viewed burnout as an extreme type of role-specific alienation with a focus on feelings of meaninglessness, especially as it applies to one's ability to successfully reach students; a result also noted by Farber (1998). A finding of a negative correlation between sense of significance found in teaching and burnout supports the relevance of an existential perspective to the case of teacher burnout (Pines, 2002). Pines (2004) suggested that when teachers no longer find significance in their work because they cannot teach, educate, influence, and inspire their students, they burn out. Similarly, LeCompte and Dworkin (1991) suggested that powerlessness in defining professional roles or negotiating agreements about one's teaching is integral to creating performance demand levels that can lead to burnout. The sense of both physical and mental exhaustion aggravated by inconsistent expectations for teachers that are constantly in flux or in conflict with previously held beliefs, has been cited by numerous researchers as influencing teacher burnout (Brown & Ralph, 1998; Bullough & Baughmann, 1997; Esteve, 2000; Hinton & Rotheiler, 1998; Troman & Woods, 2001).

That many teachers involuntarily remain in their jobs is problematic because changes in attitudes and effort, as well as a decline in performance, can be expected (Hughes, 2001; Burke & Greenglass, 1989, 1996). Hughes (2001) noted that such negative shifts cannot be ignored because they have the potential to affect both the teacher and the educational system. As a consequence, it is important to identify precursors to burnout in order to prevent such negative outcomes as reduced responsibility, emotional detachment, work alienation, and reduced work goals (Hughes, 2001). Hughes suggested that only through an aggressive intervention in the burnout process would it be possible to prevent the potential negative impact of burnout on both the teacher and the educational process.

Several studies have suggested that across industries, there is an inverse relationship between the emotional exhaustion and depersonalization dimensions of burnout and years performing a specific role, as well as years employed by the same institution (Mueller, 1997; Stanton-Rich & Iso-Ahola, 1998). Although it may be inferred from these findings that those who are able to withstand the test of time within a profession are less likely to experience burnout, other studies have suggested contradictory patterns. For example, a recent study of Turkish teachers found that more experienced subjects exhibited higher emotional exhaustion and depersonalization than their less experienced colleagues (Sari, 2004). However, Sari (2004) also found that more experienced teachers expressed feelings of higher personal accomplishment than their less experienced colleagues.

The Relationship Between Coping and Burnout

Burnout can be viewed as a prolonged response to chronic job stress (Pines & Maslach, 1978). Although much of the earlier research on burnout focused on the nature of the workplace, a number of personality factors associated with coping and stress, including low levels of hardiness, poor self-esteem, external locus of control, and an avoidant coping style, have been associated with a vulnerability to burnout (Maslach et al., 2001). Interestingly, Maslach and Leiter (1997) noted increasing interest in viewing burnout in terms of job-person fit. While the notion that career satisfaction results from a successful match of person and environment is integral to the career development literature, Maslach and Leiter (1997) note that such models often focus mainly on initial factors which predict initial job choice and satisfaction, rather than the more complex array of personality and work environments that predict burnout after the individual has worked in that setting for some time. In other words, it is one thing for an individual to select the teaching profession because of an interest in educating young people, but a healthy and successful career as an educator depends on a complicated interaction between a range of personality and workplace factors.

The dominant models of stress and coping, often referred to as transactional models, also emphasize the interaction of both person and environment in determining whether or not stress is experienced (for a review, see Lazarus & Folkman, 1984). Specially, subjective evaluations of both external demands and perceived coping resources influence whether demands become stressful. Individuals are seen as vulnerable to the physiological, emotional, and behavioral consequences of stress only when it is perceived that the demands of a situation, for example in the workplace, exceed one's resources for coping. Consequently, possession of sufficient levels of psychological coping resources is the key to avoiding many of the harmful effects of stress, including burnout symptoms (McCarthy, Lambert, & Brack, 1997).

George Albee, one of the pioneers of prevention research, noted that "it is accepted public health doctrine that no disease or disorder has ever been treated out of existence" (Albee, 2000, p. 847). Following Albee's suggestion, it is far better if the roots of teacher burnout are identified and eliminated before the syndrome develops, than to attempt to ameliorate it after it has already developed. However, far more research has been devoted to understanding and offsetting the harmful effects of stress than has been given to its prevention (Aspinwall & Taylor, 1997).

The notion that certain psychological coping resources could be useful for prevention is based on a taxonomy first suggested by Matheny,

Aycock, Pugh, Curlette, and Canella (1986) that differentiates specific psychological coping resources according to their usefulness for either combating or preventing stress. This taxonomy suggests that combative coping resources are drawn upon after a threatening event or circumstance has triggered the stress response. Such resources include the skills and abilities that are associated with traditional stress management practices, such as having the ability to self-disclose, lowering emotional arousal through relaxation procedures, and using problem-solving skills.

In contrast, coping resources that are preventive in nature allow the individual to recognize and deal with life demands so as to avoid the experience of stress in the first place (Matheny et al., 1986). Some support for the notion of proactive coping has already been found in the literature. For example, Dorz, Novara, Sica, and Sanavio (2003) noted specific approaches to coping that were predictive factors of the three components of burnout as defined by the MBI. On the one hand, they found that planning (e.g., to reflect and develop a strategy to get over a problem) and restraint coping strategies (e.g., to avoid acting impulsively, waiting for the right moment to cope with the stress) were predictive factors for personal accomplishment (PA). On the other hand, denying the problem or using humor to face the situation was more related to emotional exhaustion (EE) and depersonalization (DP).

Regarding social support, some kinds may be more useful and beneficial in moderating burnout than others (Schaufeli & Greenglass, 2001). For example, research findings from teachers confronted with high work stress suggest that practical support from one's coworkers and supervisors buffered teachers from DP (Greenglass, Fiksenbaum, & Burke, 1996). Greenglass and colleagues (1996). Practical support may result in teachers' perceptions of greater control over their work, resulting in a decrease in the teacher's need to depersonalize their students. These researchers also reported that informational support from a teacher's co-workers and supervisor buffered EE, suggesting that information support may help individuals structure their workload so that it more closely matches their resources.

The Present Study

The purpose of this study was to examine the relationship between preventive coping resources and burnout symptoms in elementary and preschool teachers. In addition, this study investigated whether entry level teachers in their first-year experienced greater burnout symptoms than

186 • C. McCARTHY ET AL.

veteran teachers, and whether teaching in a preschool versus elementary school setting was predictive of burnout symptoms.

METHODS

Participants

The sample was comprised of 148 teachers in a variety of classroom settings in North and South Carolina; private and public schools were represented as were urban and rural locations; 36 (24.32%) were preschool teachers and 112 (75.68%) were elementary teachers. All but 11 of the elementary teachers taught in Title I schools that serve a similar low-

Table 10.1. Demographic Composition of the Sample

Characteristic	Category	%
Gender	Male	2.56
	Female	97.44
Ethnicity	African American	13.16
	European American	78.95
	Other	7.89
Education level	High School	6.25
	Associates	9.82
	Bachelors	59.82
	Graduate	24.11
Years of experience	First year teacher	6.90
Setting	Head Start	24.32
	Title I elementary schools	68.24
	Other elementary school setting	7.43

Characteristics	Mean	SD
Age	38.40	13.35
Number of children in the classrool	19.39	4.92
Years of experience as a teacher	12.70	9.69
Years of experience in current school or program	7.33	7.77

Note: $n = 148$.

income population as is found in Head Start programs. Additional demographic information for the sample is included in Table 10.1

Instrumentation

The Maslach Burnout Inventory (MBI) (Maslach & Jackson, 1986) was used to assess burnout symptoms. Respondents were asked to indicate their level of agreement with statements about feelings related to their jobs. The MBI consists of 22 items and yields scores along three dimensions: emotional exhaustion (EE), depersonalization (DP), and professional accomplishment (PA). The EE scale measures the extent to which the teacher feels emotionally overextended and exhausted by their work; the DP subscale measures the extent to which the teacher interacts in an unfeeling and impersonal manner with their students; the PA subscale measures the extent to which the teacher feels a loss of personal effectiveness and goal attainment as opposed to feeling competent and successful in their work.

Each item comprising the MBI is rated on a 7-point frequency scale ranging from "never" (score 0) to "everyday" (score 6). There are 9 items comprising the EE scale of the MBI, which asks the respondent to rate how frequently they experience such things as fatigue, frustration, and interpersonal stress in their job. The DP scale is composed of 5 items, which ask the respondent to rate how frequently they have negative experiences with colleagues and clients. The PA scale is composed of 8 items, which ask the respondent to rate how frequently they have positive experiences in their job. For both MBI-EE and MBI-DP subscales, higher scores correspond to higher degrees of experienced burnout. For ease of interpretation in the context of the current study, scores on the MBI-PA sub-scale were reverse coded so that higher scores correspond to higher degrees of experienced burnout as well. The overall Cronbach's alpha for the MBI with this sample was .881, while values of .859, .630, and .623 were found for the EE, DP, and PA scales, respectively.

The Preventive Resources Inventory (PRI) was used to assess preventive coping resources. The PRI includes 5 scale scores and 18 subscale scores. Respondents were asked to indicate their level of agreement with statements about personal habits relating to the prevention of stress. The perceived control scale measures the belief that one can cope successfully with life demands and manage situations that could potentially become stressful (sample item, "I can handle most things"). The construct is further defined by its subscales: efficacy, a global belief in one's success when confronting potential stressors; mastery, confidence in specific preventive skill sets; and persistence, a willingness to remain engaged and flexible in applying preventive strategies to potentially stressful situations.

The maintaining perspective scale assesses attitudes and beliefs consistent with preventing stressful situations and keeping stress-produced emotions at manageable levels (sample item, "I am able to avoid causing myself stress by keeping things in perspective"). This construct can be more fully understood by recognizing the specific set of intentional cognitive strategies represented by its subscales: maintaining a flexible perspective, maintaining self-direction, cognitive restructuring of perspective, and knowing your limits.

The social resourcefulness scale measures the ability to draw upon a social network of caring others who can act as a buffer against life demands (sample item, "I have mutually supportive relationships"). The reciprocity in relationships subscale measures one's perceived ability to develop and maintain mutually beneficial social connections. The comfort in relationships, feedback from relationships, and assistance in relationships subscales tap into the respondent's self-assessment of the quality of their social support systems.

The self-acceptance scale measures the degree to which one can accept and overcome shortcomings, imperfections, and limitations in dealing with demanding life situations (sample item from the accepting limitations subscale, "I may not always get what I want"). In addition, the identity comfort subscale addresses a sense of acceptance and contentment with one's life circumstances while the balance subscale relates to an internalization of goals and values that contribute to a healthy and focused perception of one's circumstances.

The scanning scale attempts to measure one's perceived ability to recognize, anticipate, and plan for demands and potential stressors (sample item, "I am good at identifying things that will cause stress in the future"). The subscales help define the construct as follows: anticipation of demands, recognition of opportunities to prevent stress, planning ahead, and follow through.

Responses were indicated on a 5 point Likert-like scale ranging from "Strongly Disagree" to "Strongly Agree." Participants described the extent to which they agreed with specific prevention-related statements. The measure contains 82 items about personal habits relating to the prevention of stress. The scales, along with the Cronbach's alpha from previous research (McCarthy, Lambert, Beard, & Dematatis, 2002) and this sample respectively, were perceived control (.909 / .914), maintaining perspective (.870 / .882), social resourcefulness (.873 / .865), self-acceptance (.708 / .848), and the total preventive resources score (.949 / .973). The Cronbach's alpha for scanning, a newer scale not used by McCarthy et al. (2002), was .924 in this sample.

Statistical Analyses

The first step in the analysis involved examining the bivariate correlations between the scale scores of the PRI and the MBI. It was hypothesized that negative associations would be found between preventive resources and teacher burnout, suggesting that the teacher's ability to prevent stress may serve to temper their experience of burnout on the job. These correlations are reported in Table 10.2. Next, the MBI scale and total scores were used as the dependent variables in regression models and the PRI scales provided the predictors. Whether or not the teacher was a first-year teacher, and whether he/she was an early childhood or elementary school teacher, were used in the first step of the model, and in the second step of the model PRI scales were entered into the equation. This was done to first account for the amount of variance in burnout that might be related to being new to the profession or to the setting in which the teacher worked (early childhood or elementary). Again, it was hypothesized that a negative relationship would be found between the PRI scale scores and the MBI.

Each dependent variable was used in a hierarchical regression model. In the first step of each model, years of experience and school setting, preschool or elementary, were controlled for. Next, individual scale scores of the PRI were added to the models in an effort to detect whether any specific scale score was particularly related to the separate components of burnout. Since the scale scores of the PRI were found to be highly correlated to one another in this sample, testing them simultaneously might have been prone to disturbances in the models due to colliniarity issues.

Table 10.2. Correlation Between PRI Scale Scores and Burnout Scale Scores

Measure	*EE*	*DP*	*PA*	*BO*
Perceived control	-0.416	-0.282	-0.424	-0.449
Maintaining perspective	-0.456	-0.326	-0.459	-0.494
Social resourcefulness	-0.336	-0.237**	-0.399	-0.385
Self-acceptance	-0.495	-0.335	-0.442	-0.512
Scanning	-0.332	-0.152*	-0.352	-0346
Preventive resources	-0.536	-0.287	-0.447	-0.469

Note: $n = 148$ All correlation coefficients are statistically significant at $p < .001$ unless otherwise noted: + -NS, *-$p <. 05$, **-$p < .01$.

Therefore, in the interest of model parsimony and considering the relatively small size of the sample, theoretical considerations and the bivariate correlations between the PRI and each MBI scale score were used to select the best PRI predictor for each model. In an exploratory attempt to validate the selection of PRI scale score for each model, additional models were tested that included multiple PRI scale scores and in no case was variance accounted for increased by a statistically significant amount.

RESULTS

In the following discussion of results, all beta coefficients are reported as standardized values. In addition, all coefficients are statistically significant ($p < .05$) unless indicated by (NS). Results for all models are shown in Table 10.3. For the initial EE model, school level and first-year teacher status showed weak negative relationships ($B = -.209, -.161$, respectively, $r^2 = .065$) while the second step showed a moderately strong negative relationship with school level, first-year teacher status, and self acceptance as significant predictors ($B = -.209, .144, -.483$, respectively). The statistically significant r^2 change from the first model to the final model was .232 and the r^2 in the final model was .297.

For the initial DP model, school level and first-year teacher status were not statistically significant, while the second step showed a moderately strong negative relationship with self acceptance as a significant predictor ($B = -.336$). The statistically significant r^2 in the final model was .125.

For the initial PA model, school level showed a weak negative relationship ($B = -.307, r^2 = .105$) while the second step showed a moderately strong negative relationship with school level and maintaining perspective as significant predictors ($B = -.265, -.436$, respectively). The statistically significant r^2 change in the final model was .187, and the r^2 in the final model was .293.

Finally, for the initial model using the total scores on all three burnout scales, school level showed a weak negative relationship ($B = -.246, r^2 = .078$) while the second step showed a moderately strong negative relationship with school level and Self-Acceptance as significant predictors ($B = -.218, -.503$, respectively). The statistically significant r^2 change in the final model was .252, and the r^2 in the final model was .330.

DISCUSSION

The results of this study indicate that working in an elementary school as opposed to a preschool, having a lower level of self-acceptance, and being

Table 10.3. Regression Models for Predicting the Scale Scores of the MBI

Burnout Scales β	Step I					Step II			
	Preschool Teacher β	First Year Teacher β	Step I r^2	Preschool Teacher β	First Year Teacher β	Best PRI Predictor	PRI β	Step II r^2 Change	Total r^2
Emotional Exhaustion	-.209**	.161*	.065**	-.187**	-.144*	SAC	-.483***	.232***	.297***
Depersonalization	-.102	.060	.013	-.084	.047	SAC	-.336***	.112***	.125***
Professional accomplishment	-.307***	.130	.105***	-.265***	.099	MPR	-.436***	.187***	.293***
Burnout	-.246**	.150	.078**	-.218	.131	SAC	-.503***	.252***	.330***

Note: * = $p < .05$, ** = $p < .001$. SAC = Self Acceptance, MPR = Maintaining Perspective.

a first-year teacher, may place teachers at increased risk for burnout. Although these results are preliminary and the study was correlational using only self-report measures, a number of interesting avenues for interpretation are suggested.

First, the consistent finding that preschool teachers had lower levels of burnout symptoms than do elementary teacher suggests that environmental factors may be a contributor to burnout. Each of the preschool teachers in this sample was involved in Head Start, which may have equipped them with a variety of resources for dealing with classroom demands. In contrast, the elementary school teachers in the sample were much more variable in the amount of resources available. In addition, almost all of the elementary teachers in the sample face accountability testing, a demand not faced by the preschool teachers. The results of this study do lend support to the notion that the workplace environment in general and high stakes testing in particular are factors associated with teacher's vulnerability to stress.

The finding that first-year teacher status contributed only to emotional exhaustion is not surprising given the demands faced by these teachers. They must contend with all the rigors of starting a new job, as well as the fact that they are expected to develop lesson plans under the supervision of a mentor. The lack of relationship between first-year teacher status and DP and PA may be explained by the fact that such teachers have not been a part of the profession long enough to experience these symptoms.

While the self-acceptance scale emerged as the best predictor of burnout in three of the four analyses, it should be noted that a fairly consistent pattern of relationship between burnout scales and PRI scales was indicated. Given that self-acceptance measures the degree to which one can accept and overcome shortcomings, imperfections, and limitations, it is not surprising that this scale would be related to burnout symptoms. It is interesting to note that maintaining perspective, the scale which assesses attitudes and beliefs consistent with preventing stressful situations and keeping stress-produced emotions at manageable levels, was most associated with professional accomplishment. It is possible that an ability to put things in perspective is essential to maintaining a sense of efficacy and meaning in the workplace for teachers. Specifically, it may be those teachers that understand how and when they have influence over students and families are more capable of resisting the temptation to devalue their own accomplishments.

Given Greenglass and colleague's (1996) finding that support from coworkers and supervisors buffered teachers from DP and that that informational support from a teacher's coworkers and supervisor buffered EE, it is somewhat surprising that social resourcefulness (SR) did not emerge as the best predictor in any of the models. However, SR was negatively associated with the MBI, just to a weaker extent than other PRI scale scores. This may suggest the need for school administrators, in schools such as those in this sample, to facilitate more formalized opportunities for teachers to support each other, perhaps through structured mentoring programs and opportunities to attend off campus staff development opportunities as groups.

Implications of the Study

The results of this study, although preliminary, lend some support to the notion that teachers equipped with resources for preventing stress may be less susceptible to burnout.

Chris Kyriacou (2001), who draws from an Education Service Advisory Committee report (1998), offered a number of suggestions that may be useful in this regard, including: (a) consultation with teachers on matters, such as curriculum development or instructional planning, which directly impact their classrooms; (b) provision of clear job descriptions and expectations in an effort to address role ambiguity and conflict; (c) establishment and maintenance of open lines of communication between teachers and administrators to provide administrative support and performance feedback that may act as a buffer against stress; and (d) encouragement of professional development activities, such as mentoring and networking, which may engender a sense of accomplishment and a more fully developed professional identity for teachers. It also makes sense to focus on early detection of problems before they emerge as full-blown disorders. Studies by several researchers (cf., Brown & Ralph, 1998; Hinton & Rotheiler, 1998; Kyriacou, 2001; Troman & Woods, 2001), reported early symptoms of teacher stress and burnout as including: (a) feeling like not going to work or actually missing days, (b) difficulty in concentrating on tasks, (c) feeling overwhelmed by one's workload, (d) withdrawing from colleagues, and (e) having a general feeling of irritation regarding school.

Once teacher burnout has developed, a decision must be made as to whether the teacher can or is willing to continue his/her work (Wood & McCarthy, 2002). Troman and Woods (2001) acknowledged that a series of stressful events or a single major event may lead teachers to make what they term "pivotal decisions" to leave the teaching profession. Personal factors also loom large in a teacher's decision to stay in a school, with the current labor market, personal, financial and family obligations, and years in the field all being instrumental in the decision making process

Limitations of the Study

Given the relatively homogenous sample used in the study, cautions should be observed before generalizing the results. Caution is also warranted in the use of self-report methodology and in inferring causal relations from correlation-based studies. It will be important to test this model with experimental methods that allow for firmer conclusions about causality. Further research is also necessary on interventions to combat burnout, (Maslach, 2003). From the few studies that have been conducted, little can be concluded about the effects of burnout intervention. Currently, there is no definitive answer to the question of what kind of intervention is most effective in reducing burnout. Training in coping skills, such as cognitive restructuring and relaxation techniques, and facilitating social support have shown some effect. However, methodological shortcomings, such as lack of control groups, small study sample size, and high mortality as it relates to drop out at post-test stage, prevent firm conclusions about the intervention effects. Therefore, much about burnout intervention effects still needs to be explored.

REFERENCES

Albee, G. W. (2000). Commentary on prevention and counseling psychology. *The Counseling Psychologist, 28,* 845-853.

Aspinwall, L. G., & Taylor, S. E. (1997). A stitch in time: Self-regulation and proactive coping. *Psychological Bulletin, 121*(3), 417-436.

Bennett, K. P., & LeCompte, M. D. (1990). *The way schools work: A sociological analysis of education.* New York: Longman.

Brown, M., & Ralph, S. (1998). The identification of stress in teachers. In J. Dunham & V. Varma (Eds.), *Stress in teachers: Past, present and future.* (pp. 37-56) London: Whurr.

Bullough, R. V. Jr., & Baughman, K. (1997). *"First-year teacher" eight years later: An inquiry into teacher development.* New York: Teachers College Press.

Burke, R. J., & Greenglass, E. R. (1989). Psychological burnout among men and women in teaching: An examination of the Chemiss model. *Human Relations, 3,* 261-273.

Burke, R. J., & Greenglass, E. R. (1996). Work stress, social support, psychological burnout, and emotional and physical well-being among teachers. *Psychology,Health, & Medicine, 1,* 193-205.

Cocco, E., Gatti, M., de Mendonça L., & Carles, A. (2003). A comparative study of stressand burnout among staff caregivers in nursing homes and acute geriatric wards. *Journal of Geriatric Psychiatry, 18,* 78-85.

Dorz, S., Novara, C., Sica, C., & Sanavio, E. (2003). Predicting burnout among HIV/AIDS and oncology health care workers. *Psychology and Health, 8,* 677-684.

Dworkin, A. G. (1986). *Teacher burnout in the public schools: Structural causes and consequences for children.* New York: State University of New York Press.

Education Service Advisory Committee. (1998). *Managing work-related stress: A guide for managers and teachers in the schools* (2nd ed.). London: HMSO.

Esteve, J. M. (2000). The transformation of the teachers' role at the end of the twentieth century: New challenges for the future. *Educational Review, 5,* 197-207.

Farber, B. A. (1998, August). *Tailoring treatment strategies for different types of burnout.* Paper presented at the annual convention of the American Psychologic Association, San Francisco.

Freudenberger, H. J. (1974). Staff burn-out. *Journal of Social Issues, 30,* 159-165.

Greenglass, E., Fiksenbaum, L., & Burke, R. J. (1996). Components of social support, buffering effects, and burnout: Implications for psychological functioning. *Anxiety, Stress, and Coping: An International Journal, 9,* 185-197.

Hastings, R. P., Horne, S., & Mitchell, G. (2004). Burnout in direct care staff in intellectual disability services: A factor analytic study of the Maslach burnout inventory. *Journal of Intellectual Disability Research, 48,* 268-273.

Hinton, J. W., & Rotheiler, E. (1998). The psychophysiology of stress in teachers. In J. Dunham & V. Varma (Eds.), *Stress in teachers: Past, present and future* (pp. 95-119). London: Whurr.

Hughes, R. E. (2001). Deciding to leave but staying: Teacher burnout, precursors, and turnover. *International Journal of Human Resource Management, 12,* 288-298.

Kyriacou, C. (2001). Teacher stress: Directions for future research. *Educational Review, 53,* 28-35.

Lazarus, R. S., & Folkman, S. (1984). Coping and adaptation. In W. D. Gentry (Ed.), *The handbook of behavioral medicine* (pp. 282-325). New York: Guilford.

LeCompte, M. D., & Dworkin, A. G. (1991). *Giving up on school: Student dropouts and teacher burnouts.* Newbury Park, CA: Corwin Press.

Maslach, C. (2003). Job burnout: New directions in research and intervention. *Current Directions in Psychological Science, 12,* 189-192.

Maslach, C., & Jackson, S. E. (1981). The measurement of experienced burnout. *Journal of Occupational Behavior, 2,* 99-113.

Maslach, C., & Jackson, S. E. (1986). *The Maslach Burnout Inventory Manual* (2nd ed.). Palo Alto, CA: Consulting Psychologists Press.

Maslach, C., Jackson, S. E., & Leiter, M. P. (1996). *The Maslach Burnout Inventory-Manual* (3rd ed.). Palo Alto: Consulting Psychologists Press.

Maslach, C., & Leiter, M. P. (1997). *The truth about burnout.* San Francisco: Jossey-Bass.

Maslach, C., & Schaufeli, W. B. (1993). Historical and conceptual development of burnout. In C. Maslach, W. B. Schaufeli, & T. Marek (Eds.), *Professional burnout: Recent developments in theory and research* (pp. 1-16). Washington, DC: Taylor & Francis.

Maslach, C., Schaufeli, W. B., & Leiter, M. P. (2001). Job burnout. *Annual Review of Psychology, 52,* 397-422.

Matheny, K. B., Aycock, D. W., Pugh, J. L., Curlette, W. L., & Canella, K. A. (1986). Stress coping: A qualitative and quantitative synthesis with implications for treatment. *The Counseling Psychologist, 14*, 499-549.

Matheny, K. B., Gfroerer, C. A., & Harris, K. (2000). Work stress, burnout, and coping at the turn of the century: An Adlerian perspective. *Journal of Individual Psychology, 56*(1), 74-87.

McCarthy, C., Lambert, R., Beard, M., & Dematatis, A. (2002). Factor structure of the Preventive Resources Inventory and its relationship to existing measures of stress and coping. In G. S. Gates & M. Wolverton (Eds.), *Toward wellness: Prevention, coping, and stress* (pp. 3-37). Greenwich, CT: Information Age.

McCarthy, C. J., Lambert, R., & Brack, G. (1997). Structural model of coping, appraisals, and emotions after relationship breakup. *Journal of Counseling and Development, 76*(1), 53-64.

Mueller, K. (1997). The relationship between social support and burnout among social work caregivers of HIV/AIDs clients. *Dissertation Abstracts International Section A: Humanities & Social Sciences, 57*, 3683.

Pines, A. M. (2002). Teacher burnout: A psychodynamic existential perspective. *Teachers and Teaching, 8*, 121-141.

Pines, A. M. (2004). Why are Israelis less burned out? *European Psychologist, 9*, 69-77.

Pines, A. M., & Maslach, C. (1978). Characteristics of staff burnout in mental health settings. *Hospital and Community Psychiatry, 29*, 233-237.

Sari, H. (2004). An analysis of burnout and job satisfaction among Turkish special school headteachers and teachers, and the factors effecting their burnout. *Educational Studies, 30*, 291-306.

Schaufeli, W. B., & Enzmann, D. (1998). *The burnout component to study and practice.* London: Taylor & Francis.

Schaufeli, W. B., & Greenglass, E. R. (2001). Introduction to special issue on burnout and health. *Psychology and Health, 16*, 501-510.

Stanton-Rich, H., & Iso-Ahola, S. (1998). Burnout and leisure. *Journal of Applied Social Psychology, 28*, 1931-1950.

Troman, G., & Woods, P. (2001). *Primary teachers' stress.* New York: Routledge/Falmer.

Wood, T., & McCarthy, C. J. (2002). Preventing teacher burnout. *ERIC Clearinghouse on Teaching and Teacher Education*, ERIC Digest EDO-SP-2002-03.

Zellars, K., Hochwarter, W., & Perrewé, P. (2004). Experiencing job burnout: The roles of positive and negative traits and states. *Journal of Applied and Social Psychology, 34*, 887-911.

CHAPTER 11

THE RELATIONSHIP BETWEEN BURNOUT AND STRESS AMONG SPECIAL EDUCATORS

Stacey L. Edmonson

This chapter synthesizes the vast research on stress and job burnout among special educators in order to offer a more thorough understanding of the topic. Using procedures for quantitative synthesis, the inquiry followed a 14-stage design. In analyzing 19 effect sizes found in the literature, the author suggests that the burnout constructs of emotional exhaustion and depersonalization share extremely large positive relationships with stress. The burnout construct of personal accomplishment shares a large but inverse relationship with stress. The large population effect size and percentage of explained variance further indicate a need for additional review and study.

In its *23rd Annual Report to Congress on the Implementation of IDEA*, the U.S. Department of Education (2001) cited that almost 70,000 positions for special education teachers were open at some point during the 1999-2000 school year. Furthermore, there were 12,241 special education positions that went unfilled due to a lack of suitable candidates. Boe, Cook, Kaufman, and Danielson (1996) explain that the special education teacher

Understanding Teacher Stress in an Age of Accountability, 197–213
Copyright © 2006 by Information Age Publishing
All rights of reproduction in any form reserved.

shortage is a problem of both "quality and quantity" that has reached "pervasive and critical dimensions" (p. 2).

What part does stress play in the problems associated with burnout among special educators? Stress is often associated with teacher burnout, but how strong are the relationships between these constructs, and what do these relationships tell us about burnout among special educators? One means of understanding the interplay between stress and burnout is through meta-analysis of existing literature on these topics.

Meta-analysis of topics in special education has been encouraged by other researchers. Guskin (1984) stated that "meta-analysis is to be considered a powerful tool that has already begun to help us reduce the confusion of a growing and heterogeneous research literature" (p. 79). Because inquiry in special education often involves small groups or even individuals, meta-analysis is the tool of choice, because it allows one to synthesize the findings of numerous studies, no matter how small they are. Kavale (1984) also encouraged the use of meta-analysis with special education topics: "the variability in the findings of special education research creates a gap between past and future research, a gap that can be bridged by the intermediate step of synthesizing findings into a comprehensive whole" (p. 62). Indeed, this inquiry synthesizes the vast research on job burnout and stress among special educators in order to offer a more complete and thorough understanding of this important topic.

STRESS IN SPECIAL EDUCATORS

A common definition of stress refers to a condition a person experiences when the demands placed on him/her surpass the resources—personal or otherwise—that he/she has available to meet those demands (Lazarus, 1995). Thus, stress is seen as something that causes a person to experience emotional strain or tension. Recently stress has been viewed in a constructivist paradigm, more of a "transactional, process, contextual, and meaning-centered approach to stress" (Lazarus, 1995, p. 3) that "views stressors as environmental demands, confines, and challenges" (Gates & Boyter, 2002, p. 129). Regardless of the specific definition of stress, researchers agree that stress is not something to be feared or avoided; in fact, it is a natural, even beneficial, experience, provided that it is handled in an effective manner.

Although certainly there is stress in all areas of the educational realm, special education has its own unique and sometimes overwhelming set of stressors. In a field that guarantees all children with disabilities a "free and appropriate education" (U.S. Department of Education, 2001, p. 2), special education is highly regulated, even by education standards. Public Law 94-142 and the subsequent amendments to the Individuals with Disabilities Act require a great deal from special education teachers, including the development of individualized education plans (IEPs) for every student identified as having a disability. IEPs and the regular updating of these IEPs result in a great deal of paperwork for special educators. Mandatory IEP team meetings, formerly known as Admission, Review, and Dismissal (ARD) meetings, are also required for every special education student. In addition, these students must be educated in the least restrictive environment appropriate and must be offered any and all necessary related services that can be linked to an educational purpose. Due process is also a guarantee in special education, so the possibility of a hearing or legal proceeding is always present (Fuchs & Fuchs, 1995).

The tremendous amount of regulation is only a single aspect of the stressors cited by special education teachers. Large class sizes, unclear roles, and problems with student discipline are also cited as problem areas for special education teachers (Billingsley & Cross, 1992; Cooley & Yovanoff, 1996). Furthermore, special education teachers often endure social isolation from other professional members in schools. In addition, dealing with the highly unique needs of each student is a challenge; the difficulty of experiencing only limited success is also problematic in special education (Dedrick & Raschke, 1990; Wisniewski & Gargiulo, 1997).

In addition to the stressors mentioned above, Maslach and Jackson (1984) mention "heavy case loads, poor supervision, ambiguous rules, and resistant behavior" by students (p. 48). The authors organize their examples into four main sources of stress for special educators. These causes are lack of feedback, lack of clarity, lack of control, and lack of support. Lack of feedback refers specifically to insufficient positive feedback, which causes diminished feelings of personal achievement, confidence, and self-worth. Without appropriate coping strategies to combat such problems, these negative feelings often serve as a precursor to burnout.

In sum, in a field highly regulated by state and federal law, special educators face a job that in many ways isolates them from much of the rest of the school community. The students they educate face academic challenges that make success, at least by the standards at which success is currently defined and judged, a rarity. Reams of paperwork mandated by government agencies add to the already daunting task of educating students with disabilities. Special education is not an option for school districts, yet the job of a special educator is stressful, unique from that of other educators, and overburdened (Wisniewski & Gargiulo, 1997).

UNDERSTANDING AND MEASURING BURNOUT

Many scholars have attempted to define the construct of burnout. Originating a mere twenty-five years ago with Freudenberger's (1977) research in the helping professions, burnout remains a relatively new area of study in the social sciences (Banks & Necco, 1990; Stout, 1987). Freudenberger (1977) first coined the term "burnout," using it to describe persons who appear to be depressed with their jobs. Burnout can be identified through the appearance of fatigue, persistent colds, headaches, insomnia, and exhaustion; these signs are caused by over-exertion of a person's energy, strength, or resources. Behavioral indicators of burnout, such as anger, irritation, cynicism, paranoia, or drug use may also be apparent (Stout, 1987). Blase (1982) broadens this definition of burnout to include any adverse reaction that occurs from stress in the workplace. In fact, some researchers go so far as to make these two terms, job stress and burnout, synonymous (Male & May, 1997).

Most authors tend to agree that burnout refers to an extreme form of job stress (Cherniss, 1988; Dedrick & Raschke, 1990; Maslach, 1982; Wisniewski & Gargiulo, 1997). Beer and Beer (1992) state that burnout results from chronic stress in the workplace. Christina Maslach (1982), perhaps the most widely accepted authority on burnout and author of the Maslach Burnout Inventory, describes this condition as "one [specific] type of stress," or "a response to the chronic emotional strain of dealing extensively with other human beings, particularly when they are troubled or having problems" (p. 3).

Because Maslach's theoretical model of burnout is by far the most accepted explanation of its kind, the three constructs found in this model are also the most widely used burnout constructs. These constructs include emotional exhaustion, depersonalization, and reduced personal accomplishment. The three subscales of the Maslach Burnout Inventory are quite distinct. Emotional exhaustion refers to cases of burnout in which a person feels emotionally (or psychologically) tired or worn out, with little or no energy. Depersonalization describes a condition in which a person feels insignificant or meaningless. His or her reactions to other persons are less caring and more harsh than before. Reduced personal accomplishment is used to explain a person's feelings of inadequacy, futility, or dissatisfaction in the workplace (Crane & Iwanicki, 1986; Gmelch & Gates, 1998). All three subscales are measured according to frequency and intensity.

RESEARCH PROCEDURES

General Methodological Issues

The design of this research model was conceptualized as a 14-stage model based on the work of Thompson, McNamara, and Hoyle (1997). The model appears in Table 11.1.

Table 11.1. Design of the Inquiry

Stage	Description
Stage 1	Developing the theoretical framework
Stage 2	Specifying the population
Stage 3	Designing the classification system
Stage 4	Designing the coding system
Stage 5	Coding the data
Stage 6	Archiving the coded data
Stage 7	Constructing the research hypotheses inventory
Stage 8	Identifying the effect sizes
Stage 9	Describing the articles
Stage 10	Describing the effect sizes
Stage 11	Estimating the parameters
Stage 12	Elaborating the moderator variables
Stage 13	Assessing the stability of findings over time
Stage 14	Specifying the recommendations

The effect size indicator used for statistical analysis was the Pearson product-moment correlation coefficient. The correlation coefficient expresses the relationship between a distinct predictor variable and a distinct criterion variable and can be cumulated across studies (Hunter & Schmidt, 1990).

Cohen (1988) refers to effect size as "the degree to which the phenomenon is present in the population" (p. 9). Stated conversely, an effect size means "the degree to which the null hypothesis is false" (p. 10). For this study, then, a zero effect size was set as the null hypothesis; likewise, the alternative hypothesis describes an effect size of any nonzero value, representing the degree to which said phenomenon is present within the population under study. In this study, effect sizes are expressed through the use of Pearson product-moment correlation coefficients (r); thus, these effect sizes can be interpreted by considering the coefficient of determination (r^2), where the correlation coefficient is squared and represents the amount of variance explained by the variables being studied (Cohen, 1988). In this way, effect sizes demonstrate the potential practical significance of a relationship between two constructs.

Effect sizes as measured by Pearson r values are classified into three sizes (Cohen, 1988). A large effect size is any finding equal or greater to ±0.50. A finding between the absolute value of 0.30 and 0.49 is considered a moderate effect size, and a finding of absolute value between 0.10 and 0.29 is considered a small effect size. Any effect size smaller than the absolute value of 0.10 is negligible, demonstrating no truly measurable relationship.

Specific Methodological Stages

In Stages 1 through 3, primary studies that addressed burnout among special educators and presented empirical data suitable for quantitative synthesis were identified, and a classification system for each variable examined was developed. The researcher constructed these classification systems based on similar meta-analyses found in the literature (Thompson et al., 1997), with classification systems developed for coding burnout constructs, predictor constructs, and effect size indicators. Procedures for meta-analysis were used for classifying effect size indicators (Cohen, 1988). Initially, an exhaustive search of eight major databases using the search terms "burnout" and "special education," was conducted to identify primary studies relevant to this topic. The following databases were included in the search: ERIC, Social Sciences Abstracts, Article First, Wilson, Psyc Info, Dissertation Abstracts International, Education Abstracts, and *Educational Administration Abstracts*. A theoretical framework describing the research relating to burnout and stress was developed as well. The theoretical framework examined constructs including gender, age, years of experience, special education caseload (i.e., number of students served), and exceptionality taught (i.e., type or severity of handicapping condition identified in students). This theoretical framework was also used to help guide the search for moderator variables in Stage 12.

In Stages 4 through 6 data were reliably transferred from the synthesis population of primary studies into a SPSS data file in order to facilitate further analysis. These stages were accomplished through (1) constructing a numerical coding system developed from the classification systems found in Stage 3, (2) coding data onto specially designed coding forms, and (3) archiving the coded data into a computer data file. The reliability for these procedures was achieved through the independent analysis of behavioral researchers specially trained in meta-analysis.

Stages 7 and 8 involved the construction of the research hypothesis inventory and the identification of the effect size estimates. The research hypothesis inventory was developed from the stated or implied research hypotheses found in the synthesis population of primary studies. Primary studies in this inquiry contained anywhere from three to 216 stated or implied research hypotheses.

After an inventory of research hypotheses was constructed, effect size estimates were identified or derived. Estimates given in the form of Pearson product-moment correlation coefficients were recorded as is; estimates given in other statistical formats were converted into Pearson coefficients.

Each effect size met specific criteria suitable for quantitative synthesis (Hedges & Becker, 1986); thus, each estimate was independent, represented the same construct, and estimated the same statistical parameter.

Descriptive analyses were conducted in Stages 9 and 10. In Stage 9, the descriptive analysis of the synthesis population of primary studies took the form of univariate distributions and answered research questions one through 13. In Stage 10, the descriptive analysis of effect sizes produced univariate distributions of two sets of effect size estimates: the entire set of effect size estimates (as described by this article) and subsets of effect size estimates corresponding to research hypotheses that yielded at least eight effect sizes (as described in Edmonson & Thompson, 2002).

Stage 11 required that an independent meta-analysis be conducted for each research hypothesis that yielded at least eight effect sizes and the same unit of statistical analysis; all meta-analyses were conducted according to Hunter and Schmidt's (1990) guidelines. In these meta-analyses, effect sizes were weighted according to their corresponding sample sizes. Five estimates were then measured: the effect size estimate of the population correlation, the estimate of the variance of the observed correlations across studies, the estimate of the variance of observed correlations due to sampling error, the estimate of the variance of the population correlation, and the estimate of the standard deviation of the population correlation. From these estimates, conclusions could be drawn concerning the relationships between burnout constructs and predictor constructs.

Moderator variable analysis was conducted in Stage 12 using the guidelines laid out by Hunter and Schmidt (1990). These authors point out that moderator variables become apparent when there is true variation, not due to sampling error, in correlations across studies. When true variation does exist, Hunter and Schmidt suggest grouping the correlations into subsets and repeating the procedures for meta-analysis. Moderator variables will then evidence themselves by a mean effect size (effect size estimate of the population correlation) that varies noticeably between the subsets and a lower standard deviation of population correlations for the subsets than for the combined data.

Stage 13 involved a time series analysis for each research hypothesis used in the meta-analyses. The time series analysis required that the effect sizes be disaggregated and chronologically ordered by the studies' year of publication. No trends were found in the data from this study, and consequently these findings are not described in this paper.

Findings

Empirical studies that measured the relationship between a construct of burnout and stress in special education appeared 19 times in the synthesis population of primary studies. These studies, along with their specified research hypothesis, author, date of publication, effect size, and sample size appear in Table 11.2. In order to be included in the synthesis, each primary study had to expressly measure an empirical relationship between a construct of burnout and stress. If the relationship was not stated empirically, the study was not included; likewise, if the relationship did not measure burnout and stress, then it was excluded from the synthesis. When multiple effect sizes from a single primary study were presented, all were included in the synthesis; in such cases, each effect size represented a distinct relationship between one of Maslach's constructs of burnout and stress. All but two reported burnout constructs were measured using Maslach's Burnout Inventory (Bloom, 1992; DiCamilio, 1994; Fimian & Blanton, 1986; Freed, 1994; Lamonica, 1983; Ogden, 1992); of the others, one used a self-made questionnaire (Strassmeier, 1992) and one used the Staff Burnout Scale for Health Professionals (Beer & Beer, 1992). Stress was measured by the Teacher Stress Inventory (DiCamilio, 1994; Fimian & Blanton, 1986), the Wilson Stress Profile for Teachers (Beer & Beer, 1992; Lamonica, 1983), and self-made questionnaires (Bloom, 1992; Freed, 1994; Ogden, 1992; Strassmeier, 1992). Reliability coefficients for the burnout constructs were reported in 12 of the 19 instances; these coefficients ranged from 0.60 to 0.90, with both a median and average of 0.79. No validity coefficients were reported for burnout measures. Reliability coefficients for the stress measures were reported in four of 19 cases, with all four cases reporting a coefficient of 0.68. These same four cases reported validity coefficients of 0.50.

Every primary study included in this synthesis used some combination of Maslach's (1982) constructs of burnout. Based on the effect sizes reported in Table 11.2, this inquiry suggests that Maslach's burnout constructs of emotional exhaustion share a large positive relationship with stress, with three of the five effect sizes falling above the 0.5 level and a mean effect size of 0.6039. Depersonalization shares a much more moderate positive relationship with stress, in which three of the five effect sizes fall in Cohen's moderate range and the mean effect size is 0.3569. The burnout construct of personal accomplishment has only a negligible relationship with stress, with three of the four effect sizes classified as small. Total burnout has an overall relationship of moderate strength with stress, including two large, one moderate, and two small effect sizes for a mean effect size of 0.3025. Although the synthesis population of primary studies that treated these variables was relatively small (five or less for each individual construct), the data generated by these analyses are certainly of potential importance to practitioners.

Each of the 19 occurrences used the individual unit of analysis and thus necessarily yielded 19 effect sizes. All of these effect sizes were origi-

Table 11.2. Descriptive Analysis of Burnout Constructs Related to Stress

Research Hypothesis	Sample Size	Effect Size
Emotional exhaustion related to total stress (DiCamilio, 1994)	27	0.44
Emotional exhaustion related to total stress (Freed, 1994)	342	0.63
Emotional exhaustion related to total stress (Bloom, 1992)	23	−0.05
Emotional exhaustion related to total stress (Ogden, 1992)	143	0.68
Emotional exhaustion related to total stress (Lamonica, 1983)	89	0.6
Depersonalization related to total stress (DiCamilio, 1994)	27	0.48
Depersonalization related to total stress (Freed, 1994)	342	0.25
Depersonalization related to total stress (Bloom, 1992)	23	0.11
Depersonalization related to total stress (Ogden, 1992)	143	0.54
Depersonalization related to total stress (Lamonica, 1983)	89	0.5
Personal accomplishment related to total stress (DiCamilio, 1994)	27	0.05
Personal accomplishment related to total stress (Bloom, 1992)	23	0.16
Personal accomplishment related to total stress (Ogden, 1992)	143	0.26
Personal accomplishment related to total stress (Lamonica, 1983)	89	−0.25
Burnout related to total stress (Freed, 1994)	342	0.56
Burnout related to total stress (Beer & Beer, 1992)	33	0.22
Burnout related to total stress (Strassmeier, 1992)	716	0.06
Burnout related to total stress (Fimian & Blanton, 1986)	415	0.46
Burnout related to total stress (Lamonica, 1983)	89	0.56

nally reported as Pearson product-moment correlations. The range of correlations extended from −0.25 to 0.63, with a median effect size of 0.44. The estimated population effect size is ave (r_s) = 0.3526, indicating only a small difference between the median and the weighted average. The average correlation, using Cohen's (1988) guidelines, is a medium effect size, indicating a relationship of moderate strength between stress and burnout. The relationship is positive, meaning that as stress increases, so does burnout. Squaring the average correlation yields a coefficient of determination of 0.1244, indicating that 12.44% of the variation in burnout is accounted for by the variation in stress. These data are displayed in Table 11.3.

The analysis in Table 11.3 also reveals the estimated variance of the sample effect sizes [var (r_s)] = 0.3033, the estimated variance of the sample effect sizes due to sampling error [var (e)] = 0.0047, the estimated variance of the true population effect size [var (r_p)] = 0.29864, and the standard deviation of the true population effect size [SD (r_p)] = 0.5465. In this case, the sampling error variance (0.0047) is a relatively small component of the variance of the sample effect sizes (0.3033); specifi-

Table 11.3. Meta-Analytic Findings for the Relationship Between Burnout and Stress, by Construct

Research Hypothesis	Effect Sizes	Population Effect Size	Explained Variance %	Confidence Interval (95%) Upper	Lower
Burnout (all constructs) related to stress	19	0.3526	12.44	.2184	.4869
Emotional Exhaustion related to stress	5	0.6039	36.47	.4920	.7158
Depersonalization related to stress	5	0.3569	12.74	.2032	.5106
Personal accomplishment related to stress	4	0.0708	0.50	−.1631	.3047
Total burnout related to stress	5	0.3025	9.15	.2026	.4023

cally, it accounts for 1.5% of the variance of the sample effect sizes, meaning that 98.5% of the variance is not due to sampling error and must therefore be due to some other factor. Furthermore, because the sampling error variance is small, the variance and standard deviation of the true population effect size are relatively large, further suggesting the possibility of a moderator variable. However, because one study has a sample size that is almost double that of any other study, this variation could possibly be due at least somewhat to sample size. No other single moderator variable could be identified from the current data. Based on the guidelines of Hunter and Schmidt (1990), these data suggest that the relationship between burnout and stress is strong enough to be considered universally positive. The data supporting these conclusions appear in Table 11.3.

The effect sizes reported for stress and burnout in Table 11.2 were subjected to Hunter and Schmidt's (1990) techniques for meta-analysis, including the following statistical procedures:

Estimate of population effect size [ave(r_s)] = 0.3526

$$\text{ave}(r_s) = \Sigma[N_i r_i]/\Sigma N_i$$

Estimate of variance of sample effect sizes [var (r_s)] = 0.3033

$$\text{var}(r_s) = \Sigma N_i[r_i - \text{ave}(r_s)]^2/\Sigma N_i$$

Estimate of variance of sample effect sizes due to sampling error [var (e)] = 0.0047

$$\text{var}(e) = [1 - \text{ave}(r_s)^2]^2/[\text{ave}(N) - 1]$$

Estimate of variance of true population effect size [var (r_p)] = 0.29864

$$\text{var}(r_p) = \text{var}(r_s) - \text{var}(e)$$

Estimate of standard deviation of true population effect size $[SD\ (r_p)] = 0.5465$

$$[SD\ (r_p)] = [\text{var}\ (r_p)]^{1/2}$$

The potential for moderator variables is great in a meta-analysis of this type. For this reason, a number of variables were included in the process of data collection in order to permit further testing as needed. Potential moderator variables coded for each study included: target population (i.e., special education teachers, general education teachers, administrators, diagnosticians, first year teachers only, etc.); level of population (public K-12 schools, public and private K-12 schools, public elementary schools, level not indicated, etc.); and locale of study (if subjects were from a particular geographic location or region). The types of instruments used to measure burnout and its correlates were also coded for potential moderator effects. Other outstanding features of primary studies included in the synthesis that might have acted as a moderator variable were coded as well. Despite the probable presence of some type of moderator, no specific moderator variable was identified.

However, the inability to determine a clear moderator variable did not exclude the apparent presence of some factor causing moderation in the findings. When the mean effect sizes for burnout were run according to specific burnout constructs, differences between the mean effect size of the overall synthesis population and the mean effect sizes for each construct (emotional exhaustion, depersonalization, personal accomplishment, total burnout) were discovered. These data are reported in Table 11.3 as well. In fact, only the mean effect sizes for depersonalization and total burnout fall into the same general effect size category as the overall mean for the study. The mean effect sizes for emotional exhaustion and personal accomplishment vary widely from each other as well as from the other mean effect sizes derived from the data. When viewed in conjunction with corresponding confidence intervals, the fact that confidence intervals for each construct do not overlap further suggests the presence of moderation. For example, the confidence interval for emotional exhaustion does not overlap with the intervals for personal accomplishment, total burnout, or the mean effect size of the total study. Thus, the moderation effect of the burnout construct plays an important part of the study's overall findings. Because this study uses a relatively small number of effect sizes, the accumulation of additional studies may allow any source of moderation to become more apparent.

Educational Importance of the Study

A meta-analysis examining the relationship between stress and burnout among special educators is important for several reasons. An inquiry such as this one, which provides statistical data derived from numerous primary studies, provides the foundation for comparing and understanding the results of studies that otherwise would yield only an incomparable assortment of information. In the words of Hughlings Jackson, "we have multitudes of facts, but we require, as they accumulate, organizations of them into higher knowledge" (as cited in Kavale, 1984, p. 97). This study provides such organization. In practice, this analysis facilitates a more complete understanding than what currently exists of stress as it relates to burnout among special educators. By analyzing the correlations between stress and burnout, perhaps methods for relieving or preventing this burnout can be developed. Burnout is a very real problem among today's special educators, particularly for its relationship to teacher retention and attrition (Cooley & Yavonoff, 1996). Thus, a complete understanding of burnout and its relationship to stress is vital to effectively overcoming this educational challenge.

Implications for Research

Stress accounted for almost 13% of the variance in burnout, which indicates that the relationship between these two constructs is important and deserves further study. When a single variable, such as stress, can explain a large amount of variance in another single variable, burnout, then the relationship indeed should be examined in depth. Studies that examine the interplay between stress and burnout should be conducted in order to discover how the two constructs work together to impact special education teachers. This type of study could potentially impact such important factors as job satisfaction or teacher efficacy, and the implications of such findings could reach into areas of teacher preparation, staff development, retention, and even student performance. While quantitative studies that empirically define this relationship are useful, qualitative research that involves a thorough and comprehensive examination of special educators' perceptions would be valuable for filling in the gaps that quantitative relationships do not explain.

Likewise, further study is needed to identify and understand other constructs that help explain burnout among special education teachers. For example, does the type or severity of disability that students have make a difference in whether or not special educators experience burnout? Previous meta-analyses have found that demographic factors, such as age, experience, and gender, have little relationship with burnout (Edmonson & Thompson, 2002), yet obviously there are variables that impact burnout in special educators. Identifying what these variables are and what kind of relationship they have with burnout is imperative to helping relieve this problem.

The operationalization of constructs in the research is, at best, inconsistent and should be pursued much more stringently. Burnout, for example, is defined in a number of ways. Some authors describe burnout as a form of job stress (Cherniss, 1988; Dedrick & Raschke, 1990; Maslach, 1982; Wisniewski & Gargiulo, 1997), which could be one explanation for the large amount of explained variance between these two constructs. Others researchers describe burnout as a reaction to stress (Greer & Greer, 1992) or as a number of physiological and psychological symptoms (Gold, 1989; Guglielmi & Tatrow, 1998; Hudson & Meagher, 1983). Likewise, stress is also widely defined in the literature (Gates & Boyter, 2002; Lazarus, 1995); while the definitions of stress are more consistent than those for burnout, they are still quite broad when trying to study the construct in depth or draw conclusions. More clearly defined constructs would increase the validity and reliability of all research, particularly research using meta-analysis and/or techniques of quantitative synthesis.

The coefficient of determination is used to describe the amount of explained variance in a study (McNamara, 1991). The amount of explained variance can therefore be used as an indicator of potential practical significance: a large amount of explained variance indicates a greater strength of association between two constructs, whereas a small amount of explained variance—meaning that a large amount of variance is unexplained by the variable being studied—would indicate a lesser strength of association. Indicating the amount of explained variance in a study, then, would be beneficial to understanding the potential importance of research findings to practitioners.

Implications for Practitioners

Special education is a field that offers numerous challenges to its teachers and administrators. Professional educators in special education are sorely needed, even though the field continues to grow rapidly (U.S. Department of Education, 2001). Although burnout is not the sole reason for this shortage of teachers, the prevention of burnout could help retain the teachers who currently serve in this critical-needs field. An understanding of the relationship between burnout and stress is one step in learning how to prevent and/or alleviate burnout among special educators.

One way that special educators may deal with stress is through the development of coping strategies (Gmelch & Gates, 1998). Coping strategies are implemented by persons who experience stressors but believe they can successfully handle and/or overcome these problems. Coping strategies in general are either active and problem-focused or passive and emotion-focused. Problem-focused strategies attempt to change the cause of the stress, whereas emotion-focused strategies work to reduce a person's reaction to stress (Folkman & Lazarus, 1988). According to Gmelch and Gates (1998), stress can be task-based, role-based, conflict-mediating, or boundary-spanning. Likewise, the coping mechanisms that a person develops to deal with these stress types are classified into the same four categories. When a person experiences stress but can develop or use a coping strategy to deal with this stress, then burnout is less likely to occur. McCarthy, Lambert, Beard, and Dematatis (2002) point out specifically that the development of effective coping strategies is critical in educational environments and offer mechanisms for helping educators meet this need. Just as coping strategies are used in handling stress, they may prevent or relieve burnout in the same way. Knowing that stress and burnout are strongly related allows educators to encourage the use of appropriate coping strategies.

Furthermore, there are areas of educator preparation programs that should address burnout as well. Ensuring that prospective special education teachers are prepared for their jobs—including the stress that will likely occur—should be an important part of any preparation program. Similarly, providing future special education teachers with the tools to develop or enhance their coping skills, conflict mediation skills, and self-awareness skills is also a valuable consideration (Gmelch & Chan, 1995; Gmelch & Torelli, 1994). Adequate preparation for the varied tasks that will face a future special educator is critical to preventing job burnout among these professionals.

CONCLUSION

This study demonstrates that the relationship between burnout and stress among special education teachers clearly exists. Thus, school administrators should be aware that teachers who experience a great deal of stress may be likely to experience burnout. This study also found that while 13% of the variance in burnout is due to stress, a great deal of variance is not explained by this single factor. In other words, focusing all our attention to alleviating stress among special educators will not by itself prevent burnout. Although recognizing stress is important, special education professionals must also look for other factors that have strong relationships to burnout. As the picture between burnout and its related factors becomes more clear, special educators can learn more precisely how to deal with burnout in their chosen field.

REFERENCES

Banks, S. R., & Necco, E. G. (1990). The effects of special education category and type of training on job burnout in special education teachers. *Teacher Education and Special Education, 13*(3-4), 187-191.

Beer, J., & Beer, J. (1992, December). Burnout and stress, depression and self-esteem of teachers. *Psychological Reports, 71*(3), 1331-1336.

Billingsly, B. S., & Cross, L. (1992). Predictors of commitment, job satisfaction, and intent to stay in teaching: A comparison of general and special educators. *The Journal of Special Education, 25*, 453-471.

Blase, J. J. (1982). A social psychological grounded theory of teacher stress and burnout. *Educational Administration Quarterly, 18*(4), 93-113.

Bloom, J. (1992). *Parenting our schools: A hands-on guide to education reform.* Boston: Little, Brown and Company.

Boe, E. E., Cook, L. H., Kaufman, M. J., & Danielson, L. C. (1996). Special and general education teachers in public schools: Sources of supply in national perspective. *Teacher Education and Special Education, 19*(1), 1-16.

Cherniss, C. (1988). Observed supervisory behavior and teacher burnout in special education. *Exceptional Children, 54*(5), 449-454.

Cohen, J. (1988). *Statistical power analysis for the behavioral sciences.* Hillside, NJ: Erlbaum.

Cooley, E., & Yovanoff, P. (1996). Supporting professionals at-risk: Evaluating interventions to reduce burnout and improve retention of special educators. *Exceptional Children, 62*(4), 336-355.

Crane, S. J., & Iwanicki, E. F. (1986). Perceived role conflict, role ambiguity, and burnout among special education teachers. *Remedial and Special Education, 7*(2), 24-31.

Dedrick, C. V. L., & Raschke, D. B. (1990). *The special educator and job stress.* Washington DC: National Education Association.

DiCamillo, M. P. (1994). An investigation of stress and burnout factors in special educators and regular educators (Master's thesis, California State University, Long Beach, 1994). *Master's Abstracts International, 33-01*, 0041.

Edmonson, S. L., & Thompson, D. (2002). Burnout among special educators: A meta-analysis. In G. Gates & M. Wolverton (Eds.), *Toward wellness: Prevention, coping, and stress* (pp. 151-177). Greenwich, CT: Information Age.

Fimian, M. J., & Blanton, L. P. (1986). Variables related to stress and burnout in special education teacher trainees and first-year teachers. *Teacher Education and Special Education, 9*(1), 9-21.

Folkman, S., & Lazarus, R. S. (1988). Coping as a mediator of emotion. *Journal of Personality and Social Psychology, 54*, 466-475.

Freed, E. H. (1984). The relationship of social support, occupational stress, burnout, and job satisfaction among special education teachers (Doctoral dissertation, Temple University, 1984). *Dissertation Abstracts International, 55-04A,* 0909.

Freudenberger, J. (1977). Burnout: Occupational hazard of the child care worker. *Child Care Quarterly, 6,* 90-98.

Fuchs, D., & Fuchs, L. S. (1995, March). What's "special" about special education? *Phi Delta Kappan, 76,* 522-530.

Gates, G., & Boyter, G. (2002). A study of Texas school board president stress: Struggling with duties of the presidency. In G. Gates & M. Wolverton (Eds.), *Toward wellness: Prevention, coping, and stress* (pp. 127-142). Greenwich, CT: Information Age.

Gmelch, W. H., & Chan, W. (1995, September). Administrator stress and coping effectiveness: Implications for administrator evaluation and development. *Journal of Personnel Evaluation in Education, 9*(3), 275-285.

Gmelch, W. H., & Gates, G. (1998). The impact of personal, professional, and organizational characteristics on administrator burnout. *Journal of Educational Administration, 36*(2), 146-159.

Gmelch, W. H., & Torelli, J. A. (May, 1994). The association of role conflict and ambiguity with administrator stress and burnout. *Journal of School Leadership, 4*(3), 341-356.

Gold, Y. (1989). Reducing stress and burnout through induction programs. *Action in Teacher Education, 11*(3), 66-70.

Greer, J. G., & Greer, B. B. (1992). Stopping burnout before it starts: Prevention measures at the preservice level. *Teacher Education and Special Education, 15*(3), 168-174.

Guglielmi, R. S., & Tatrow, K. (1998). Occupational stress, burnout, and health in teachers: A methodological and theoretical analysis. *Review of Educational Research, 68*(1), 61-99.

Guskin, S. L. (1984). Problems and promises of meta-analysis in special education. *The Journal of Special Education, 18*(1), 73-80.

Hedges, L. V., & Becker, B. J. (1986). Statistical methods in the meta-analysis of research on gender differences. In J. S. Hyde & M. C. Linn (Eds.), *The psychology of gender: Advances through meta-analysis* (pp. 14-30). Baltimore: John Hopkins University.

Hudson, F., & Meagher, K. (1983). *Variables associated with stress and burnout of regular and special education teachers: Final report.* Lawrence, KS: Kansas University. (ERIC Document Reproduction Service No. ED 239 471)

Hunter, J. E., & Schmidt, F. L. (1990). *Methods of meta-analysis.* Newbury Park, CA: Sage.

Kavale, K. A. (1984). Potential advantages of the meta-analysis technique for research in special education. *The Journal of Special Education, 18*(1), 61-72.

Lamonica, A. (1983). An investigation of factors related to psychological stress and burnout in teachers of severely handicapped children (Doctoral dissertation, Hofstra University, 1983). *Dissertation Abstracts International, 45-02A,* 0676.

Lazarus, R. (1995). Psychological stress in the workplace. In R Crandall & P. Perrewe (Eds.), *Occupational stress: A handbook* (pp. 3-14). Washington, DC: Taylor & Francis.

Male, D. B., & May, D. S. (1997, September). Burnout and workload in teachers of children with severe learning disabilities. *British Journal of Learning Disabilities, 25*(3), 117-121.

Maslach, C. (1982). *Burnout: The cost of caring.* Englewood Cliffs, NJ: Prentice Hall.

Maslach, C., & Jackson, S. E. (1984). Burnout in organizational settings. *Applied Social Psychology Annual, 5,* 133-153.

McCarthy, C. J., Lambert, R. G., Beard, M., & Dematatis, A. (2002). Factor structure of the preventive resources inventory and its relationship to existing measures of stress and coping. In G. Gates & M. Wolverton (Eds.), *Toward wellness: Prevention, coping, and stress* (pp. 3-37). Greenwich, CT: Information Age.

McNamara, J. F. (1991). *Surveys and experiments in education research.* Lancaster, PA: Technomic.

Ogden, D. L. (1992). Administrative stress and burnout among public school administrators in Georgia (Doctoral dissertation, Georgia State University, 1992). *Dissertation Abstracts International, 53-05A,* 1349.

Stout, L. C. (1987). Attitudes toward paperwork and the relationship to conditions of burnout, locus of control, and pupil control ideology (Doctoral dissertation, East Texas State University, 1987). *Dissertation Abstracts International, 48-03A,* 0534.

Strassmeier, W. (1992, September). Stress amongst teachers of children with mental handicaps. *International Journal of Rehabilitation Research, 15*(3), 235-239.

Thompson, D. P., McNamara, J. F., & Hoyle, J. R. (1997, February). Job satisfaction in educational organizations: A synthesis of research findings. *Education Administration Quarterly, 33*(1), 7-37.

U.S. Department of Education. (2001). *Twenty-third annual report of Congress of the implementation of the Individuals with Disabilities Act.* III-36.

Wisniewski, L., & Gargiulo, R. M. (1997). Occupational stress and burnout among special educators: A review of the literature. *The Journal of Special Education, 31*(3), 325-346.

CHAPTER 12

HELPING TEACHERS BALANCE DEMANDS AND RESOURCES IN AN ERA OF ACCOUNTABILITY

Christopher McCarthy and Richard Lambert

Recent studies of teacher stress are reviewed in the context of the transactional model of stress and coping. Emerging themes are outlined that represent both the occupational demands of the educational environment and the resources and strategies teachers use to cope with these demands. Implications for the teaching profession and the future of teacher stress research are presented.

Given the demands inherent in today's educational workplace, this book was devoted to examining the factors that exacerbate and protect teachers from harmful levels of stress in their profession. As is clear from the preceding chapters, uniform standards of accountability for student performance, such as those delineated in the No Child Left Behind Act developed and applied by politicians and administrators who are often far away from the classroom, represent perhaps one of the most significant sources of stress for today's teacher. Such standards are typically instituted as an external method of evaluating whether or not schools, teachers, and administrators are performing at least at minimal levels of competence. As such, they represent something of a "free-market approach" approach to education: at least in theory, the results of standardized testing provide consumers (i.e., parents and guardians) objective information about whether or not their children attend quality schools. Presumably at least, schools that do not "measure up" in the market place will be forced to either improve or be replaced as parents choose to send their children to other schools.

In *The Costs of Living*, Schwartz (1994) analyzed the complex ways in which a free market economy impacts human welfare, both to our advantage and detriment. Although the free market brings many benefits to its participants in terms of efficiency and consumer choice, he argued that an emphasis on competition and profits can also undermine much of what is "good" in life and in many occupations. Perhaps most relevant to this book is his notion that in such a system, there are three ways in which occupations can be approached: as a job, in which the main motivation is money, as an occupation, in which both money as well as the opportunity for advancement, recognition, and prestige are important, and as a calling, in which the value of one's work is what is important, even if it does not result in material reward or recognition. Schwartz (1994) pointed out that most of us think that teaching should be a calling, in which educators are motivated not by money or personal recognition, but by the belief that are doing something that is important and worthwhile. A central question therefore is whether standards of accountability based on high-stakes testing, a free market tool for evaluating performance, undermines the notion of teaching as a calling. Teachers who view their profession as a calling should be motivated at least as much by the welfare of their students as by standards of accountability: if accountability standards and the interest of students are in conflict, teacher (and of course student) stress can be the result.

Balancing demands and resources are therefore central to understanding teachers' welfare in accountability systems. Before reviewing the main themes that emerged from the studies presented in this book, we will first briefly revisit the theoretical model of stress which predominated in this book, namely transactional models of stress that assume when a potentially threatening event is encountered, a reflexive, cognitive balancing act ensues in which the perceived demands of the event are weighed against one's perceived capabilities for dealing with it (Lazarus & Folkman, 1984).

TRANSACTIONAL MODELS OF STRESS

Most of the research in this book focuses on teachers' perceptions of their workplace environment in one form or another. Richard Lazarus (1981) was among the first stress researchers to focus on the pivotal role of "appraisal" in human stress, a term he used to refer to the subjective evaluations we all make when encountering potentially stressful events. Lazarus and Susan Folkman (1984) developed the theoretical notion that we conduct two fairly automatic, mental operations when we encounter any event or situation in our environment. First, we take stock of the potential threat an event represents, which is called a primary appraisal. As can be seen in this volume, teachers face myriad demands—it is safe to say that every day in a teachers' career brings unique demands and challenges.

Second, once we encounter a demand, we conduct a sort of mental inventory of our coping resources, which is called a secondary appraisal. Aspects of each situational demand (e.g., the degree of threat it represents and the perceived consequences of our failure to deal successfully with it) and of our resources coping (e.g., their appropriateness for the demand and their sufficiency) are therefore taken into consideration in appraising the seriousness of the situation (Folkman & Lazarus, 1984). Teachers who feel equipped to meet the challenges of the classroom will likely experience their jobs as energizing and rewarding.

However, events perceived as outstripping our resources can be viewed as potential threats that trigger the stress response, a series of physiological and psychological changes that occur reflexively whenever coping resources are threatened (Hobfoll, 1988a, 1988b). Obviously, these physiological changes would be worth the toll they exact from our bodies if they prevented us from even greater harm. Although extremely adaptive for human ancestors who faced daily threats to their very survival, today the body's stress response is poorly suited to the psychosocial nature of modern demands. Teachers who do not feel able to meet the needs of their students, who perceive a lack of support by administrators, and otherwise experience their jobs as under-resourced will not only suffer in their teaching, they will likely suffer physically and emotionally. It is therefore important to consider what we know about the nature of demands faced by teachers and the types of resources employed to cope with them.

DEMANDS FACED BY TEACHERS

It seems clear from the contributions in this volume that teachers experience administrative demands as a key feature of their work lives, particularly because they experience these demands as taking them away from the instructional process and their work with children. Administrator requests concerning noninstructional duties of various kinds take an increasing amount of time and energy. Teachers want their administrators to protect them from unnecessary interruptions to the instructional process and hope to rely on administrators for technical assistance when attempting to improve in their areas of weakness. However, many teachers report a general lack of support from their administrators and see it as a demanding aspect of their jobs (Lambert, Kusherman, O'Donnell, & McCarthy, 2005). Many of these same demands were identified as critical to teachers in Turkey (Kiziltepe, in this volume). And, special education teachers in particular found documentation and paperwork requirements to be very burdensome (Edmonson, in this volume).

The central administrative or policy-driven demand on teachers comes from accountability programs. Teachers feel confined within administrative requirements that range from pacing guides to scripted lesson plans (Mathison & Freeman, in this volume). Accountability programs make strong causal inferences about teacher impact on student achievement and do so using only aggregated test scores as indicators of teacher quality, without the use of validated measures of the quality of classroom processes or any study design features that allow for causal inferences. Teachers therefore feel responsible for everything that happens when the tests are given and have lost a sense of partnering with parents and children to impact achievement and learning. Mathison and Freeman (in this volume) noted the perception of many teachers that standardized testing drives many of the activities in the classroom, and many feel compelled to teach to the test. Webb (in this volume) outlined the experience of teachers who report internal conflicts between the mandated curriculum and demands of the accountability programs on one hand, and their own professional diagnosis of what individual children need on the other. All of these factors work together to impair creativity and lead teachers to feel underappreciated and treated as less than professional.

The multicultural classroom presents the teacher with many wonderful opportunities for creative instruction, and yet as the linguistic diversity of students increases so do the demands on teachers and schools to facilitate the assimilation and language acquisition process for children. For example, while previous waves of immigration to America presented a strong familial focus on assimilation and the acquisition of English, and it was a status symbol for families to have children who had assimilated, assimilation today is much more of a two way street, placing more of the burden on the school (Nassar-McMillan, Karvonen, & Young, in this volume).

A perceived lack of parental support is another major area of concern for teachers. Preschool teachers reported that all types of communication with parents including conferences can be very demanding (Lambert,

Kusherman, et al., in this volume). Teachers bear much of the impact of a cultural shift that has seen parents transition from allies of the teacher into advocates for their children, even to the point in some cases of being adversaries of the teacher and school. Rather than regarding the school as a community resource, a support in the parenting process, and an extension of parental authority, parents often model for their children a lack of respect for authority as they resist the teacher and principal themselves.

In support of this point, my coeditor on this volume (RGL) learned during the course of a research study about an experienced and committed teacher who was placed on administrative leave for intervening in a physical confrontation between two students. The teacher was placed on leave because one of the students' legal guardians complained vigorously to the school principal about how the teacher handled the situation. The teacher became disillusioned with how the situation was handled that he decided not to return to the urban school system the following year. He now teaches in a suburban system shere he reports having more resources, fewer behavior problems, and greater administrative support.

It is impossible to completely evaluate the actions of any of the participants in this study without all the details. However, at least two points seem readily apparent. First, both the teacher and the administrator worked in a very demanding, high stress environment with limited rewards. Second, it is hard to find a positive outcome to the story. Although this case may not be typical and does not directly involve national accountability standards, it illustrates several of the themes that appeared in this book. Throughout this volume, teachers from various contexts have reported in various ways their perceptions of the same demands the teacher experienced: child behavior problems, lack of administrative support, lack of parental support, and lack of instructional resources.

Managing student behavior has been widely recognized as the most consistently mentioned theme when teachers are asked about the demanding aspects of their work. Children with behavior problems were perceived as the most demanding feature of the preschool classroom. The only difference in classroom structural characteristics between teachers at risk for stress and their less stressed colleagues was the number of children with problem behaviors (Lambert, Kusherman, et al., in this volume). Firth, Frydenberg, and Greaves (in this volume) noted that students with learning disabilities are particularly likely to lead to teacher stress as such students are more likely to engage in problematic behaviors and use non-productive coping strategies. In addition, student behavior problems were found to be a significant source of demotivation for teachers (Kiziltepe, in this volume).

Despite the low salaries and lack of professional recognition inherent in the teaching profession, economic factors were not reported by teachers as a major source of demotivation. Rather, a lack of instructional resources was mentioned as a demanding feature of the workplace (Kiziltepe, in this volume). Preschool teachers reported that a lack of resources was moderately demanding, yet rated it as the least demanding negative feature of their jobs as compared to the other areas discussed above (Lambert, Kusherman, et al., in this volume). However, Segumpan and Bahari (in this volume) did find some evidence that stress levels were higher for teachers with lower incomes.

Special education teachers also experience many of the same demands outlined above, and they tend to be one of the subgroups of teachers most likely to experience the stress response. Higher levels of stress among special education teachers tend to be associated with higher levels of burnout, especially characterized by emotional exhaustion and low levels of a sense of professional accomplishment. Furthermore, both burnout and stress have been shown to be contributors to the shortage of special education teachers (Edmonson, in this volume).

THE RESOURCES NEEDED TO HANDLE THE DEMANDS OF TEACHING

Given the demands that teachers face everyday, how can they be equipped to better handle their jobs and be less likely to experience stress, burnout, and the desire to leave the profession? What resources do teachers report that they need? The chapters in this volume have offered some answers to these questions. Not surprisingly, the themes that emerged followed a similar pattern to those identified as demands. Teachers feel a need for more administrative support, instructional materials, specialized resources targeted at demanding children, parental support, and professional recognition.

Grant and Hill (in this volume) made a persuasive case based on a series of studies for student-centered learning strategies. The flexibility of such an approach, its emphasis on problem-solving, creativity, and the use of technology has the potential to help teachers feel more empowered in their roles as educators. In other words, student-centered pedagogy has the potential to be a powerful resource for both students and teachers given an appropriate educational context. Much to their credit, Grant and Hill (in this volume) note that this form of instruction also carries challenges for teachers and students, which may be exacerbated by the current climate of high-stakes testing.

With respect to administrative support, preschool teachers were asked to rate how helpful a wide range of resources were to their daily work lives in the study by Lambert, Kusherman, et al. (in this volume). The support of experienced teachers, particularly when structured and supported by administrators in the form of mentoring programs, was regarded as one of the most helpful resources. Professional development opportunities, particularly when they offer engaging activities, were also rated as very helpful. The resources they reported clustered into three areas: general program resources which included instructional materials and administrative support, specialized program resources designed to help teachers handle demanding children, and the support of parents. The former two categories were rated as very helpful while parental support was rated as only moderately helpful (Lambert, Kusherman, et al., in this volume). Teachers in Turkey reported a need for administrators to provide more instructional materials and to develop more innovative resources to enhance professional recognition as a way to bolster motivational levels (Kiziltepe, in this volume).

With respect to specialized resources targeted at demanding children, several themes emerged from the study of teacher multicultural competencies (Nassar-McMillan, et al., in this volume). Teachers reported that they were provided inadequate resources to handle linguistic and cultural diversity, and inadequate training to prepare them for the diversity contained in their classrooms. Teachers also reported that while they would like to include all cultures in their classrooms as a part of the instructional process, they needed the help of parents to do so and felt it was difficult to gain that support. This study pointed out the need to provide teachers with specific resources, multicultural competencies, materials, and training, to help them handle the diversity of their classrooms.

Edmonson (2005) reported that special education teachers need to acquire conflict mediation skills, stress coping strategies, and self-awareness or reflection skills to be successful in their roles as the primary resource for children with special needs. Toward this end, Firth et al. (in this volume) presented a well-studied program aimed at helping both students with learning disabilities and their teachers cope with problematic student behaviors. Although it seemed that the program served mainly to limit nonproductive coping, instead of the hoped for increase in productive coping strategies, the intervention seemed worthy of future research.

Several studies identified innovative resources for handling the demands of the classroom that have emerged from teachers themselves. McCarthy, Yadley, Kissen, Wood, and Lambert (in this volume) found that higher levels of the preventive coping resource of self-acceptance were associated with lower levels of burnout symptoms. When the daily lives and perceptions of teachers in a low wealth school setting in a state with a potentially punitive accountability program were profiled, teachers were observed developing policy brokering strategies as a coping resource. They found ways to alter, modify, adapt, and even resist aspects of the accountability programs, all in the context of finding strategies for enhancing their feelings of effectiveness in working with demanding children (Webb, in this volume). Finally, many teachers simply spend money out of their own pockets for materials, bringing their own resources to the classroom as a strategy for meeting demands (Lambert, Kushner et al., in this volume).

IMPLICATIONS FOR FUTURE RESEARCH

This volume has reinforced prior notions that that teaching is a potentially high stress occupation (Dunham & Varma, 1998; Kyriacou, 2000; Kyriacou, 2001; Kyriacou & Sutcliffe, 1977; Travers & Cooper, 1996). Teacher's perceptions of demands are substantial, and they paint a picture of persistent and frequently occurring challenges that can take various forms. For many teachers, their perceptions of the available resources are not sufficient to prevent the stress response, leaving burnout and attrition as public policy issues that impact the entire educational system. Nevertheless, future research is needed to document the demanding conditions within which teachers perform, understand the resources they find most helpful, and evaluate interventions that can bring new resources to them in an effective manner. For those who remain in the profession, the question becomes how can we educate the general public about the realities of the teaching profession in order to influence public policy? One of the important steps toward that end is a concerted effort to remind the citizenry that although teaching has always been a stress prone profession, there are compelling reasons to believe that the demands on teachers have increased in recent years in several salient ways.

First, classrooms have become increasingly diverse, both culturally and linguistically. Globalization has created many wonderful opportunities for the international exchange of capital, ideas, and human resources. However, with these systemic shifts, teachers have been asked to simultaneously address the educational needs of children from a wide array of cultural backgrounds. Similarly, a high level of technological sophistication is now integral to the educational process. Advances have been made in the capability and availability of computer technology in general and instructional technology in particular. Yet these changes are both a blessing and a curse for teachers. They are a blessing in the sense that teachers can take advantage of free access to a seemingly infinite array of resources available through the Internet. They can share resources with like-minded teachers from all over the world. They can use technology to offer their students engaging and interactive activities. Technology is, however, a curse for teachers as well. Preparing lessons that effectively incorporate technology can be very time consuming and demanding and can require new skill sets. Furthermore, teachers are expected to compete with the increasingly technological world of children, feeling pressures to be just as engaging and entertaining as the last electronic game or gadget to grace the youth culture. Children who have grown up in a technological society often bring a shorter attention span and a more passive approach to the learning environment than did their parents and grandparents, many of whom experienced the play of childhood differently because they had to entertain themselves using their own imaginations.

The second sense in which the working conditions for teachers are more demanding is centered on the nature of family structure. Fewer children today have a parent who does not work outside the home. Therefore, these same American children may spend at least some part of their day in out-of-home care. To meet the demand for childcare, schools are evolving into critical components of the economic infrastructure of our society and indispensable support systems for the families that rely on their services. Society in general and families with children in particular are expecting more of the school than ever before. The school is expected to be social change agent as well as provide care before school and after school (Lambert, Abbott-Shim, & Sibley, 2005). These demands are added onto several other relevant features of many families: mobility, transience, crowded schedules, and a tendency to live apart from extended family support structures. Children may come to school with much less sleep than they did a generation ago and are raised by parents who also are getting much less sleep than their parents did. Furthermore, as mentioned earlier in this chapter, parents are much more likely to see themselves as adversaries of the teacher rather than allies. It could be argued that parents understand less about the daily life of teachers while expecting more from them.

Third, the accountability phenomenon is far reaching in scope and impact. Wide scale testing programs have been a part of the educational landscape for over a century. However, in the United States, the role of the federal government in educational policy, reaching from Washington down to the local system level, is not only unprecedented but potentially unconstitutional (McColl, 2005). Furthermore, testing programs are more punitive and detrimental to teacher morale than they have ever been. Teachers report a sense of competition has hurt collegiality as it has crept into the schools, bringing a tendency for teachers to blame each other for short falls in accountability goals. School administrators feel pressures to play "the test score game." Teachers report administrative emphases on the children near the cut scores for on grade level performance, as opposed to valuing growth for all children, and a high value placed on direct instruction and test preparation over teaching higher order thinking skills (Webb, in this volume).

SUMMARY

While it has widely been recognized that teaching is a demanding, and often stressful, occupation, at the same time the role of the educator is both prized and essential in modern democracies. Schwartz's (1994) notion that teaching is a calling in which the value of their work takes precedence over financial reward helps explain why many teachers stay in their profession despite the many demands of today's classroom. However, the notion of a calling means that teachers are at least partially motivated by their own internal standards and values about what it means to educate younger persons. To the extent that accountability standards undermine teachers' autonomy and creativity for working with individual students, teachers will likely continue to face unacceptable levels of stress in many settings. In the long run, this may lead to talented professionals leaving the field, to the detriment of our schools, children, and society as a whole. It is our hope that this volume will shed light on this issue and spur further research and dialogue aimed at improving the lives of teachers and their students.

REFERENCES

Dunham, J., & Varma, V. (Eds.) (1998). *Stress in teachers: Past, present, and future.* London: Whurr.

Hobfoll, S. E. (1988a). Conservation of resources: A new attempt at conceptualizing stress. *American Psychologist, 44,* 513–524.

Hobfoll, S. E. (1988b). *The ecology of stress.* Washington, DC: Hemisphere.

Kyriacou, C. (2000). *Stress busting for teachers.* Cheltenham, England: Stanley Thornes.

Kyriacou, C. (2001). Teacher stress: Directions for future research. *Educational Review, 53,* 27–35.

Kyriacou, C., & Sutcliffe, J. (1977). Teacher stress: A review. *Educational Review, 29,* 299–306.

Lambert, R., Abbott-Shim, M., & Sibley, A. (2005). Evaluating the quality of early childhood educational settings. In B. Spodek & O. Saracho (Eds.), *Handbook of research on the education of young children* (2nd ed., pp. 457-475). Mahwah, NJ: Erlbaum.

Lazarus, R. (1981). The stress and coping paradigm. In C. Eisdorfer, D. Cohen, A. Kleinman, & P. Maxim (Eds.), *Models of clinical psychopathology* (pp. 177–214). New York: Spectrum.

Lazarus, R. S., & Folkman, S. (1984). *Stress, appraisal, and coping.* New York: Springer.

McColl, A. (2005, April). Tough call: Is No Child Left Behind constitutional? *Phi Delta Kappan, 86,* 604–610.

Schwartz, B. (1994). *The costs of living: How market freedom erodes the best things in life.* New York: W. W. Norton.

Travers, C. J., & Cooper, C. L. (1996). *Teachers under pressure: Stress in the teaching profession* London: Routledge.

ABOUT THE AUTHORS

Fazli B. Bahari holds a master of business administration from Universiti Utara Malaysia. He was with the *Institut Kota Melaka*, Malacca, Malaysia as an academic executive before joining Binary University College as a lecturer and program coordinator. Mr. Fazli obtained his chemical engineering undergraduate degree from Universiti Kebangsaan Malaysia, Bangi, Malaysia. His current research interests are on higher education and entrepreneurship.

Stacey Edmonson is an associate professor of educational leadership and coordinator of the doctoral program at Sam Houston State University in Huntsville, Texas. She received her EdD in educational administration from Texas A&M University–Commerce in 2000. Her research interests include school law, special populations, and efficacy and burnout issues among educators. She has had experience in Texas public schools as a teacher, principal, and director of special programs. Dr. Edmonson is the president of the Texas Council of Professors of Educational Administration and an executive board member of the National Council of Professors of Educational Administration.

Huub Everaert is currently teaching statistics and methodology at the Faculty Of Education of the University of Professional Education of Utrecht, where he is also a member of the Research Group Behavioral Problems in Schools. He received his degree in anthropology at the University of Amsterdam. His dissertation at the same university dealt with male-female relationships among slaves on sugar plantations in the former Dutch colony of Suriname. His research interests, apart from general methodology and applied statistics, are stress and coping among teachers, historical demography, and event history analysis.

Nola Firth was originally a secondary school teacher who specialized in teaching and supporting students who had learning difficulties. She is currently cofounder and specialist consultant at The Learning Difficulties Project, Swinburne University in Victoria, Australia. In this capacity she undertakes research, and designs and delivers teacher professional development in regard to supporting students who have learning disabilities. Nola is also a consultant with Learning Difficulties Australia where she is a recent past president. She has published "Taking Charge," which is an assertiveness program designed for students who have learning disabilities. Nola is conducting doctoral research at The University of Melbourne into interventions that enhance effective copy by students who have learning disabilities.

Melissa Freeman is assistant professor in the qualitative research program, Department of Lifelong Education, Administration, and Policy at the University of Georgia. She is currently doing research on the effects of high-stakes testing on teaching and learning in elementary and middle schools in upstate New York as well as on fourth and eighth grade students' perceptions of those effects.

Erica Frydenberg is a psychologist and fellow of the Australian Psychological Society. She is an associate professor and head of the Educational Psychology Unit at the University of Melbourne. She has authored over 60 journal articles in the field of coping, authored or coauthored five books relating to coping, published psychological instruments to measure coping, and produced a cd-rom to teach coping skills. Her most recent volumes are *Morton Deutsch: A Life and Legacy of Mediation and Conflict Resolution* and *Thriving, Surviving Or Going Under: Coping With Everyday Lives*.

Michael M. Grant is an assistant professor in the instructional design and technology program at the University of Memphis. His research interests include methods to help educators implement technology integration, and the ways in which students represent their learning with computer technologies. He is currently exploring project-based learning in K–12 schools, as well as Internet video and two-way audio and video. Dr. Grant earned his PhD from The University of Georgia in Instructional Technology and was recently selected for the American Educational Research Association Special Interest Group for Instructional Technology's 2005 Young Researcher Award.

Daryl Greaves is a senior lecturer in the Department of Learning and Educational Development at the University of Melbourne in Australia. His main interest is in the contribution that educational psychology can make to students and classroom teachers, in particular, providing parents and teachers with a deeper understanding of their child's educational needs. Currently, his main focus of research is the assessment of individuals with learning disabilities. In the past he has examined programs to deal with stress such as that provided by Rational Emotive Behavior Therapy.

Janette R. Hill is an associate professor of instructional technology in the College of Education at The University of Georgia. Dr. Hill has been working in the instructional technology field for 12 years, teaching and doing research in a variety of areas and contexts. Dr. Hill served as a faculty fellow at NASA's Johnson Space Center and was recently selected to attend the Summer Institute for Women in Higher Education Administration. Her current research focuses on Web-based learning environments, specifically exploring how we make connections in virtual environments with a variety of resources (people, places, things).

Meagan Karvonen is an assistant professor in the Department of Educational Leadership and Foundations at Western Carolina University, where she teaches graduate level research methods courses. She received her PhD in educational psychology and research from the University of South Carolina. Her interests are in mixed methods research and evaluation, large-scale assessment of students with significant disabilities, and school-based health and mental health programs.

Debra Kissen a business consultant in the field of organizational performance improvement, recently returned to academia to pursue a PhD in counseling psychology at the University of Texas in Austin, where she combines her passion for growth and development with her knowledge of organizational challenges and opportunities. Debra's research interests are stress, coping, and the potential for mindfulness to enhance overall well-being. Debra hopes to bring the construct of mindfulness training into the organizational arena so individuals as well as entire entities can benefit from the clarity, awareness, and nonjudgmental attention obtained through daily mindfulness practice.

Zeynep Kiziltepe finished American Robert College in Istanbul and received a BA in English language and literature, a teachers' certificate, and an MA in psychology from Bogazici University, Istanbul. She received her PhD from the University of Exeter, England in linguistics. She has been working as an assistant professor in Bogazici University, Faculty of Education since 1996 where she teaches courses on educational psychology, psychology of learning, classroom management, and applied research in education. She has papers published in Turkey, Belgium, Japan, and now the United States, and a course book published on educational psychology in Turkey.

Jennifer Kusherman is currently working as the project coordinator for the Preschool Curriculum Evaluation Research grant in the Educational Leadership department at the University of North Carolina at Charlotte. She received her BS in early childhood education from the University of Georgia and was an early childhood educator for 7 years. She then earned her MEd in instructional systems technology from the University of North Carolina at Charlotte.

Richard Lambert received his PhD in research, measurement, and statistics from Georgia State University in 1995. He is now an associate professor in the Department of Educational Leadership at the University of North Carolina at Charlotte. His research interests include stress and coping, teacher stress, evaluating programs for young children, and applied statistics.

Sandra Mathison is a professor and head of the Department of Educational and Counseling Psychology and Special Education, University of British Columbia. Her research is in educational evaluation and her work has focused especially on the potential and limits of evaluation to support democratic ideals and promote justice. She is currently doing research on the effects of government-mandated testing on teaching and learning in elementary and middle schools. She is editor of the *Encyclopedia of Evaluation* and coeditor of *Defending Public Schools: The Nature and Limits of Standards-Based Reform and Assessment*.

Christopher McCarthy received his PhD in counseling psychology from Georgia State University in 1995. He is now an associate professor in the Department of Educational Psychology at the University of Texas at Austin. His research interests include stress and coping, teacher stress, health psychology, parental attachment processes, and group counseling.

Sylvia Nassar-McMillan is an associate professor of counselor education at North Carolina State University. Her scholarship and service revolve around ethnic and gender diversity, specifically around issues ethnic and other aspects of identity development. As both an educator and practitioner, she develops initiatives to facilitate cross cultural understanding and communication. She has been involved with the professionalization of counseling, both domestically and internationally, for over 15 years, and currently serves on the board of directors of the National Board for Certified Counselors.

Megan O'Donnell is currently working as a project coordinator for the Preschool Curriculum Evaluation Research Grant from the U.S. Department of Education in the Department of Educational Leadership at the University of North Carolina at Charlotte. She earned her MA in counseling from UNC Charlotte and a BS in psychology and exercise science from Elon University.

Reynaldo Gacho Segumpan, EdD, is associate professor and deputy director at the Executive Development Center, Universiti Utara Malaysia, Sintok, Kedah, Malaysia. He has also been deputy director of the University Teaching and Learning Center. He teaches organizational behavior and human resource management at the university's master's programs and leadership studies at the doctoral program. Dr. Segumpan has researched and published on areas related to higher education, psychology, public management, and personnel management, among others. Dr. Segumpan holds a bachelor's degree in education (Magna Cum Laude) and three master's degrees in administration and supervision, science education, and public management.

P. Taylor Webb is an assistant professor at the University of Washington, Bothell. Dr. Webb studies and teaches about the politics of education policy and the role of inquiry in policy making, including the politics of knowing. Dr. Webb's research has examined the discontinuities between macropolicy influences and the microrealities of educational implementation. He is particularly interested in the ways educators participate in the formal and informal leadership roles within schools, and within various accountability contexts. Dr. Webb is also interested in how the social construction of race, gender, and class affect educators' and policymakers' beliefs about educational practice.

Kees van der Wolf is a professor emeritus of psychosocial stress in children and youth at the University of Amsterdam. He now holds a professorship at the Utrecht University of Professional Education. He is the chairman of the Dutch Research Foundation for Psychosocial Stress. His research deals with topics like stress in teachers and learners and teaching students at risk in regular classrooms and schools.

ABOUT THE AUTHORS

Teri Wood earned a bachelor's degree in environmental design from Texas A&M University in 1984 and completed the coursework for a teaching certification in English through Texas State University in 1989. She taught English and AP English at the secondary level for 7 years. An interest in understanding factors that impact student learning led her to complete a master's degree in educational psychology at the University of Texas in 1998. Since completing this degree, she has worked as an elementary school counselor in Austin, Texas. Currently, she is a PhD candidate in educational psychology at the University of Texas.

Lauren J. Yadley received an MA in empirical psychology and a BA in psychology from Wake Forest University. There, she built a solid foundation in the discipline and studied gender and development in a cross-cultural context. She conducted her thesis research on sex stereotypes in Mexico City. She is currently pursuing a PhD in counseling psychology at the University of Texas in Austin. She is interested in the empirical investigation and application of mindfulness therapy. Lauren defines health and happiness holistically and hopes to spread both of these in her future personal and professional endeavors.

Cheryl Young is currently an assistant professor in special education at the University of North Carolina at Charlotte. She has earned a PhD in special education from the University of Texas, MA in bilingual special education from the University of Arizona, and BA in special education from South Connecticut State College. Her research interests include dyslexia, secondary students with reading difficulties, ELL, and reading.

Printed in the United States
51565LVS00002B/11